3D Game Textures

Luke Ahearn

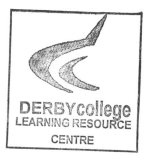

ELSEVIER

AMSTERDAM • BOSTON • HEIDELBERG • LONDON
NEW YORK • OXFORD • PARIS • SAN DIEGO
SAN FRANCISCO • SINGAPORE • SYDNEY • TOKYO

Focal Press is an imprint of Elsevier

Focal
Press

Acquisitions Editor: Becky Golden-Harrell
Project Manager: Andrew Therriault
Assistant Editor: Robin Weston
Marketing Manager: Christine Degon-Veroulis

Cover and interior design by the author with assistance from Eric DeCicco

Focal Press is an imprint of Elsevier
30 Corporate Drive, Suite 400, Burlington, MA 01803, USA
Linacre House, Jordan Hill, Oxford OX2 8DP, UK

 Recognizing the importance of preserving what has been written, Elsevier prints its
books on acid-free paper whenever possible.

Library of Congress Cataloging-in-Publication Data
Application submitted.

British Library Cataloguing-in-Publication Data
A catalogue record for this book is available from the British Library.

ISBN 13: 978-0-240-80768-3
ISBN 10: 0-240-80768-5

For information on all Focal Press publications
visit our website at www.books.elsevier.com

06 07 08 09 10 11   10 9 8 7 6 5 4 3 2 1

Printed in Canada

Contents

To Julie, Ellen, and Cooper.

Acknowledgments

Becky Golden-Harrell at Focal Press.

Brian Grabinski, Mark Birge-Anderson and Jose Vazquez, the concept artists.

Ann Sidenblad, a great friend and one of the best digital artists I know, for providing her invaluable feedback.

Nick Marks for his initial input on this book and for being the crazy fresh pimp of game art.

NVIDIA—Doug Rogers, Kevin Bjorke, Gary King, Sébastien Dominé, Carrie Cowan, and Derek Perez, for information and help developing the shader section.

Alkis "Atlas" Roufas for the Genetica2 demo on the desk.

Michael S. Elliott for the use of the Tengwar-Gandalf font.

Introduction

Game development is booming! In the past few years many books have been written, more information than ever is available on the Internet, and many colleges are offering courses—even degrees—in game development. And of all the numerous topics that fall under the large umbrella of game development, texture creation is among the most important and fundamental. Yet to my knowledge, among all those classes and books, there has never been a thorough treatment of texture creation. The big picture of texture creation involves much more than learning to use the Offset Filter in Photoshop. The subject truly deserved a book.

I wrote this book after having held many positions on various game projects, from president and art director to an in-the-trenches artist working through crunch. I worked with many artists on numerous projects, and no matter what their education or background, their knowledge of game development came largely from actually doing it. No one school or book can adequately train you for an industry that changes so fast and requires a rather large set of skills to function in. Even an experienced game developer must face the learning curve quite frequently. The reality is that most game projects are one-time, unique ventures that are never to be done the same way twice. Things change too fast—technology, processes, the marketplace. And the industry is still a bit transitory, so you may find yourself in a new town, with a new company, at work on a new genre of game and with tools you have never before used. You would think that writing a book about something that is so constantly changing and affected by so many variables would be impossible. But given all the change and evolution in our industry, there are some core skills and practices that don't change year to year. My goal with this book is not only to show you how to create textures, but also to give you a basis for understanding the larger picture of game development as it pertains to texture creation. The difference between a good artist and a good artist that can function as a member of a high-performance game development team is the ability to do good work fast and efficiently—and contribute to the forward momentum of the project. I approached each of the projects in the book with all this mind and tried to give you a feel for the various situations you may find yourself in as a game artist.

I also developed the exercises in this book to rely heavily on Photoshop. I did this for several reasons:

- The only way to really get to know Photoshop well is to use it a lot and to use it with real-world examples, not just a limited three-step tutorial on the Offset Filter.
- When you get to know your way around Photoshop, you will be more impressed by it. Every day I learn some new trick or feature that saves precious time.
- When you are truly proficient in Photoshop, you will develop a *feeling* for the best way to accomplish a task. When you develop this feeling, you know that you have left the learning curve far behind you. You can then focus on getting better and faster at Photoshop until it becomes an extension of you. You will be less hindered in creating what you are envisioning.
- When you get to know the capabilities of Photoshop, you will be able to create anything you want and will be less dependent on resources that may not be available everywhere you go such as pre-made texture sets, digital cameras, and other software.

When you are able to use other resources to create your textures, they will be much better, and not only visually. Your source files will be more flexible, better organized, and much easier to work with. This is very important because creating game art is a balancing act. You are always making decisions that involve not only aesthetics, but also efficiency and technological limits. Having files that are easy to find and can be quickly altered is as important as how good they look. The best-looking texture in the world is useless if you can't find it or it won't run in a game engine. And on a development team you will most likely not be the only person using a file. If your layers are not named, grouped, and organized, the next person's job will be much, much harder. One of the biggest challenges in game development is not breaking any of the fragile connections between the thousands of parts of a typical game. A poorly organized file is one of the things that will threaten to break those connections; many poorly organized files will almost assuredly cause a break. These connections are called dependencies.

The development team must function smoothly and efficiently as a whole because usually certain tasks and goals must be reached by one group, or individual, in order for the other team members to move forward with their work. A good number of poorly organized or missing files will cause the guilty party to take longer to complete his work and cause the dependent party to wait before starting her work. This snowballs, delays cause more delays, and the schedule starts to slip dramatically. The project may even grind to a dead standstill. What's worse is having no schedule and not knowing (until it's way too late) that the game you had hoped (or are contractually obligated) to develop is an impossibility given the lack of time and resources you have so late in development. The worst case is that this will cause the project to get cancelled. At best, this is where most of the infamous *crunch time* is created. Crunch is those last few months where the development team lives in the office day and night to finish a game. One day developers are going to realize that the reason they are crunching is because the project wasn't planned properly. Someone at a higher level didn't do his job a year or two earlier, and the developers end up paying for it.

So, beyond creating a wood or metal texture, the greater goal is to learn to create assets in an efficient, organized, and flexible way. To work on a game development team, speed, accuracy, and flexibility are critical. The process in which you handle assets is called the pipeline. From concept to creation to in-game asset—tens of thousands of files pass through the pipeline. So things like where you save your files, what you name them, how you name, group, and organize the layers in a Photoshop file are all important details. You don't want to be the person responsible for losing or overwriting a file that took someone else hours or days to create. Not only will you create the loss of precious man-hours of work, but potentially you could be responsible for delaying the entire project.

I hope you enjoy the book.

What This Book Is NOT

There is much confusion when it comes to the vocabulary of game development. This book does not cover careers, characters, animation, lighting, modeling, NURBS, shader programming, or character skinning and is not a vague overview of "all" game art. This book is focused on creating 2D textures for various 3D game environments.

Whom This Book Is For

This book is for game developers, architects, simulation developers, web designers, and anyone who needs to create 2D imagery for a 3D computer application. I have come across two general types of individual in the art departments of game development teams: the artistically challenged technical person and the technically challenged artistic person. Most people are trained and/or simply more proficient at thinking in one of those ways. There's no shame in being a great programmer who can't draw a bloody talon or in being a great artist who can't do all that complex code stuff. This book will help the beginner get started in game texturing, but it will also help the technically oriented professionals who are artistically challenged create textures (in a way they can relate to), and it will teach the technically challenged artists to create their art in a fashion that will allow them to set up their work with an eye toward the important aspects of game development. There is no shame in being an artist who has focused solely on creating beautiful art, and not on the technical issues of game development, but it is limiting. The good news is that the creation of beautiful art is the hard part. All you have to do now is set up your art in a way that allows you to quickly find, alter, and output your textures for use in a game.

Chapter Overview

One: A Basic (Game) Art Education

The basis of computer art is art itself, so in Chapter 1 we will discuss the most basic and important aspects of visual art. While teaching you traditional fine art skills is beyond the scope of this book, it is critical to have an understanding of some basic aspects of visual art in order to create game textures. The basic aspects of visual art we will focus on are shape and form, light and shadow, texture, color, and perspective.

Two: A Brief Orientation to Computer Graphic Technology

We will talk technology very briefly. You will eventually need to learn a good deal about the technical side of computer art to make the various decisions technology will present to you, but a brief orientation of technology is all you will need to start painting textures. While creating art on a computer can be limiting, frustrating, and confusing for many people, once you understand the limits placed on you and learn to work within them, you are much more likely to create impressive work. The aspects of technology that we will look at are common features of graphic file formats, the power of two and the grid, UV mapping, and shader technology for artists.

Three: A Quick Overview of Photoshop for Game Artists

Photoshop is the right hand of the game artist. While there are many 3D applications, Photoshop pretty much stands alone as the 2D application of choice for game developers. This chapter is an "orientation" to the aspects of Photoshop that are most useful to the texture artist. This is not a tutorial chapter or a user's manual. While I mention some specifics about how certain aspects of Photoshop can be used in game development, they are only mentioned in this chapter and put into practice throughout the rest of the book. This chapter is written based on version 7 of Photoshop with notes on the updates and differences that exist in Photoshop CS. I figured this approach would be most useful to the users of both versions of Photoshop.

Four: Prepping for Texture Creation

In this chapter we will look at the various sources of digital resources for texture creation and each of the steps in the process of gathering, preparing, and storing your assets. While the focus of this book is the creation of textures using Photoshop, so you develop strong Photoshop skills, in reality it is more common, easier, and more effective to use photo reference in texture creation. We will be using photo reference later in the book, and the DVD contains a good collection of photo reference for you to use in your work.

Five: The Sci-fi Setting

This is the first tutorial chapter. The sci-fi scene looks complex due to the geometry and effects present, but in actuality the texture set is very simple. We will start by taking from the concept sketch ideas for the base materials we will create for the scene and from that base build a simple and versatile set of textures. This method produces textures that can be used in various ways and are designed to be used with the newer technology coming out (shaders like bump and normal mapping, etc.).

Six: The Urban Setting

In this chapter we will learn to work more faithfully to the detail in a concept sketch or any reference material that may be given to us. When you create textures for a game environment, you are usually creating them for a world that has been thought out, detailed, and developed to the point that showcasing your creativity is not the primary goal of your work. You are showcasing your talent and ability to recreate what you see in the materials in front of you. We will build a set of textures as they were traditionally created, in sets: base, wall, floor, and ceiling. This chapter focuses on breaking out not only the base materials that need to be created for a scene, but also the detail textures as well. Even though this approach is falling by the wayside due to technological advances, it is still an applicable skill to many games and applications and a good skill to have when you are required to work with more advanced technology. We always start with the basics to build a material (shape, color, texture) and build detail on top of that. What you end up with is a full texture set that is easily altered and built upon. By the end of the chapter you will have created all the textures needed for the urban environment as seen in the concept sketch.

Seven: The Fantasy Setting

This is a long chapter, so be ready to pace yourself. This chapter combines the creation of many high-detail textures that are used in a high polygon-count scene. We will use the Path Tool in Photoshop to create the fancy curves you see in the scene, and we will do some basic hand painting that will produce great results. Finally, we will look at the process of creating the textures used in a shader.

Eight: The Outdoor Setting

In this chapter we will create a set of textures for a forest that can be altered to look spooky, friendly, or fanciful. Using the basic approach presented here to break out the elements of an outdoor scene, you can also create a similar set of textures for any outdoor environment; jungle, desert, etc. I will also introduce the use of photo source in texture creation. I mentioned in the very beginning of the book that the use of photo source to create textures is not only common but preferred. It makes your job faster and easier and gives your textures an extra layer of richness that can take a lot of time to achieve otherwise. While working with overlays may take the most time and tweaking, they are generally added later in the creation process, after a good foundation is laid. Using digital imagery will greatly enhance and speed up your work, but you don't want it to be a crutch that you will always lean on. We will also look at the ways the sky is typically handled in a game.

Nine: Game Effects

Games are full of visual effects, probably even more than you realize. These effects are important, not just as eye candy, but for giving the player clues and information on what is happening in the game world. These effects also add a great deal to the level of immersion a player will experience in a game. Typically, if you shoot at any surface in a game—wood, metal, concrete, and their variations—you will see and hear a different effect for each surface. Effects also include the glow around a candle, light shafts from a window, even rain drops. The assets for these effects are fairly easy to create. Actually, asset creation is the easy part of creating effects in a relative sense. It does take work to create the art and it must look good, but it's the systems that run the effects that can be complex and challenging to work with. Generally, you will often create three types of effects: Static, Animated, and Particle.

Have fun!

The Concept Artists

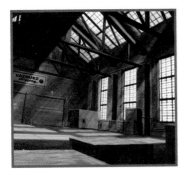

The Urban Setting
Jose Vazquez

Jose was born in Mexico and raised in Chicago, IL, from the age of three. He still keeps a close connection to his Mexican heritage. Jose has a B.A. in Illustration from Columbia College and a B.A. in Media Arts and Animation from the Illinois Institute of Art. Jose has over 15 years of professional experience that began with graffiti then grew into contracted large-scale murals. Dabbling in airbrush art, portraits, and paintings of all media, Jose has a strong traditional art background, but due to his animation education all of his current works are digital. Jose currently develops characters in the video gaming industry. You can contact Jose at www.sephseer.com.

The Sci-fi Setting
Brian Grabinski

Brian was born and raised in Illinois, He graduated from the Chicago-based American Academy of Art in 1997. Upon graduation he started working freelance and has worked as a full-time illustrator/graphic designer for 8 years now. Brian has also worked as a full-time concept artist for the video game company Rainbow Studios / THQ based out of Phoenix, AZ, and for the Chicago area Animation Studio, Dreamation / Cineme. Brian continues to work freelance for various clients and is employed full-time at the Hoffman Estates, IL, based video game company High Voltage Studios as a full-time concept artist. You can contact Brian Grabinski via e-mail at briangrabinski@aol.com or brian.grabinski@high-voltage.com

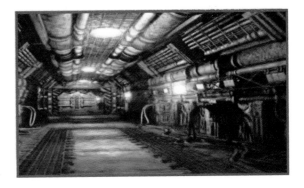

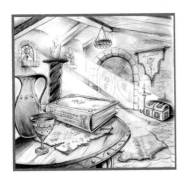

The Fantasy Setting
Mark Birge-Anderson

Mark attended the Layton School of Art and Design in Milwaukee, WI, and The Art Academy of Cincinnati. He works in advertising in Chicago, coming up with original concepts and designs. He has also done concept art for an animation studio in Chicago and plans to pursue that exciting field. Mark does freelance illustration as well and can be reached at mark@matrix1.com.

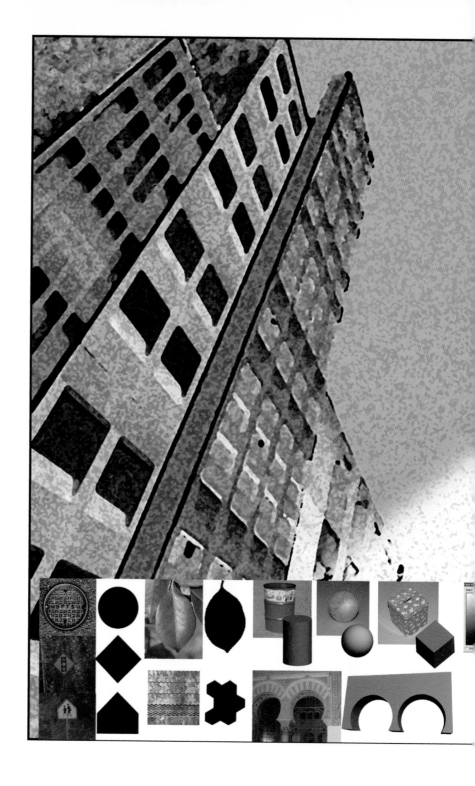

Chapter 1

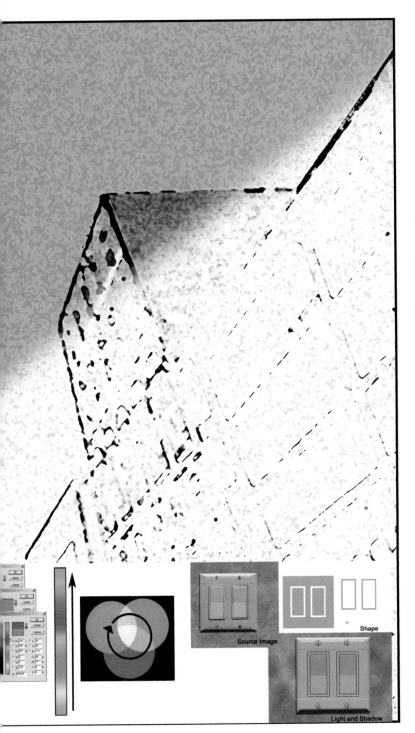

Source Image

Shape

Light and Shadow

Introduction

The basis of computer art is art itself, so before we dive into any technical issues we must first discuss the most basic yet most important aspects of visual art. While teaching you traditional fine art skills is beyond the scope of this book, it is critical to have an understanding of some basic aspects of visual art in order to create game textures. Fortunately, these basic aspects of art are fairly easy to present in book form. By studying these basics of art, you will learn to see the world as an artist does, understand what you see, and then be more able to create a texture set for a game world.

A Basic (Game) Art Education

Art is born of the observation and investigation of nature.

Cicero
Roman author, orator, and politician (106 BC–43 BC)

The basic aspects of visual art we will focus on are:

- Shape and form
- Light and shadow
- Texture
- Color
- Perspective

Learning to observe the basic visual aspects of the world around you is a strong beginning in the process of seeing the world like an artist, communicating with other artists, and creating great game textures. Technology is, of course, critical to the larger picture of game textures, but the actual basics of art is where great textures begin. Too often would-be game artists are thrown into a discussion on tiling, or even game engine technology, when what is most important for the creation of game textures is the ability to understand what you are seeing in the real world and to recreate it on the computer. Often a texture artist is required to break a scene down to its core materials and build a texture set based on those materials, so learning this ability is essential. While you don't need to have an advanced degree in art to create great textures, let's face it: almost anyone can learn what buttons to push in Photoshop, but the person who understands and skillfully applies the basics of art can make a texture that stands out above the rest.

There are many types of art and aspects of visual art that you should further explore in order to develop as a game artist. Some of the things you can study and/or practice are:

- Figure drawing
- Still-life drawing
- Photography
- Painting (oil, watercolor, etc.)
- Lighting (for film, still photography, the stage, or CG)
- Color theory and application
- Sculpture
- Drafting and architectural rendering
- Anatomy
- Set design

It is even worth the time to study other areas of interest beyond art including science, particularly the behavior of the physical world. Light, for example, is becoming processed more and more in real time and not painted into the texture to the extent it was just a few years ago. The more you understand and are able to reproduce effects such as reflection, refraction, blowing smoke, etc., the more success you will find as a game artist. We presently have emerging technologies that reproduce the real world to a much greater extent than ever before, but it still takes an artist to create the input and adjust the output for these effects to look their best. The areas of study that will help you when dealing with real-world behaviors are endless. You can start by simply observing the world, how water drips or flows, the variations of light and shadow on different surfaces at different times of the day, how a tree grows from the ground. Straight like a young pine or flared at the base like an old oak—you will soon be staring at the cracks in the pavement and photographing the side of a dumpster while the world stares at you. An excellent book for this type of activity is *Digital Texturing & Painting* by Owen Demers. You can also take tours of museums, architectural tours, nature walks; join a photography club, or a figure drawing class . . . there is no end to the classes, clubs, disciplines, and other situations you can expose yourself to that will open up your mind to new inspirations and teach you new tools and techniques for texture creation. And, of course, playing games, watching movies, and reading graphic novels are the food of the game artist.

Chapter Overview

- Shape (2D) and Form (3D)
- Light and Shadow
- Texture: tactile vs. visual
- Color
- Perspective

While there are many elements of traditional art, we will narrow our focus to those elements that are most pertinent to texture creation. We will start with shape and form.

Shape and Form

A **shape** is simply a two-dimensional (height and width) outline of a form. A circle, square, rectangle, and triangle are all examples of shape. Shape is what we first use to draw a picture before we understand such concepts as light, shadow, and depth. As children we draw what we see in a crude way. Look at the drawings of very young children and you will see that they are almost always composed of pure basic shapes: triangle roof, square door, circle sun. Even as adults, when we understand shadows and perspective, we have trouble drawing what we see before us and instead rely on a whole series of mental notes and assumptions as to what we think we are seeing. There are exercises to help develop the ability to draw what we actually see. Most notably, the book *Drawing on the Right Side of the Brain* offers many such exercises.

One of the most famous of these exercises involves the drawing of a human face from a photo. After you have done this, you then turn the photo upside down and draw it again. The upside-down results are often far better than the right-side up, first try. This is due to the fact that once you turn the image upside down your brain is no longer able to make any mental assumptions about what you think you are seeing; you can only see what's really there. Your brain hasn't yet developed a set of rules and assumptions about the uncommon sight of an upside-down human face. One of the first skills you can practice as an artist is trying to see the shapes that make up the objects that surround you. Figure 1-1 has some examples of this ranging from the simple to the complex. This is a very important skill to acquire. As a texture artist you will often need to see an object's fundamental shape amidst all the clutter and confusion in a scene so you can create the 2D art that goes over the 3D objects of the world.

Form is three-dimensional (height, width, and depth) and includes simple objects like spheres, cubes, and pyramids. See Figure 1-2 for examples and visual comparisons. You will see later that as a texture artist you are creating art on flat shapes (essentially squares and rectangles) that are later placed on the surfaces of forms. An example can be seen in Figure 1-3 as a cube is turned into a crate (a common prop in many computer games). When a shape is cut into a base material in Photoshop and some highlights and shadows are added, the illusion of form is created. A texture can be created rather quickly using this method. See Figure 1-4 for a very simple example of a space door created using an image of rust, some basic shapes, and some standard Photoshop Layer Effects.

Of course, mapping those textures to more complex shapes like weapons, vehicles, and characters gets more complex, and the textures themselves reflect this complexity. Paradoxically, as the speed, quality, and the complexity of game technology increase, artists are actually producing more simplified textures in some cases. The complexity comes in the understanding and implementation of the technology. Don't worry—you will gradually

Figure 1-1
Here are some examples of shapes that compose everyday objects. These shapes range from simple to complex.

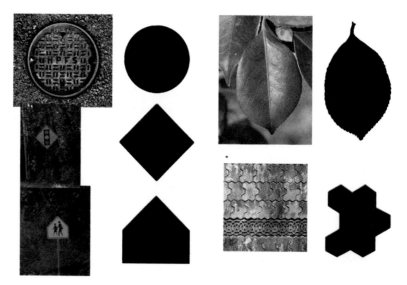

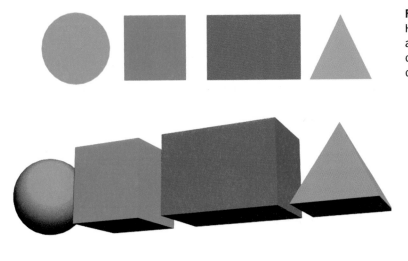

Figure 1-2
Here are examples of shapes and forms. Notice how it is only shadow that turns a circle into a sphere.

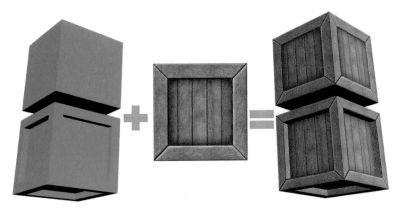

Figure 1-3
A game texture is basically a 2D image applied, or mapped, to a 3D shape to add visual detail. In this example a cube is turned into a crate using texture. And a more complex 3D shape makes a more interesting crate while using the same 2D image.

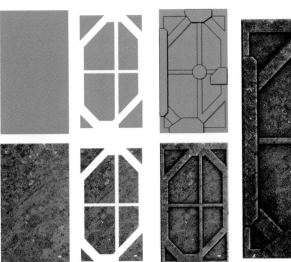

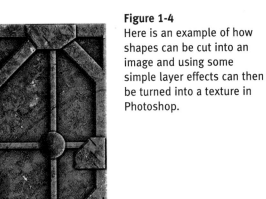

Figure 1-4
Here is an example of how shapes can be cut into an image and using some simple layer effects can then be turned into a texture in Photoshop.

Figure 1-5
Here are some examples of
the forms that make up the
objects around you.

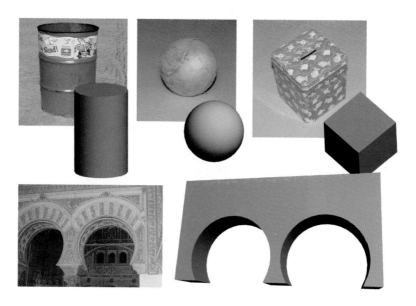

be introduced to this complexity until it culminates with the sections on Shader Technology.

As in the above section, you can practice looking for the forms that make up the objects around you. In Figure 1-5 you can see some examples of this.

Light and Shadow

Of all the topics in traditional art, this is arguably the most important due to its difficulty to master and its importance to the final work. Light and shadow give depth to and, as a result, define what we see. At its simplest, light and shadow are easy to see and understand. Most of us are familiar with shadow; our own shadow cast by the sun, making animal silhouettes with our hands on the wall, or a single light source shining on a sphere and the round shadow that it casts. That's where this book will start. Light and shadow quickly get more complicated, and the examples in this book will get more complex as well. The book will start with the ability to see and analyze light and shadow in this chapter, move up to creating and tweaking light and shadow in Photoshop using Layer Styles for the most part, and finally look at some basic hand tweaking of light and shadow. If you desire to master the ability to hand paint light and shadow on complex and organic surfaces, then you are advised to take traditional art classes in illustration, sketching, and painting.

We all know that the absence of light is darkness, and in total darkness we can obviously see nothing at all, but the presence of too much light will also make it difficult to see. Too much light blows away shadow and removes depth and desaturates color. In the previous section we looked at how shape and form differ. We see that difference primarily as light and shadow as in the example of the circle and a sphere. But even if the sphere were lit evenly with no shadows and looked just like the circle, the difference would become apparent when rotated around the vertical axis. The sphere would always look round if rotated, whereas once you began to rotate the circle it would begin to look like an oval until it eventually disappeared when completely sideways. In the previous example, where a shape was cut into an image of rusted metal and made to look like a metal space door using Photoshop Layer Effects, the highlights and shadows were faked using the various tools and their settings. In Figure 1-6 you can see the same door texture rotated from front to side. Notice the complete lack of depth in the image on the far right. The illusion is shattered.

Understanding light and shadow are very important in the process of creating quality textures. We will go into more depth on this topic as we work through this book. One of the main reasons for dwelling on the topic is not only due to the importance of light and shadow visually, but you will see that many of the decisions that need to be made are based on whether light and shadow should be represented using texture, geometry, or technology. To make this decision intelligently in a serious game production involves the input and expertise of many people. While what looks best is ideally the first priority, what runs best on the target computer is usually what the decision boils down to. So keep in mind that in game development you don't want to make any assumptions about light and shadows—ask questions. We cover different scenarios of how light and shadow may be handled in a game in this book. It can be challenging to make shadows look good in any one of the situations. Too little and you lack depth, too much and the texture starts to look flat. Making shadows too long or intense is an easy mistake. And unless the game level specifically calls for that, on rare occasion, don't do it. Technology sometimes handles the highlights and shadows. This is challenging because it is a new way of thinking that baffles many people who are not familiar with computer graphics. This method can also be a bit overwhelming because you go from creating one texture for a surface to creating three or more textures that all work together on one surface.

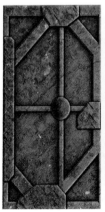
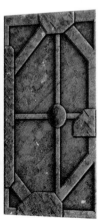
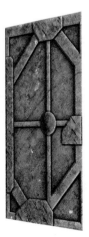
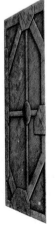

Figure 1-6
Here is the same door texture from the previous section. Notice the complete lack of depth as we look at it from angles other than straight on. The illusion of depth is shattered.

Naming and storing those textures can get confusing if you let it get away from you.

Overall you want your textures to be as versatile as possible, and that includes, to a great degree, the ability to use those textures under various lighting conditions. See Figure 1-7 for an example of a texture where the shadows and highlights have been improperly implemented and one that has been correctly created. For this reason we will purposely use highlight and shadow to a minimalist amount. You will find that if you need more depth in your texture than a modest amount of highlight and/or shadow, then you most likely need to create geometry or use a shader—or consider removing the source of shadow! If there is no need for a large electrical box on a wall, then don't paint it in if it draws attention to itself and looks flat. If there is a need and you are creating deep and harsh shadows because of it, you may need to create the geometry for the protruding element. You may find that as game development technology accelerates, things like pipes, door knobs, and ledges are no longer painted into the texture but modeled in geometry. Many texture surface properties are no longer painted on. Reflections, specular highlights, bump mapping, and other aspects of highlight and shadow are now processed in real time.

Figure 1-7
The crate on the left has conflicting light sources. The shadow from edge of the crate is coming up from the bottom, is too dark, is too long, and even has a gap in it. The highlights on the edges are in conflict with the shadow cast on the inner panel of the crate, and they are too hot, or bright. The crate on the right has a more subtle, low-contrast, and diffuse highlight and shadow scheme and will work better in more diverse situations.

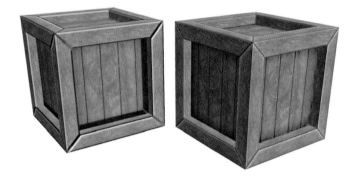

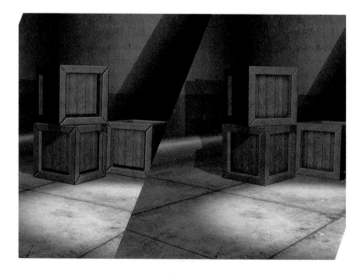

In the rest of this book we will take various approaches to light and shadow using both Photoshop's Layer Effects to automate this process and other tools to hand paint highlights and shadows. One of the main benefits to creating your own highlights and shadows in your textures is that you can control them and make them more interesting as well as consistent. Nothing is worse than a texture with shadows from conflicting light sources; harsh, short shadows on some elements of the texture and longer, more diffuse shadows on others. See Figure 1-8 for an example of this. The human eye can detect these types of errors even if the human seeing it can't quite understand why the image looks wrong. One of the artist's greatest abilities is not only being able to create art, but also being able to consciously know and verbalize what he is seeing. In Figure 1-9 you can see the various types of shadows created as the light source changes. This is a simple demonstration. If you ever have the opportunity to light a 3D scene or movie set, you will discover that the range of variables for light and shadow can be quite large.

Highlights also tell us a good bit about the light source as well as the object itself. In Figure 1-10 you can see another simple illustration of how different materials will have different highlight patterns and intensities. These materials lack any texture or color and simply show the highlights and shadows created on the surface by one consistent light source.

For a more advanced and in-depth discussion on the subject of light and shadow for 3D scenes, I recommend *Essential CG Lighting Techniques* by Darren Brooker.

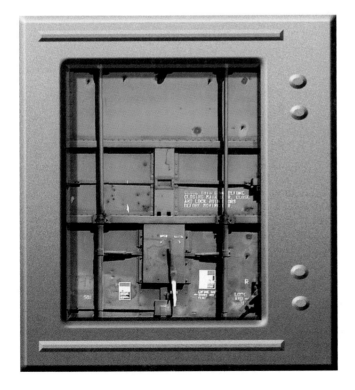

Figure 1-8
Here is a REALLY BAD texture created from two sources. Notice the difference in the shadows and highlights. The human eye can detect these errors even if the human seeing it can't understand why the image looks wrong.

Figure 1-9
With one light source and a simple object you can see the range of shadows we can create. Each shadow tells us information about the object and the light source, such as location, intensity, etc.

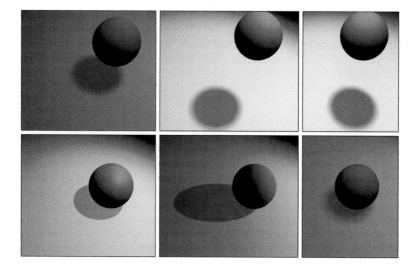

Figure 1-10
With one light source and a simple object with various highlights on it, you can see that the object appears to be created of various materials. Keep in mind that what you are seeing is only highlight and shadow. How much does only this aspect of an image tell you about the material?

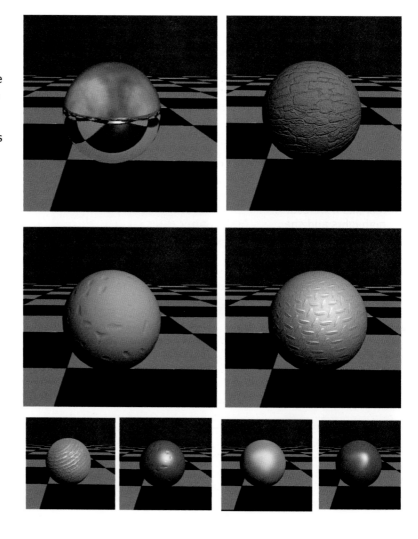

Texture

In the bulk of this book, as in the game industry, we will be using the term "texture" to mean a 2D static image. What we refer to as textures in this book are also sometimes called materials, or even tile sets (from older games), but we will stick to the term texture. The one exception in this book is that in this section we will talk about the word texture as it is used in traditional art: painting, sculpture, etc. A side note on vocabulary: keep in mind that vocabulary is very important and can be a confusing aspect of working in the game industry. There is much room for miscommunication. Different words can often mean the same thing, and the same words can often mean many different things. Acronyms can be especially confusing; RAM, POV, MMO and RPG all mean different things in different industries. POV means point-of-view in the game industry and personally-owned vehicle in the government and also stands for persistence of vision. So to clarify, the term "texture," while usually meaning a 2D image applied to a polygon (the face of a 3D object), in this section of this chapter it will refer to an aspect of an image and not the image itself. We draw this distinction for the following conversation on traditional art.

In traditional art there are two types of texture: tactile and visual.

Tactile texture is when you are able to actually touch the physical texture of the art or object. Smooth and cold (marble, polished metal, glass) is as much a texture as coarse and rough. In art this applies to sculptures and the like, but many paintings have thick and very pronounced brush or palette knife strokes. Vincent Van Gogh was famous for doing this. Some painters even add materials to their paint like sand to add more physical or tactile texture to their work.
Visual texture is the illusion of what the surface's texture might feel like if we could touch it. Visual texture is composed of fine highlights and shadows. As computer game texture artists, we deal solely with this aspect of texture. So, for example, an image on your monitor may look like rough stone, smooth metal, or even a beautiful woman and if you try and kiss that beautiful woman she is still just a monitor—not that I have ever tried that, mind you.

There are many ways to convey texture in a two-dimensional piece of art. In computer games we are combining 2D and 3D elements and must often decide which to use. With 2D we are almost always forced to use strictly 2D imagery for fine visual texture. And while the faster processors, larger quantities of RAM, and the latest crop of 3D graphic cards allow us to use larger and more detailed textures and more geometry, a great deal of visual texture is still static, and noticeably so to a trained artist. This limitation is starting to melt away as complex Shader Systems are coming into the mainstream of real-time games. The real-time processing of bump maps, specular highlights, and a long list of other more complex effects are adding a depth of realism to our game worlds not even dreamed of in the recent past. This book will teach you both the current method of building texture sets and the ever-increasing method of building material sets that use textures and shader effects together. We will discuss this more at length later in the book, but for now you can see some visual examples of these effects. In Figure 1-11 you can see how in the 2D strip the object rotates but the effects stay static on the surface, while on the 3D strip the object rotates and the effect moves realistically across the surface.

The game artist's job is often considering what tools and techniques we have at our disposal and choosing which best accomplishes the job. We are often trading off between what looks good and what runs well. As you begin to paint textures, you will find that some of the techniques of traditional art don't work in the context of game texturing. As a traditional artist we usually do a painting that represents one static viewpoint, and we can paint into it strong light sources and a great deal of depth, but that amount of depth

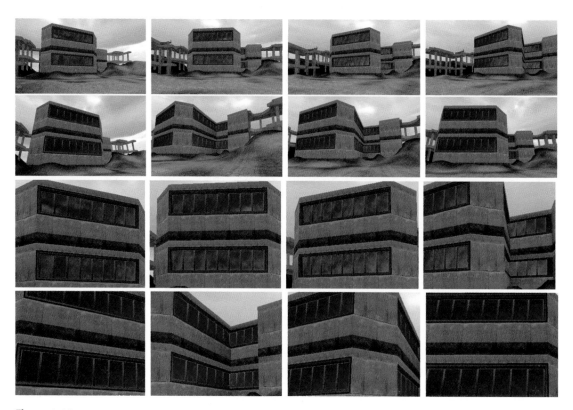

Figure 1-11
Visual texture is composed of fine highlights and shadows. A shader allows for the real-time processing of visual texture, among other effects, and adds much more realism to a scene as the surface reacts with the world around it. In this example I used a specular map. These effects are best seen in 3D, but you can see here that the windows in the building on the top row have a reflection of the sky in them and that reflection moves as the players does. The windows in the building on the lower row are painted textures and stay the same no matter where the player walks. The bottom two rows are close-ups to help you see the effect. If you pick one window in the close-up images and look closely, you will see that the cloud reflections are in different places in each frame.

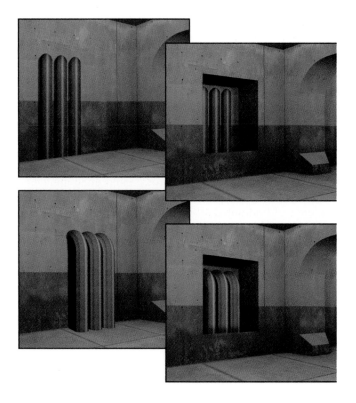

Figure 1-12
There are several possibilities when dealing with overt depth representation. **Upper left:** the pipes are painted into the texture and totally lack any depth; notice how they dead end into the floor. **Upper right:** restricting the players' ability to move around the texture can alleviate some of the problem. **Lower left:** adding actual geometry for the parts of the texture that cause the overt depth is the best solution if possible (this method uses less texture memory but more polygons). Finally, **lower right:** adding the actual geometry into the recess is an option that looks pretty interesting and actually allows for a reduction of geometry. The removal of polygons from the backsides of the pipes more than offsets the added faces of the recess.

representation goes beyond tactile texture and becomes faked geometry and looks flat in a dynamic, real-time 3D world. As mentioned earlier in this chapter, this will not work in a 3D game where a player can move about and examine the texture. Once again we must choose what to represent using a static 2D image, what can be processed in real time using a shader, and what must be represented using actual geometry. There are many solutions for this problem; among them are restricting the players' ability to move around the texture, removing the element of overt depth representation, or adding actual geometry for the parts of the texture represented by the overt depth representation (see Figure 1-12).

Color

We all know what color is in an everyday fashion, "Get me those pliers. No, the ones with black handles . . . I said paint the house green—I didn't mean neon green!" That's all fine for the civilian discussion of color, but when you begin to speak with artists about color, you need to learn to speak of color intelligently and that takes a little more education and some practice. You will also learn to choose and combine color, too. In games, as in movies, interior design, and other visual disciplines, color is very important. Color tells us much about the world and situation we are in. While I was at CMP, we developed a massively multiplayer game that started in the town—saturated green grass, blue water, butterflies—you get the picture, this was a nice and safe place. As you moved away from town, the colors darkened and lost saturation. The grass went from a brighter green to a less saturated brownish-green. There were other visual clues as well. Most people can look at grass and tell if is healthy, dying, kept up, or growing wild. Away from town the grass was also long and clumpy, dying, and growing over the path. But even before we changed any other aspect of the game—still using the same grass texture from town that was well trimmed—we simply lowered the saturation of the colors on the fly and you could feel the life drain from the world as you walked away from town. As you create textures you will most assuredly have some form of direction on color choice, but maybe not. You might need to know what colors to choose to convey what is presented in the design document and what colors will work well together.

This section lays out a simple introduction to the vocabulary of color, color mixing (on the computer), and color choices and their commonly accepted meanings. I decided to skip the complex science of color and stick to the practical and immediately useful aspects of color. Color can get very complex and esoteric, but you would benefit from taking your education further and learning how color works on a scientific basis. While this chapter will be a strong starting point, you will eventually move on from working with only the colors contained in the texture you are creating to how those colors interact with other elements in the world, such as lighting. To start with, however, a game texture artist needs the ability to communicate, create, and choose colors.

First, we will address the way in which we discuss color. There are many color models, or ways of looking at and communicating color verbally. There are models that concern printing, physics, pigment, and light. They each have their own vocabulary, concepts, and tools for breaking out color. As digital artists, we use the models concerning light since we are working with colored pixels that emit light. A little later we will take a closer look at those color systems from the standpoint of color mixing, but for now we will look at the vocabulary of color. In game development you will almost always use the RGB color model to mix color and the HSB color model to discuss color. You will see that Photoshop allows for the numeric input and visual selection of color in various ways. When you discuss color choices and changes and then go to enact them, you are often translating between two or more models. Don't worry; this is not difficult and most people don't know they are doing it.

First, we will look at the HSB model, which stands for **Hue, Saturation**, and **Brightness** since this is the most common way for digital artists to communicate concerning color. These three properties of color are the main aspects of color that we need to be concerned with when discussing color. In Figure 1-13 you can see examples of these aspects of color.

- Hue is the name of the color (red, yellow, green).
- Saturation (or Chroma) is the strength or purity of the color.
- Brightness (or Value) is the lightness or darkness of the color.

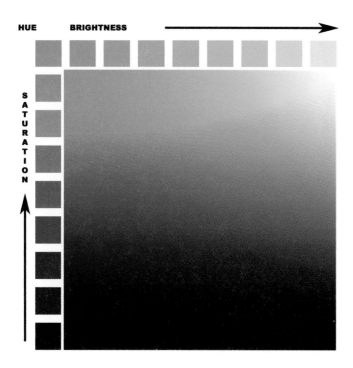

HUE   **BRIGHTNESS**

S A T U R A T I O N

Figure 1-13
In this image you can see a representation of HSB—Hue, Saturation, and Brightness.

Hue

Most people use the word "color" when referring to hue. While there are many, many colors, there are far fewer hues. Variations of saturation and brightness create the almost unlimited colors we see in the world. Scarlet, maroon, pink, and crimson are all colors, but the base hue for all of these is red.

Understanding color and its various properties is best done with visual examples. The most often used method is the Color Wheel developed by Johannes Itten. We will look at the Color Wheel a little later. In Photoshop you will recognize the Color Picker, which allows for various methods for choosing and controlling color, both numerically and visually. The Color Picker has various ways to choose color, but the most commonly used is RGB (Red, Green, Blue)—Figure 1-14.

Saturation

Saturation quite simply is the amount of white in the color. In Figure 1-15 you can see the saturation of a color being decreased as white is added. If you have access to a software package like Photoshop and open the color picker, you can slide the picker from the pure hue to a less saturated hue and watch the saturation numbers in the HSB slots go down as the color gets less saturated. Notice how the brightness doesn't change unless you start dragging down and adding black to the color. Also, you may want to look down at the

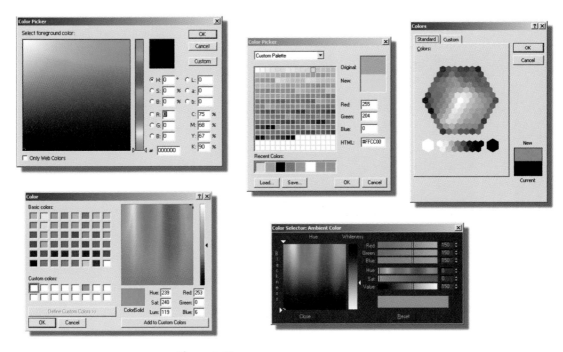

Figure 1-14
Here are Color Pickers from various applications.

Figure 1-15
The saturation of the color red at 100% and decreasing to 0% by adding white.

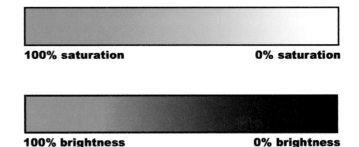

100% saturation   **0% saturation**

Figure 1-16
The brightness of the color red at 100% and decreasing to 0% by adding black.

100% brightness   **0% brightness**

RGB numbers and notice how the red in RGB doesn't change, but the green and blue do.

Brightness

Brightness is the amount of black in the color. In Figure 1-16 you can see the brightness of a color being decreased. As in the previous example discussing saturation, you can open the color picker in Photoshop and this time, instead of decreasing the saturation, you can decrease the brightness by dragging down. You can look at the HSB and the RGB slots and see the brightness numbers decreasing. Also notice that this time in the RGB slots the red numbers decrease, but the blue and green are already at zero and stay there.

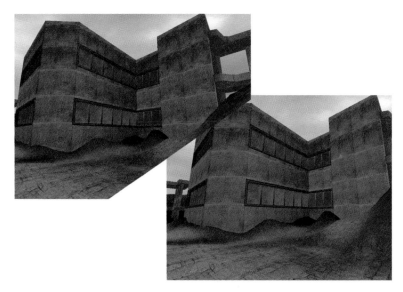

Figure 1-17
Here is an example of a texture that may have looked okay in Photoshop, but needed to be corrected to fit in the scene correctly. This is a subtle example. Notice the patch of exposed stone in the concrete on the building that repeats?

Like most other aspects of color, brightness is affected by other factors. What colors are next to each other? What are the properties of the lights in the world? Another job the texture artist needs to do is to make the textures in the world are consistent. That involves balancing the hues, saturation, and brightness of the color in most cases. Figure 1-17 depicts an example of a texture that may have looked okay in Photoshop, but needed to be corrected to fit the scene. You can see that a great deal of contrast and intensity of color makes tiling the image a greater challenge.

Color Systems—Additive and Subtractive

There are two types of color systems, additive and subtractive. Subtractive color is the physical mixing of paints, or pigments, to create a color. It is called "subtractive" due to the fact that light waves are absorbed (or subtracted from the spectrum) by the paint and only the reflected waves are seen. A red pigment, therefore, is only reflecting red light and absorbing all the others. In the subtractive system you get black by mixing all the colors together— theoretically. It is a challenge to mix pigments that result in a true black or a vibrant color. That is one of the reasons art supply stores have so many choices when it comes to paint. One of our advantages of working in the additive system is that we can get consistent and vibrant results with light. We won't dwell on the subtractive system since we won't be using it.

The additive system is when light is added together (like on a computer screen) to create a color, so naturally we deal with the additive system as computer artists as we are working with projected light. In Figure 1-18 you can see how the additive system works. I simply went into Max and created three spotlights that were pure red, green, and blue and created my own Additive Color Wheel, or a visual representation of how the colors interact. Black is

Figure 1-18
The additive system works by adding lights. Black is the absence of light (the area outside of the spotlights), White is all light (the center area where all three lights overlap each other). The combination of red, green, and blue is the additive system.

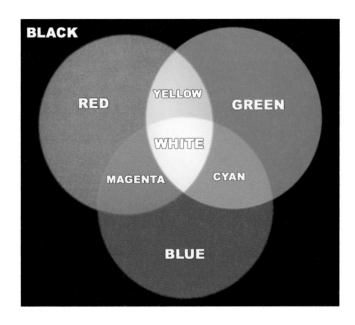

the absence of light (the area outside of the spotlights), White is all light (the center area where all three lights overlap each other)—the combination of red, green, and blue is the additive system. If you look at the Color Picker in Photoshop (Figure 1-19) you will see a vertical rectangle of color graduating from red through the colors and back to red. This allows you to select a Hue and use the Color Picker Palette to change the value and intensity.

Primary Colors

The three primary colors in the additive color system are red, green, and blue (RGB). They are referred to as primary colors because you can mix them and make all the other colors, but you can't create the primary colors by mixing any other color. Many projection televisions use a system where you can see the red, green, and blue lens that project the three colors (RGB) to create the image you see using the additive method.

Secondary Colors

The secondary colors are yellow, magenta, and cyan. When you mix equal amounts of two primary colors together, you get a secondary color. You can see that these colors are located between the primary colors on the color wheel and on the Photoshop Color Picker vertical strip.

Color Emphasis

Color is often used for emphasis. Look at Figure 1-20. All things being equal, the larger shapes dominate, but the small shapes

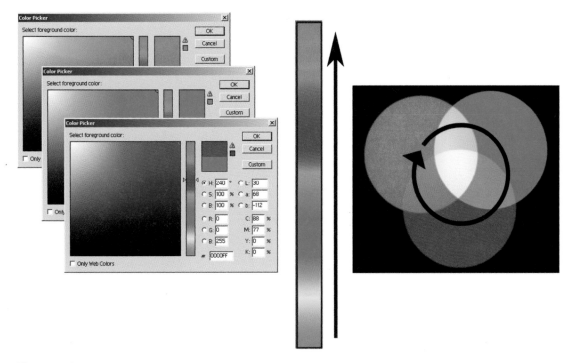

Figure 1-19
The Color Picker in Photoshop has a vertical rectangle of color graduating from red through the colors and back to red. This allows you to select a hue and use the Color Picker Palette to change the value and intensity.

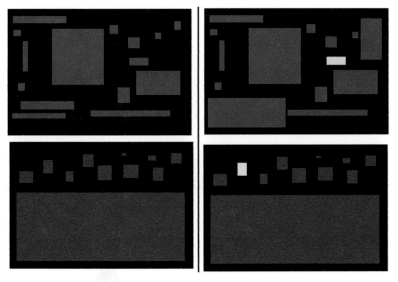

Figure 1-20
The larger shapes dominate, but the small shapes demand your attention once color is added.

demand your attention once color is added. Of course, there are many other forms of emphasis you can use in creating art, but color can be the most powerful—and the most overused. Ever come across a web page that has a busy background and every font, color, and emphasis devised by man splashed across it? There is almost no emphasis as all the elements cancel each other out. Often, less is more.

In another example using a photograph, in Figure 1-21, you can see that in the first black and white photo, your eye would most likely be drawn to the dark opening of the doghouse and you would most likely assume that the subject of this picture is the doghouse. In the second version the colorful flower draws the primary interest, it still competes with the doghouse entrance for attention, but you would probably make the assumption that the focus of this picture was the flower.

In a game scene you can see the use of color drawing the attention of a player to an important item. Look at Figure 1-22. In the first version of the scene you are drawn to the fire and then look around at all the items in the shadows. In the second version the red crate draws your attention and clearly means something. Depending on the world logic of the game you are playing, that could simply mean that you can interact with the object, or it could mean the item is dangerous. That decision brings to our next topic, color expression.

Figure 1-21
Your eye is most likely drawn to the opening of the doghouse in the black and white photo, but add color, and the flower draws the primary interest.

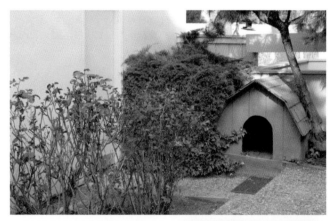

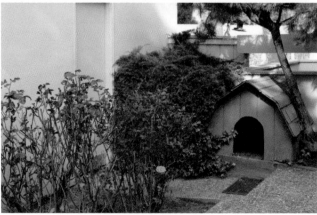

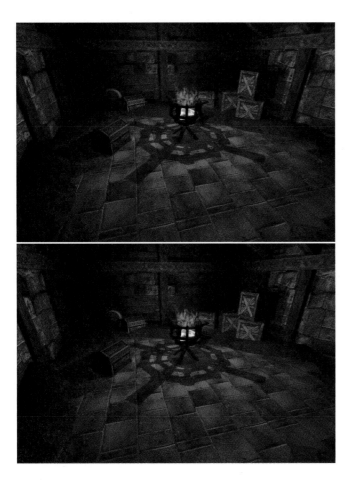

Figure 1-22
In a room full of normal objects, the players' eyes will be drawn to the fire and then equally to the objects. In a room full of normal objects, a red crate draws attention, especially given the fact that there are other normal crates around it.

Color Expression or Warm and Cool Colors

When you start painting textures and choosing colors, you will want to know how they react together in terms of contrast, harmony, and even message. There is a lot of information on this topic and once again, Johannes Itten (the guy who did the color wheel) enters the picture. Itten has provided artists with a great deal of information on how color works and how they work together. He was among the first people to look at color, not just from a scientific point of view, but from an artistic and emotional point of view. He was very interested in how colors made people feel. From his research we get the vocabulary of warm and cool colors.

We all are familiar with this convention as it is mostly based on the natural world. When asked to draw a flame, we reach for the red or orange crayon, ice is blue, the sun yellow. Each warm and cool color has commonly associated feelings for them, both positive and negative. The brighter or more pure the color, the more positive the association. Darker and duller colors tend to have the negative connotations associated with them.

The warm colors are red and yellow, while the cool colors are blue and green. Children will color the sun yellow and ice blue and use the black crayon to scratch out things they don't like. Traffic lights are hot when you should stop or be cautious (red and yellow) but cool when it is okay to go (green). Red and orange are hot and usually associated with fire, lava, coals. How many red and black shirts do you see at the mall? Red and black generally symbolize demonic obsession. Red by itself can mean royalty and strength as well as demonic. Deep red can be erotic. Yellow is a hot color like the sun, a light giver. Yellow is rich like gold as a pure color. A deep yellow (amber) window in the dark of a cold night can mean fire and warmth. But washed out or pale yellow can mean envy or betrayal. Calling a person yellow is an insult, meaning he is a coward. Judas is portrayed as wearing yellow garments in many paintings. During the Inquisition, people who were considered guilty of heresy were made to wear yellow. Moving into green, we think of lush jungles teaming with life. As green washes out, we get a sense of dread and decay (zombie and orc skin). Vibrant green in a certain context can be toxic waste and radioactive slime. Blue in its saturated state is cold like ice, fresh like water and the sky. Darker blues are misery. Purple is mysterious and royal.

Keep in mind that color is context-sensitive. Water is generally blue; would you drink dark green water? But not just any blue will do. In the real world, if we come across water that is a saturated blue that we can't see through, we get suspicious. Was this water dyed? Are there weird chemicals in there? If anything lives in that, then what could it be?! Blood is generally red, but what if an enemy bled green? What if the game you are playing is about an alien race taking over earth and one of your companions bleeds green from an injury during combat? In a fantasy game you might come across coins. Which coin do you take, the bright yellowish metal or gray-green metal? With no previous information on the color of coins in this world, most people would pick the brighter yellow. Look at Figure 1-23. What are some of the assumptions you might make about these three scenes?

Looking at color in this way may make it seem a bit mechanical, but it still takes a talented artist to make the right color choices. You can memorize all the information in the world, but it usually comes down to having a good eye and being able to convey that vision in your work and to your coworkers.

Perspective

We discussed earlier in this chapter that dramatic perspective (Figure 1-24) is usually not used in the creation of a game texture, although sometimes perspective is present and needs to be understood. In addition, understanding perspective is not only a valuable artistic tool to have available, but understanding perspective will help you when you are taking digital reference images and when you are cleaning and straightening those images. We will look at the artistic aspects of perspective now and later on

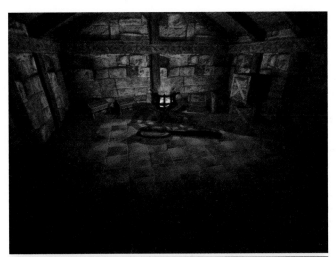

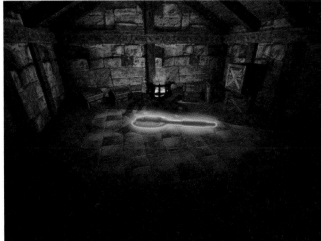

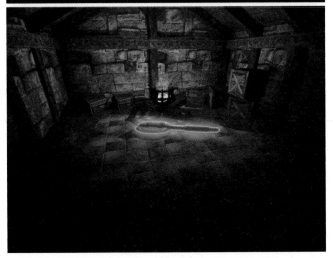

Figure 1-23
These three scenes are the same, except for the ax. What questions and/or assumptions run through your mind looking at each version?

Figure 1-24
While dramatic perspective is used in traditional art, it is not used in a game texture, but there is some notion of perspective so it is best to understand the concept.

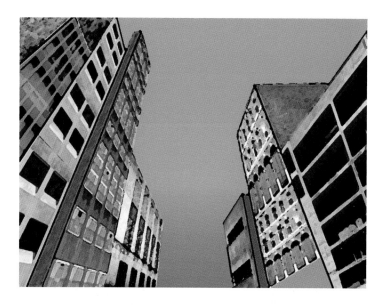

in the chapter on cleaning and storing your assets we will talk about fixing those images.

Quite simply, perspective is the illusion that something far away from us is smaller. This effect can be naturally occurring as in a photo, or a mechanically created illusion in a painting. You can see samples of this in Figure 1-25. In 2D artwork perspective is a technique used to recreate that illusion and give the artwork a three-dimensional depth. Perspective uses overlapping objects, horizon lines, and vanishing points to create a feeling of depth. You can see in Figure 1-26 an image with the major lines of perspective as they converge on one point called the vanishing point. There are several types of perspective used to achieve different effects.

One-Point Perspective

One-point perspective is when all the major lines of an image converge on one point. You can see this effect best illustrated when looking down a set of straight railroad tracks or a long road (see Figure 1-25). The lines of the road and track, although we know they are the same distance apart, seem to meet and join together at some point in the far distance—the vanishing point. In one-point perspective all the lines move away from you (the z-axis) and converge at the vanishing point. Vertical and horizontal or up and down and right and left lines (X and Y) remain straight, as seen in the Figure 1-27.

Two-Point Perspective

One-point perspective works fine if you happen to be looking directly at the front of something or standing in the middle of some railroad tracks, but what if the scene is viewed from the side? Then

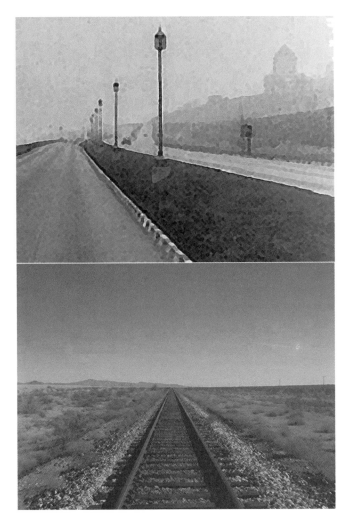

Figure 1-25
Perspective is the illusion that something far away from us is smaller. Are the street lights actually getting smaller in this image? Are the train tracks really getting closer together?

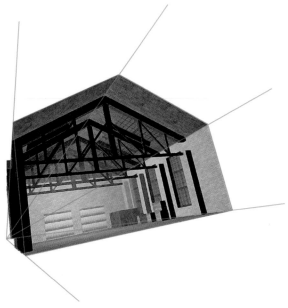

Figure 1-26
In 2D artwork perspective is a technique used to recreate that illusion and give the artwork a three-dimensional depth.

Figure 1-27
In one-point perspective all the lines that move away from the viewer seem to meet at a far point on the horizon. This point is called the vanishing point.

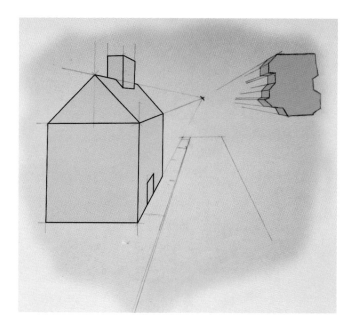

Figure 1-28
Two-point perspective has two vanishing points on the horizon line. All lines, except the vertical, will converge onto one of the two vanishing points.

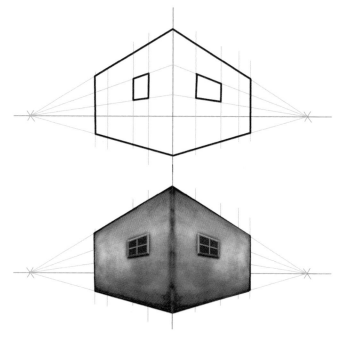

you shift into two-point perspective. Two-point perspective has two vanishing points on the horizon line. All lines, except the vertical, will converge onto one of the two vanishing points. See Figure 1-28.

Three-Point Perspective

Three-point perspective is probably the most challenging of all. In three-point perspective every line will eventually converge on one of

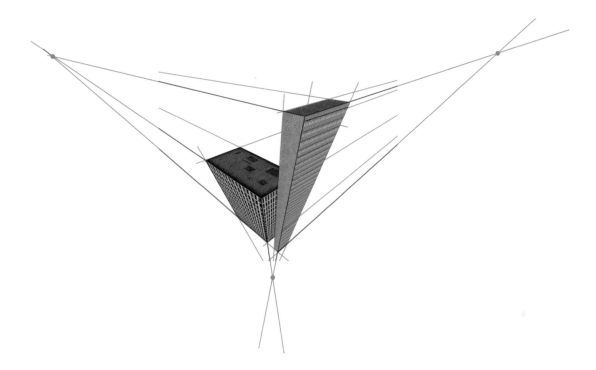

three points. Three-point perspective is the most dramatic of all and can often be seen in comic books when the hero is flying over buildings or whooping butt in the alley below as the buildings tower above. Figure 1-29 shows some three-point perspective.

Perspective, from the texture artist's point of view while photographing surfaces for game art, can be the enemy. We will look at that in a coming chapter when we talk about collecting and cleaning your images. From the art education point of view, knowing what perspective is and what it looks like is enough.

Figure 1-29
In three-point perspective every line will eventually converge on one of three vanishing points.

Quick Studies of the World Around You

The following pages are some quick studies I did of random objects. I tried to work through each of them as a game artist might to give you some quick and general examples of various how a game artist might break them down. We will do this type of exercise in more depth throughout the book, but in the tutorial portions of the book those breakouts will be more specific and focused to the goal at hand. This is a general look and introduction to the thought process of recreating surfaces and materials in a digital environment. I covered all that was introduced in this chapter: shape and form, light and shadow, texture, color, as well as considering other aspects of the object or material. I didn't touch on perspective in these exercises because I wanted to limit the exercise to recreating 2D surfaces (textures), and perspective is not as critical as the other concepts in this chapter. In the following pages, Figures 1-30 to 1-35 will each have a caption that discusses the particulars of each study.

Figure 1-30

The upper left-hand image is a digital photo of some simple concrete stairs. You may have an art lead email you an image like this and tell you she wants a texture based on these stairs. Fortunately, this is a rather simple form; not a lot of color or detail to distract us. Look at the simple recreation of the stairs to the right showing the basic light and shadow patterns on the stairs. The lower left image shows the 2D texture created in Photoshop to be applied to a 3D model of the stairs. If you look at the yellow stripe on the stairs and compare it to the stripe on the texture, you can see the highlights painted in the texture where the edge of the step is and the shadow under the lip of the edge. If you were able to examine the original digital image of the stairs closely, you would see an almost infinite amount of detail. Part of the texture artist's job is to know when to draw the line. Here I didn't include every scuff and mark from the original stair image because it wouldn't work. You will learn in coming chapters that such details usually stand out and draw attention to the repeating pattern of a texture, or in the case of fabrics and fine meshes can create noise or static in the texture. I created this texture pretty quickly; given more time, I would experiment with the chips and wear on the edge of the steps to add more character.

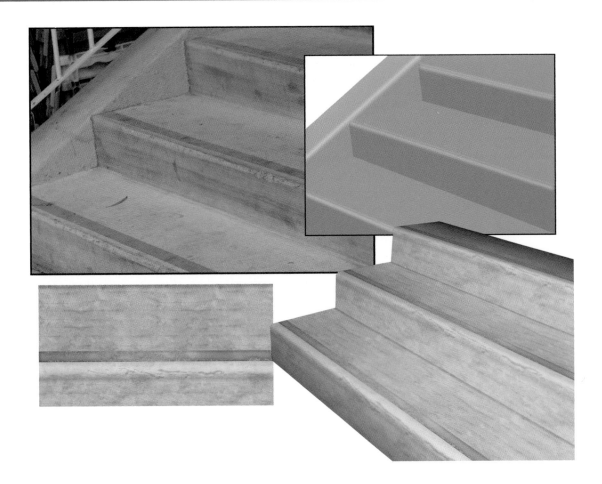

Figure 1-31

This is a straight-on photo of an interior plaster wall. I included this obviously unexciting image to demonstrate that even in such a simple surface there can be complex highlight and shadow going on. Look at the color swatches of the highlight, shadow, and mid-tone. Notice that the colors are not simple black, white, and gray. The highlight is not pure white or light gray, but a very pale green. Look at the close-up of the image. You can clearly see the consistent behavior of light as it highlights the upper ridges of the plaster and shadow falls from the lower edges. Once you start studying such seemingly commonplace things, like a wall you may walk by a hundred times a day, you will start to notice, understand, and remember how various lights, materials, and other factors affect a surface. Do you convey that simple raised pattern in the texture, using geometry, or a shader? Of course, that depends on many factors, and hopefully by the end of this book you will know what questions to ask to determine the answers.

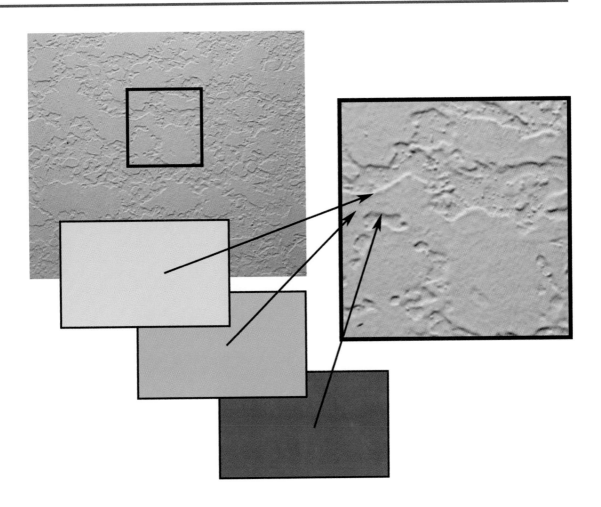

Figure 1-32
This image simply shows the world that I need to wash my car. Seriously, look at the various parts of complex objects and you will see a variety of surface behaviors. Notice how the paint is highly reflective and mirrors the world around the car. The metal is not flat like a mirror, so notice the distortion of the reflected image. The windows, while reflecting the surrounding world as well, are translucent so you can also see what's behind the window and on the other side of the car. The window also has a patina of dirt and spots on it. If you needed to recreate this as realistically as possible, you would have to take all those aspects into consideration and determine the best way to achieve the effect. Look at the close-up of the rim. You can see that the highlights are not mirror-like in their accuracy, but rather they are a diffuse notion of highlight. Looks simple to paint, but wheels rotate and will instantly look bad if not painted properly. Using a real-time process for highlights eliminates this problem. While the tires are flat black and reveal only a faint notion of highlight, depending on the detail level, you may be dealing with complex mapping and shader effects here, too. While all of this seems obvious, taking the time to examine the object you are recreating and understanding what you are seeing and how to verbalize it helps when turning the object into game art. If you were to make materials or textures for this vehicle, you would need to know many things about the technology and how the car will be used in the game. Can we have real-time environmental reflections? Can we fake them using a Shader? Do we have to carefully paint in a vague notion of metallic highlights that work in all situations the car may be in? And the windows. Can we do a translucent/reflective surface with an alpha channel for dirt? If the car is used in a driving game where the vehicle is the focus of the game and the player gets to interact up close and personal with the car, then I am sure a lot of attention will be given to these questions. But if this car is a static prop, sitting on a street that the player blazes past, then over-the-top effects may only be a waste of development time and computer resources.

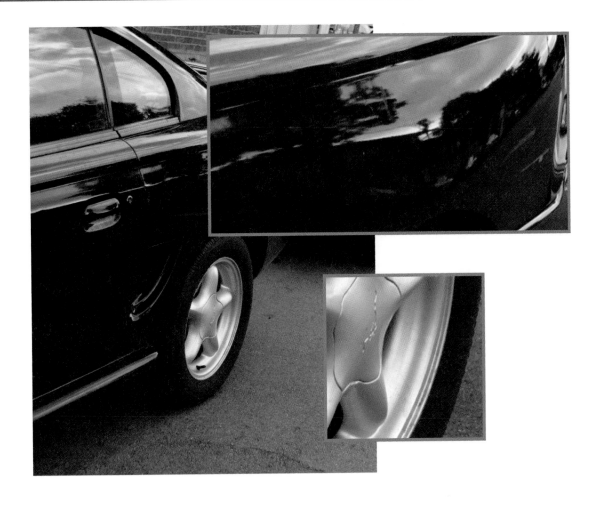

Figure 1-33

This sewer intrigued me; a simple shape of a common item that many may overlook as not worthy of serious attention. Some may have the attitude that it is only a sewer grate, so make it and move on. But a shiny new sewer grate with clean edges would stand out in a grungy urban setting. Look at this sewer grate. It is made of iron and looks solid and heavy. It was probably laid down decades ago and has had thousands of cars drive over it, people walk over it, millions of gallons of rain water pour through it. On the image at the upper left you can look at the iron and see how it is rusted, but so well worn that the rust is polished off in most places. Dirt has built up in the cracks between the grate, the rim, and the concrete. Even little plants have managed to grow. Look at the close-up at the upper right and you can see just how beat up this iron is and how discolored it has become. At the lower left I desaturated and cleaned up a portion of the image to see just how the light and shadow are hitting it and to get a feel for the quality of the surface. In this image you can more clearly see the roughness of the cement and the metal, and while the circular grate looks round from a distance, up close there are no straight edges and smooth curves. All this detail can't be depicted 100% in a game texture, but knowing it's there and understanding what you are seeing will allow you to convey a richer version of the grate as you will learn to focus on those details that add realism and character. On the lower right is a texture I did, and you can see that I was able to quickly achieve a mottled and grungy look for the metal and the edges. There are a few places at the top where I started the process of eating away at the concrete and the metal a bit.

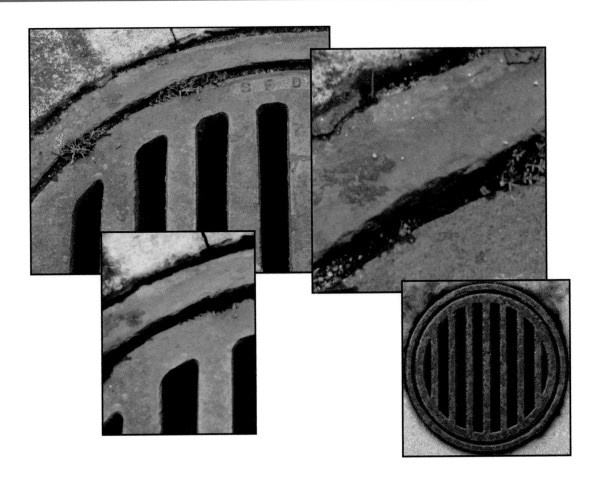

Figure 1-34

This image is similar to the sewer in approach. Here I wanted to point out how a simple shape can be turned into an ornate hinge with little effort. The top image is the original digital photo of the hinge. I drew the shape of the hinge in Photoshop. You may notice that I drew the screws separately. This is because you need the shapes separately to work with them in Photoshop; you will see why later in the book. In Photoshop I applied and adjusted the Layer Effects and then colored the hinge close to the overall color of the original. After that it was a matter of applying the right filters and doing some hand work to get the edges looking right. We will be doing this type of work throughout the book. And I will remind you from time to time that while the best approach may be to use photo source, or any one of the other methods available, the focus of this book is to help you develop a set of Photoshop skills that will allow you to not depend on any one method. These skills will improve your abilities when working in any of the other methods.

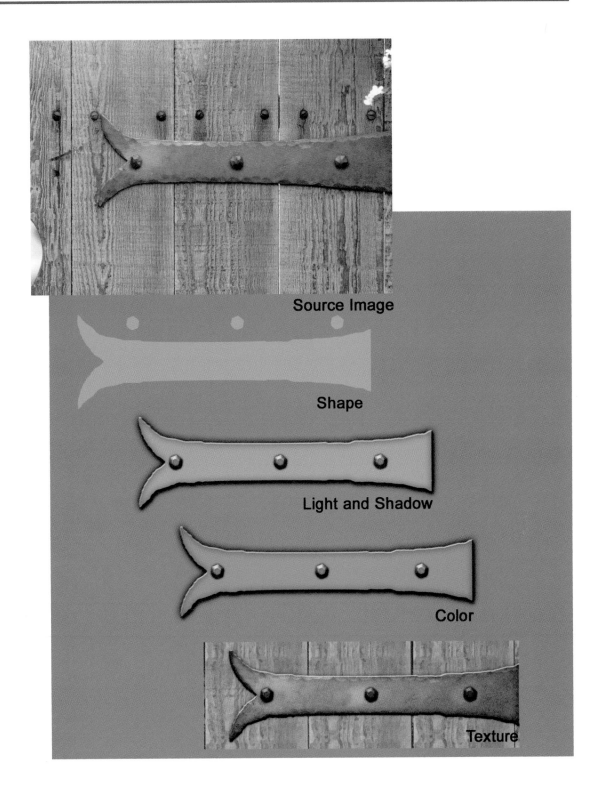

Source Image

Shape

Light and Shadow

Color

Texture

Figure 1-35
This light switch is a common object you may need to create. Instead of taking the time to clean up and manipulate a photo, you can just make one quicker from scratch. The switch is composed of simple shapes with the layer effects applied. The wall behind the switch was a quick series of filters run to add a base for this exercise.

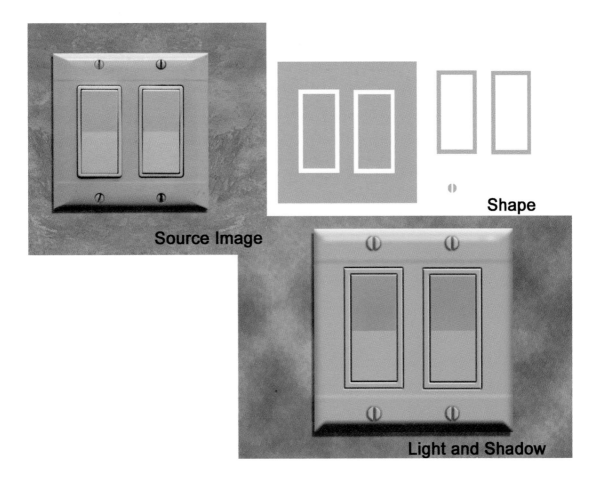

Source Image

Shape

Light and Shadow

Conclusion

This chapter was an overview of the most basic, but critical, aspects of traditional art. Understanding the concepts in this chapter, and further exploring them on your own, will make you a much better texture artist. We are now ready to get more technical and look at the mechanical issues of creating game textures.

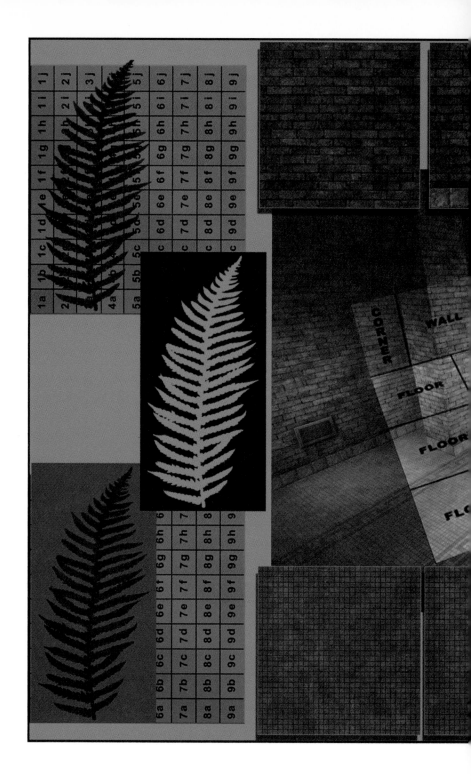

Chapter 2

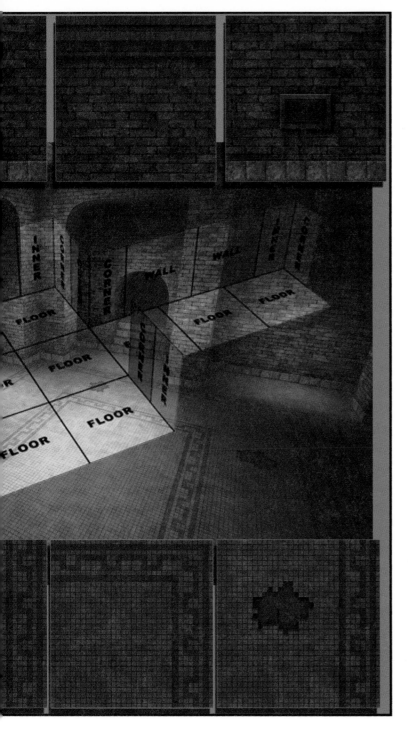

Introduction

Now it's time to talk technology, but very briefly. You will eventually need to learn a good deal about the technical side of computer art to make the various decisions technology will present to you, but a brief orientation of technology is all you will need to start painting textures. I could have gotten away without including this chapter at all and instead launched directly into painting textures, but I believe that orienting you to this small bit of information is critical to your long-term success as a texture artist. Learning to button-push from a tutorial may get you good results, but it won't give you the tools to eventually attack your own unique problems when asked to create a texture that will be used in a certain context—genre, platform, etc. Understanding why textures are constructed the way they are, and why there are certain limits and restrictions placed on the game artist, will help you avoid a lot of wasted time. Later, as you are exposed to more information, complexity, and unique development situations, you will more easily assimilate that information and be able to use it more creatively.

A Brief Orientation to Computer Graphic Technology

"Everything should be made as simple as possible, but not simpler."

Albert Einstein
1879–1955

While creating art on a computer can be limiting, frustrating, and confusing for many people, once you understand the limits placed on you and learn to work within them, you are much more likely to create impressive work. One of the first things you will run into is file formats. There are many graphic file formats, and each has many options and features. Each is designed for different purposes, and their complexity and range of options reflect that. We will look not at the formats themselves so much as the options and features most used by the texture artist. I find that starting with the gross oversimplification that I am just dealing with colored dots somehow helps me keep my mind wrapped around concepts and techniques that can get very complex in their implementation. Keep in mind that at the core, as a game artist you are always working with pixels—colored dots—and a file format is simply the way in which those pixels are stored, even in the case of the PSD file format, which we will look at later. The PSD, or Photoshop Document, saves a great deal of information, but mainly it stores information about pixels and how they interact with each other. I am not trying to oversimplify a very complex subject and application such as Photoshop, but I am trying to tell you that you should not be intimidated by all of the complexity. You can start very simply and assimilate, rather than be overwhelmed all at once.
Just remember: there is always more to learn, there is always a better, faster way to do something, and you should be having fun. Photoshop, with all of its powerful tools and options, is simply giving you an almost unlimited number of ways to adjust the hue, saturation, brightness, and transparency of pixels in an image to achieve many different results. One concept, which we will look at in more detail in Chapter 4, is layer blending modes. In addition to being able to layer images on top of each other in Photoshop, you can control how the pixels in each layer blend with each other. Blending modes are very useful and often used in building textures. Quite simply, when you choose a blending mode you are changing the way in which a pixel reacts with the pixels below it, thus affecting its hue, saturation, brightness, and/or transparency. The end result on screen is one pixel of a specific hue, saturation, and brightness.

We will look at image size, too. This is pretty straightforward, as we will talk about height and width, but knowing how big to make your images involves a bit of knowledge about the technology used, the method in which the world is being built, and how the texture will be used in the world. A texture that is huge, but on a small sign the player will never go near, is a waste of texture memory. Likewise, a texture that covers 80% of the walls of your level, which the player will spend most of his time running past, probably warrants a much larger image.

And we will talk about the grid. The grid is a bit of a throwback to games that required ridged geometry placement for various technical reasons. Nowadays, in most cases, we can literally build levels any way we like with no regard to right angles and grids, but if we do that we run into problems. The grid is still very important for many reasons and makes building easier. Laying out textures on a grid makes them fit perfectly together, not just one texture tiling with itself, but a set of textures that will fit together when combined in the game world. When you are using a set of many textures you built on the grid, in a game world built on the same grid, things will match up perfectly and look solid. When the textures and world elements are both built on the same grid, we can also more easily keep track of relative proportions of objects in the world as we work.

We will look at UV mapping. While we won't be doing any UV mapping in the book, it makes texture creation a little easier, and the process will make more sense, if you understand how your textures will be applied to the surfaces of the 3D game world. You will see how the textures you create in this book are applied to the 3D scenes they are decorating.

Finally, a brief introduction to shaders comes at the end of this chapter. Shaders allow a level of realism in games that is stunning and getting better all the time. Very simply, a shader is a mini-program that processes graphic effects in real time. Shaders are used for image effects like hair, fire, shadows, water, reflections, and so on, While shaders play a huge role in game development, you still need to know basic texture creation to get the best results. Later in the book we actually build the assets for a shader.

Even though this book is focused on creating game textures, it is important to introduce some technical concepts. But looking at every conceivable graphic file format or aspect of technology would be counterproductive, so I will keep it brief.

Chapter Overview

- Common features of graphic file formats
- The power of two and the grid
- UV mapping
- Shader technology for artists

Common Features of Graphic File Formats

I will discuss graphic formats from a functional point of view rather than list every graphic file format available. Knowing the most common options typically available and used by the game artist is really what you need to know.

Vector and Bitmapped Files

There are basically two types of graphic files: vector and bitmapped. A bitmapped file is the native format for the Windows environment and contains pixels (or colored dots). When you zoom into a bitmapped image, you can see the pixels. While bitmapped is a type of image, there are many formats of the bitmapped image. Game developers deal almost exclusively with bitmapped images and the options associated with them, so they will naturally be our focus.

Source and Output Files, Distinctions

There is a distinction between the format of the output file (game-ready art) and the format of the original (source) file. The source file is what the game artists creates in Photoshop using large image sizes and many image options. They will then output a copy of that image and resize, convert, and optimize it. In actual production you will almost certainly work in Photoshop's proprietary file format (PSD) as the source file; these files get very large. Your source image will always be larger and of higher detail than the output file for reasons discussed earlier in the book. The PSD file format is very flexible and saves a large amount of information. The output file, the game-ready art, is much smaller.

This book is focused on the creation of the flexible source file in the PSD format. When the time comes to output any of these images for use as a texture in a game, you will determine the size, format, and other details about the final image. The image you see in a game may only be 256 by 256 pixels (you can often see the pixels if you look) but is most certainly a smaller and more optimized copy of the original PSD file. While the smaller, compressed game image may be 40k in file size, the original PSD file may easily be 40 Megabytes or larger. Photoshop saves lots of other data specific to the PSD format and useful in image creation such as layers, levels, alpha channels, adjustment layers, layer effects, text layers, layer sets—and a great deal more, even audio files and attached notes. Don't let all this confuse you; you will be introduced to the PSD file later.

Warning: One mistake many new artists make is to work in Photoshop on a source image, forget they are editing the source, and then resize and convert the original and save it. Once you do that and close the file, you can't go back. When you are later asked to alter that image, you only have the small, low-detail version to work with. You will see exactly what I am talking about in this chapter with the introduction of layers.

Choosing a File Format

There are four criteria I know of for choosing which file format you will output:

- **What looks best.** This is the most important consideration from the artist's point of view but often changes as a result of the other equally important criteria.
- **What the development technology requires.** Quite simply, if you don't generate assets to the specifications the game engine requires, it may not run at all.
- **What the target user system requires/will support.** Making a game that will only run on the most powerful computer that money can buy will severely limit your audience. If you are id Software (the creators of DOOM, Quake, etc.—I don't have to tell you that, do I?), you can pull this off as people will actually upgrade their systems to play your game. I literally just spent $1,600 building a new computer so I could play a $50 game. But that is of course the exception and not the rule. Most developers must determine what computers their audience will most likely be using when their game is released. Console developers know almost exactly what they are developing for in terms of hardware configuration, while PC developers have to make complex decisions that always leave someone unhappy. Due to the vast variations in power, configuration, and compatibility of all the PCs in the world, it often requires developing significant amounts of technology and additional assets to deal with these differences by offering the user many configuration options. Or you develop to the least common denominator, knowing that you are not creating the best game you can because you are not developing for the cutting-edge hardware. But game play is king, so often a low-tech game will break out on the sales charts.
- **What your boss tells you to use.** I am not trying to be flip with this fourth one. There may be circumstances when a superior tells you what format an asset needs to be, and usually the reason is logical. You can ask why or simply obey, but I don't advise ignoring the instructions.

Format Options

Here are some of the most commonly used and critical features of graphic formats game artists use most. As you work on different teams using different development technologies, you will learn about the numerous file formats available and the options specific to each format. But the core functionality of these files will be fundamentally the same. So understanding the basic information presented here will make the adoption of those varying formats and their options much easier.

Compression

Compression is simply making a file smaller in size. It's easier said than done for a programmer. Creating compression routines that don't ruin visual quality is of course a complex programming task, but as artists we deal with compression primarily on a visual basis, judging whether or not we like the quality of the compressed image. We will make sure our file meets the technical requirements and

Figure 2-1
Here are some examples of
what compression can do to
an image. On the **upper left**
is the original uncompressed
image, in the **middle** is a
moderately compressed
image, and on the **right** is a
highly compressed image.
Below are close-ups of the
three images. Notice how the
middle image appears to
have a pattern of squares
over it. This is due to the
compression scheme. The
image on the right has had
many colors stripped out so
the image is very small, but
lacking many colors looks
blotchy. You need to know
how close the player will get
to this image to determine
how small and compressed
you can make it.

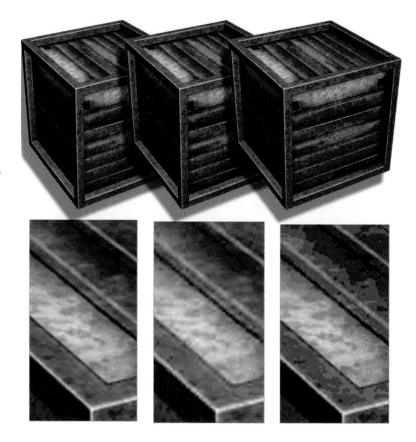

then press "Save As" and we are done. Most game artists will learn
more about the various compression schemes and their options so
they can create the smallest file size with maximum image quality.

Some image formats use absolutely no compression and preserve
the image in its original state and lose no data. These are called
"lossless," whereas a "lossy" format will allow compression that
strips out and reorganizes data in various ways and results in data
loss for a smaller file size at the cost of visual quality to varying
degrees. Compression is almost exclusively used on the output file
and not used on the source asset since it degrades quality. In Figure
2-1 you can see some examples of what image compression can do
to an image.

Alpha Channels

Alpha channels are simply black and white or grayscale images.
These images can be used in different ways, but typically they
are used for transparency or masking. In other words, an alpha
channel can make a portion of an image completely transparent or
(depending on the quality of the alpha channel) semi-transparent. In
Figure 2-2 you can see a very common use for the alpha channel—

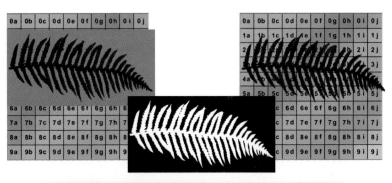

Figure 2-2
An alpha channel is typically used to make parts of an image transparent. Here you can see how a few polygons and one image can make these ferns look complex and organic due to the fact that we can make parts of this image transparent.

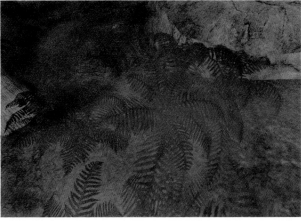

foliage. The use of the alpha channel extends to other objects as well, objects that have details that would be better created using the alpha channel method rather than modeling the detail. Wire fences, tree branches, and other real-world objects are often created using alpha channels and so are effects like muzzle blasts and scorch marks. Since alpha can give a semi-transparent property to a model, they have been used on ghosts, water, fire, and other ethereal effects. Look at the ferns in the previous example. The use of alpha channels allows for much more complex and realistic shapes than can be efficiently created in 3D in some cases. If you modeled each fern in 3D, there would need to be so many polygons as to be impractical, the other option being terribly "geometric"-looking ferns if modeled using a low number of polygons.

When "Saving As" or "Exporting" an image from Photoshop, you need to make sure the format you are saving to supports alpha channels, or that information may be lost. Typically, alpha channels are preserved in many formats, but not all formats. Keep in mind the distinction between exporting to a format, which typically means you are creating another version of that file, and saving a file. As mentioned previously, if you resize and degrade your source asset and save the file, you will lose the ability to easily alter and re-export the asset. Usually the "Save As" or "Exporting" function will warn you about the potential for loss, or tell you the options available to you in that format. In Figure 2-3 you can see on the

Figure 2-3
Typically, "Saving As" or "Exporting" in Photoshop will warn you about information that may be lost such as this file being saved as a JPEG. The warning is that layers and alpha channels will not be preserved.

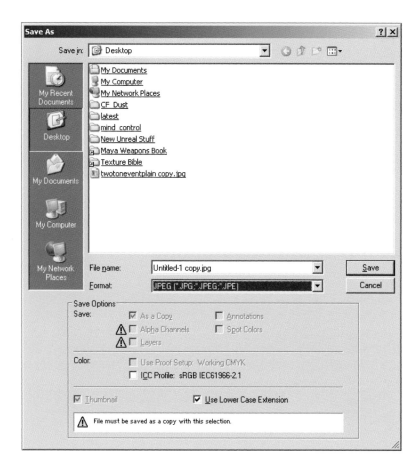

"Save As" window that this file being saved as a JPG is warning the user that layers and alpha channels will not be preserved.

Sometimes the alpha channel or mask is part of the file format, and sometimes it is a separate image. In low-quality transparency schemes, it is sometimes only a certain color in the image itself that determines what part of the image is see-through, and there is no separate mask or alpha channel. You can see examples of these types of alpha in the very next section—DDS Format and DXTC.

DDS Format and DXTC (Output Format)

This is a common file format game developers output, so I want to specifically mention it. DDS stands for *Microsoft DirectDraw® Surface* file format. This format stores textures as well as a lot of other information that is used in-game for various reasons that are both technical and visual in nature. While DDS is the file extension, the compression scheme is referred to as *Direct X Texture Compression* (DXTC). Several tools allow you to save in the DDS format using DXTC. Douglas H. Rogers, in the Developer Relations group at NVIDIA, develops Texture Tools that support DXTC and stores textures in the DDS format. The developer pages on the NVIDIA web site contain many useful texture manipulation tools and a mountain of information for programmers and content creators.

NVIDIA's developer web site
http://developer.nvidia.com/

Texture tools
http://developer.nvidia.com/object/nv_texture_tools.html

Figure 2-4 shows the NVIDIA DDS tools interface. This is an easy–to-install plug-in that allows the exporting of the DDS file format from Photoshop. After you select "Save As" in Photoshop and select the DDS format, the NVIDIA tool activates. On the Texture Tool interface you will see a lot of options available for the output format of the image and tools to view the choices you make. There are options for compression, MIP map filtering, sharpening, fading, normal map creation, and more. We will only discuss the compression options here because the other options are out of the scope of this book. Suffice it to say, you have a lot of control with this tool. Among the

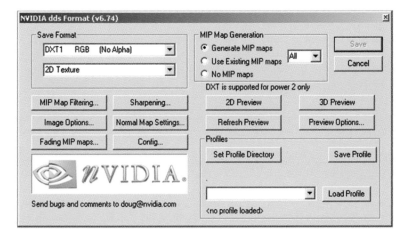

Figure 2-4
This is the NVIDIA DDS tools interface, an easy-to-install (and very useful) plug-in that allows the exporting of the DDS file format from Photoshop. After you select Save As in Photoshop, there are many options and tools to view various versions of the file before committing to the version of the file you want to export.

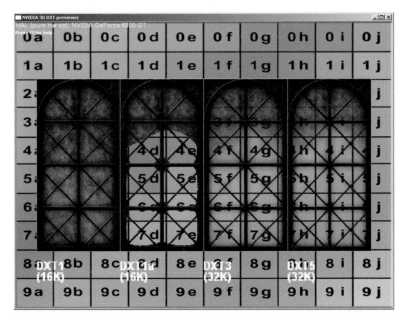

various options, the two you will be most concerned with are compression and the alpha channel. You can decide to compress an image a great deal (8:1) if you can get away with it visually, or use no compression if you want the highest possible quality. There is also a 3D preview window so you can see various versions of the texture before you save the image to disk. You can zoom, rotate, and move the image in the window, and you can even assign a background color or background image to the preview window. By choosing the background you can see your textures in context. It only makes sense that if you are developing a texture with an alpha channel, the bars of a cage for example, that sits in front of another texture, maybe a dark stucco wall or bright canvas tent, it helps to see the two textures together. This makes workflow much faster as you can see what you are getting before you commit to exporting the file, checking the results, exporting again, and guessing each time as to whether you made the proper adjustments to the image.

The DXT compression scheme can reduce texture size eightfold (fourfold if there is an alpha channel). In my experience they still look really good, especially considering the reduction in file size. You must examine both the visual and technical results of any file you output, and that's where the NVIDIA tools really come in handy. In general, the DDS format allows for the highest quality and most efficient output of assets and gives you the tools to make that balancing act much easier. There are many options, but most likely you will use four main compression options: DXT1 (w/no alpha), DXT1 (w/alpha), DXT3, and DXT5 (both with alpha).

DXT1 with no transparency is the most compressed of the choices and results in the smallest file size.

DXT1 with alpha transparency offers a simple version of alpha with an on/off alpha transparency scheme (not supported by some game engines). In this scheme the pixel is either completely transparent or completely opaque and results in jagged edges in the image. Consequently, this compression scheme has limited uses.

DXT3 and DXT5 have more refined alpha channels, and both result in a larger file size. You can see in the previous figure of the DDS Viewer that the file size and compression scheme used are displayed below the image. These image sizes are larger due to the fact that this format saves the alpha channel as a separate image inside itself. In case there is any confusion, you are effectively doubling your image file size because of the alpha but not the pixel dimensions of the image. Both these schemes result in the same file size. Then why the two choices? While each has the same color compression scheme, they have different compression schemes for the alpha channel. They will each generate good or bad results depending on the texture. You should visually compare how the alpha looks in each format to choose the right one, but when given the choice it is safe to say that you will be using DXT5 the most. The tool makes this visual comparison very easy. The example in Figure 2-5 shows a window with fine granularity in the alpha channel so it requires DXT3 or DXT5. You can see that the less refined alpha

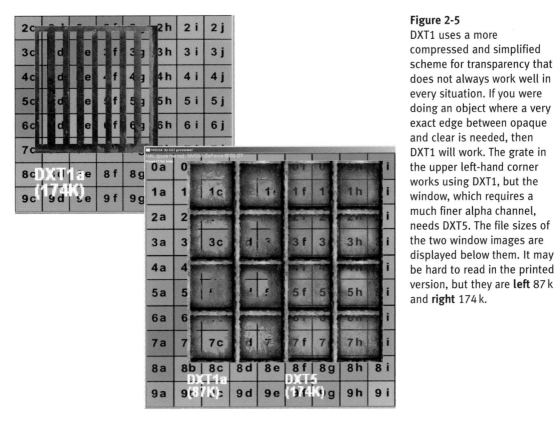

Figure 2-5
DXT1 uses a more compressed and simplified scheme for transparency that does not always work well in every situation. If you were doing an object where a very exact edge between opaque and clear is needed, then DXT1 will work. The grate in the upper left-hand corner works using DXT1, but the window, which requires a much finer alpha channel, needs DXT5. The file sizes of the two window images are displayed below them. It may be hard to read in the printed version, but they are **left** 87 k and **right** 174 k.

scheme of DXT1 simply will not work on the window. But if you were doing a texture, such as a grate or vent, where a very exact edge between opaque and clear exists, then DXT1 will do the trick. These formats are still "lossy" compression schemes, meaning some data are lost from the original image.

In general, when using the NVIDIA texture tools, you should always try to compress your textures as much as possible. Use the tool and compare the various images side by side. You will find that DXT1 compression is very good for a lot of images and can save a ton of your texture memory budget, thus allowing you to possibly use more textures in the game. Of course, if you need an alpha channel, use DXT5 or DXT3.

Explore the options in the texture tools if you like; you will find a lot of them. Don't let yourself get overwhelmed though. You know what you need for now and 80% of what you will most likely need to know in the near future.

PSD Format (Production Format)

PSD, as mentioned earlier, is the native file format for Photoshop and usually the production format of choice for game developers. This format's file size can get quite large as it retains a lot of information in a very flexible way so the artist can easily go back and tweak, or even drastically change, the art and re-output a new file quickly. One of the features of the PSD format that makes it so large and flexible a format is layers. We will look at layers in more detail in a coming chapter (as well as many of the other numerous tools and features available in Photoshop) and will also use Photoshop layers quite extensively throughout the book. Here is a quick introduction to the concept.

Layers is one of the first options you will come across in Photoshop. This is an option increasingly available in other formats used by high-end 2D paint programs. Storing an image in layers means you can effectively store many images on top of each other and control how each layer affects the one under it. Imagine one image being a megabyte in size and storing a stack of those images on top of each other. That is one reason that this file size can get so large. In Figure 2-6 you can see the Layers Window as it appears in Photoshop. This is the window that lets you move and manipulate layers and is not the actual image. The stack of layers on the right is an illustration of the concept of layers and doesn't actually appear in Photoshop that way. What you see in the Photoshop image window, the actual

Figure 2-6
At the **upper left** is the Layers Window as it appears in Photoshop. This tool allows you to move and manipulate layers. The stack of layers on the **right** is an illustration of the concept of layers and doesn't actually appear in Photoshop that way.

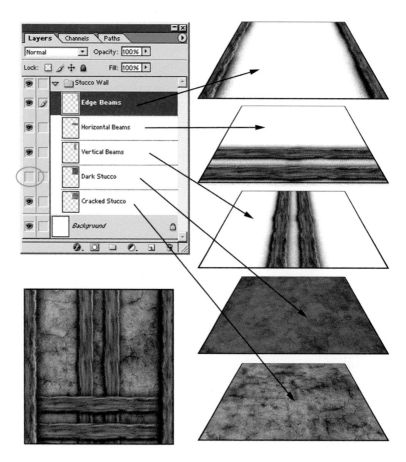

image you are editing, is what the final image will look like whether it is in layers or flattened.

Flattened means what it sounds like. When all the layers are reduced to one layer, the image becomes one layer—one image. When this happens (if you save your file and can't undo the Flatten operation), you lose all flexibility. Notice that in the Layer Window the layer named "Dark Stucco" is turned off (there is no eye icon next to it like the others) so this layer, while actually in the file, is not visible and not part of the final texture as a result. Also notice that the layer "Horizontal beams" is on top of the layer "Vertical beams" and these beams have that relationship in the final texture. I output the final texture and you can see it at the lower left of the figure. Layers are critical in texture creation because they allow you to build textures in an easy and effective way and to keep the layers separate so the texture can be adjusted and modified and quickly output again. In Figure 2-7 you can see several examples of how layers are used in Photoshop. Imagine if this layer was flattened and I wanted to remove an element that is part of the final image such

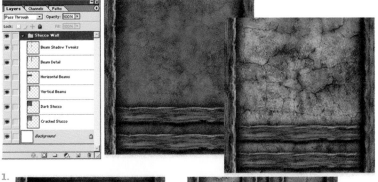

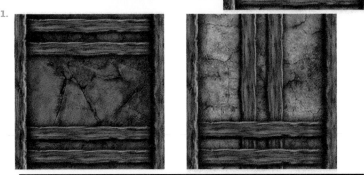

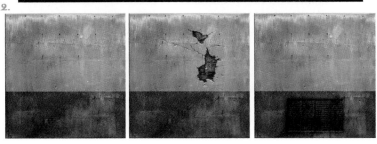

Figure 2-7
Here you can see two examples of how various textures were built up using layers in one file and, furthermore, how layer control allows for the modification and quick output of a texture.

as the horizontal or vertical beams, or the cracks. It would be tough: I would essentially have to rebuild the texture instead of clicking a layer on and off.

The Power of Two and The Grid

Now we will speak a bit about working with 2D images that are meant to be used in a 3D space, like a game world. Most game art books talk a lot about image resolution, and that is an important topic, but for now all you need to know is that you are restricted in most games to a certain image size. When you create a 2D image for a game, you will always have parameters, restrictions, and rules that you must follow, and they can range in number from a few to many. Where you are working, what technology you are using, and even what type of game you are making all contribute to determining those specific parameters and guidelines. The most basic and general requirement for game art is that you must make your textures a power of two in size, which means that the images must be a specific number of pixels in height and width. These sizes are typically:

- 16×16
- 32×32
- 64×64
- 128×128
- 256×256
- 512×512
- 1024×1024
- Next-generation games now under development are commonly using 2048×2048 maps.

Note that a 512×512 image is four times as large as a 256×256 image, just as a 256×256 image is four times larger than a 128×128 image. Sometimes the fact that the power of two numbers are twice as big as the previous number throws some people off. The fact that $256 \times 2 = 512$ makes it seem logical on the surface. But look at Figure 2-8 for a visual representation of this concept. Understanding that concept, you can see that a 512×512 has four times the pixels of a 256×256 image. Not long ago a 512×512 image was considered a large texture. For the next-generation games (2 to 3 years out), we are already using 1024×1024 images as a standard size and frequently go up to 2048×2048. Add to that hardware and software advances and the jump in visual quality of a game is simply incredible. Maybe more so to those of us who have watched game technology creep along at first, explode, and then keep growing exponentially. The advances are across the board and most contribute directly to the visual quality of a game: rag doll physics, more complex and refined animation tools, improved AI, more complex yet easier to use particle systems—the list is very long.

Back to the power of two and the first question that most people ask—"Why must we make our textures a power of two?" The

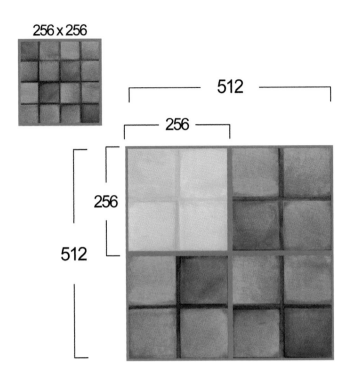

256 x 256

512

256

256

512

Figure 2-8
A 512 × 512 image is four times as large as a 256 × 256 image, not twice as large. The fact that the number 512 is twice as big as 256 sometimes throws people off. I used an image of some tiles so you can see the relationship. The 256 image overlaid takes up one fourth of the area of the 512 image.

simplified answer is that most computer game engines and 3D cards require a texture to fit certain criteria because they can process and display them faster. Most game engines do not restrict texture size to a perfect square. Rectangular sizes like 256 × 512 and 128 × 1024 are usually acceptable. I started the above list at 16 × 16, but most game engines today don't even use textures smaller than 32 × 32, and that's usually for particles and small decals. Plugging in an asset with the wrong parameters can cause an error message, the asset will be ignored, and some engines will even crash. Some engines/game tools might even take the asset and alter it so it will work: changing size, format, color depth, etc.

The "power of two" limit actually doesn't exist in the code of many 3D graphics engines but is still commonly imposed on game developers for various reasons. I believe that you can already use non-power of two textures in certain engines, but I would still stick to the grid for most of the work unless I hit the uncommon situation where I need to use a non-power of two texture. Maybe I am biased and simply used to working on the grid, but I believe that it makes building a game easier for everyone involved from the texture artist to the level designer. That takes us to the next point about the grid. Aside from technical reasons to use the power of two and a grid, there are productivity issues.

So your images need to be certain pixel dimensions for technical reasons (they won't work in most game engines if they aren't exact at present), but it also helps in production to work with these standard sizes. Most major game-world editors (the tool you use to build the game world) use a grid system based on the same power of two dimensions. If you lay out a hall with a floor that is 256 units wide in the world and place a 256-pixel image on that floor, you are going to get a perfect fit. You can also make the texture 512 and scale the UV mapping down by exactly 50%, and once again you will get a perfect fit. You can use an image of a tile that is only 128 pixels and UV that across the floor in a repeating pattern and get a perfect fit, too. This makes everyone's life easier because you are not guessing, eyeballing, and trying to calculate how to make various-sized images fit in odd-sized spaces.

When working in Photoshop, you can use the grid tool to lay a grid over your workspace to subdivide a power of two texture into smaller power of two units. We will talk about how to do that later on in the book, but for now just know that Photoshop allows for the placing of grids and guidelines over your image that are not part of the art, but are tools that help you keep things straight. For a game developer this functionality is very useful, you just have to remember to set your grid spaces to the power of two. In the commonly used 3D packages like Max and Maya, you can also set up a custom grid to these dimensions. The result is that the models, textures, and world space are all built on a standard grid, giving the developer consistent units and sizes. A simple example would be the creation of an object for a game decoration, say a doorway arch. If the texture artist creates a texture for the arch that is 512×1024 and the modeler makes the model of the arch on a grid and creates the arch model 512×1024, the image will fit perfectly over it. I left out the third dimension of depth in the model for this example to keep things simple. That textured model will then fit perfectly in a 512×1024 doorway that was built on the grid in the game world. Figure 2-9 shows the visual for this example.

Other reasons for creating visual elements within a texture on the grid are so they line up with each other even if they are on different textures. For example, in many first-person shooters the height of a stair is 16 units (a power of two). Therefore, if you make a wall texture with a floor molding 16 units high, it will look much neater when the wall molding runs into the stairs. Even though the real world is often put together in a way that defies these guidelines, that is no excuse to allow those mistakes in a game. In a game those are mistakes and they are noticeable and not looked upon as a faithful recreation of reality. In the real world you will see wallpaper that wasn't hung correctly and the seams don't meet up with each other, or a brick wall that was repaired with bricks that don't match in color, grass that has been laid down in squares by a landscaper and actually tile, and other messy real-world examples. In Figure 2-10 you can see a simple texture set applied to a game setting and see how all the various textures fit with each other on the various surfaces of the room.

While some artists view the grid as a limit, others appreciate it as a tool. And given the fact that we are not bound to it nearly as much as we were just a few years ago, it is more of a tool now than a restraint. Working on the grid helps the world stay consistent and

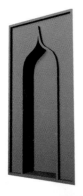 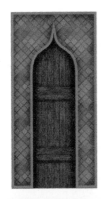 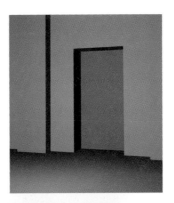

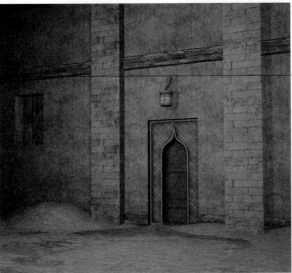

Figure 2-9
A texture created on a grid will fit perfectly on a model created on the same grid, which in turn will fit perfectly into a game world built on the same grid. In this case the arch model (**left**) is 512 × 1024, the texture (**middle**) is also 512 × 1024, and the boring doorway (**right**) we are trying to fill in the game world is of the same dimensions. You can see all the elements together in the image at the bottom.

look better, and frankly you can work much faster. This is called modular design. Modular design is very important when you work on a computer game. A computer game requires efficiency and organization. No matter how powerful computers get, you always want to squeeze out every ounce of performance you can. The best way to do that is to use only the textures you need, no more and no less.

Modular Design

In the context of texture creation, modular design is the art of designing and creating your textures so that they will all fit together. This starts with simple tiling and moves into the next realm of advanced tiling, which we will, of course, cover in the chapter *Prepping for Texture Creation*. In the real world a great example of modular design is office furniture. You can buy the core desk and add hutches, lighted cabinets, extensions, and on and on. All these parts are designed to fit together, allowing you the ability to create hundreds of combinations, thus ending up with a desk very unique

Figure 2-10
This texture set of eight textures was built off two base textures: tiles and bricks. Building everything on the grid in Photoshop and Max allowed for the seamless tiling of the entire set. Notice the pattern that runs through the floor and how it meets at every turn. I was able to rotate the tile with the corner pattern on it and have it still match up to the others. It is pretty easy to tile tiles, I admit, but by making sure they met up properly in Photoshop, I was able to use one corner pattern tile instead of four.

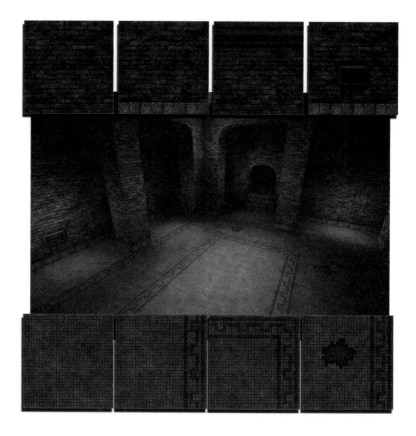

and fit for you. Add to that the ability to swap textures . . . I mean, select the color and finish you want, and you end up a huge variety of options.

Earlier you saw an example of texture modularity with the set of textures based on a brick and tile with variations that all fit together. The base brick wall covers most of the surface of the game world. To make that space interesting, I added trim, cracks, a baseboard, a vent, and other details. As we progress you will become very familiar with the concept of modularity. Modularity extends to all aspects of game design, and 3D modelers are often creating modular chunks of a game world that can be copied and arranged. Typically, modelers start with the large common and repetitive chunks like floor panels, wall panels, ceiling panels, and other repetitive large world geometry, then move into decorations such as columns, lamps, and special case meshes. They may even create versions of the large modular chunks with damage like cracks or holes in them. The power of two and the grid are both limits and tools for creating clean, solid levels. In Figure 2-11 you can see the base 3D parts of simple level set; in Figure 2-12 the parts are assembled into a room and hall, and in Figure 2-13, the room and hall are textured. In Figure 2-14 you can see an additional example of modular design. The castle wall is actually two pieces: one undamaged and one damaged.

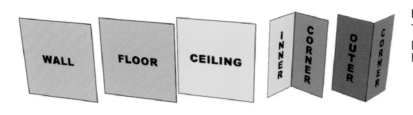

Figure 2-11
These are the basic 3D pieces of geometry for building a modular level.

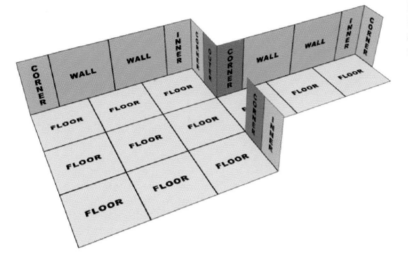

Figure 2-12
Here the base pieces are assembled into a simple room and hall.

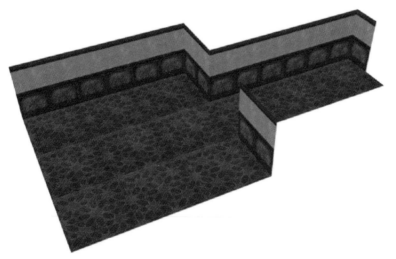

Figure 2-13
The simple room and hall textured.

As you create textures on a specific project, you will find that in most instances there are many other parameters to consider besides the grid, but these concern the final output file more than the source file. While the grid must be considered as you build, things like the largest and smallest file size that the engine can handle, the total texture memory you are allotted, and other technical details are pretty much reserved for after the texture is created and pertain to the output file.

Figure 2-14
Here is an example of a modular piece of geometry. There are two sections of castle wall: one is undamaged and one has a gaping hole in it. They were built on the grid so they meet up perfectly. The wall here is several normal wall sections lined up with a damaged section in the middle.

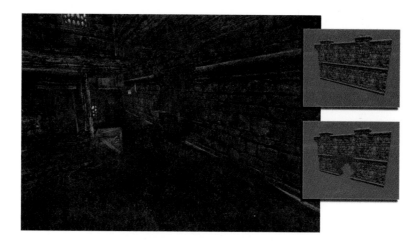

As a side note on technical limits, just because there is a maximum texture size a game engine can handle doesn't mean that you should use a lot of textures at the maximum size. A large image on a small object, or one that a player never sees close up, is just a waste of resources. In fact, while some game engines demand very specific input parameters, others allow for multiple color depths, variable file sizes and resolutions, and even differing formats. Knowing your engine is important, because you can cut file sizes significantly with little to no loss of visual quality simply by knowing what options you have.

There are always going to be limits imposed on you by development technology, game design, target audience, or even genre. Certain texture size is just one of those limits. Most importantly, knowing those limits and what you can do to work around them makes you more valuable than just a great artist. If you are able to experiment with file size, compression, color depth, etc. and are able to get twice the number of textures into the game, you will not only free yourself up to do more as an artist, you will be much more valuable as a developer.

UV Mapping

All the textures you create will end up being mapped onto a 3D object. UV mapping at its simplest is the process of placing of a 2D texture on a 3D mesh. We will look at the various ways textures can be placed on a 3D object.

Note that there is a distinction between a texture and a skin. A skin is the art that goes on a more complex model such as a character, monster, or weapon. Skins are generally not tileable and are created for a specific mesh. A texture is generally the art that covers the game world surfaces: grass, floor tiles, walls, etc., and UV'ing these surfaces is much simpler than skinning an organic model. You will not be applying your textures to any 3D meshes in this book, but you should understand the various UV mapping types since it can affect how you create your textures in some cases.

Mapping Types

Planar

Planar mapping works like a projector. The texture is projected onto the 3D surface from one direction. This can be used on walls and other flat planar surfaces but is limited and can't be used on complex objects since the process of projecting the texture in one direction also creates smearing on the sides of the 3D model that don't face the planar projection directly. See Figure 2-15 for an illustration of the planar UV mapping type.

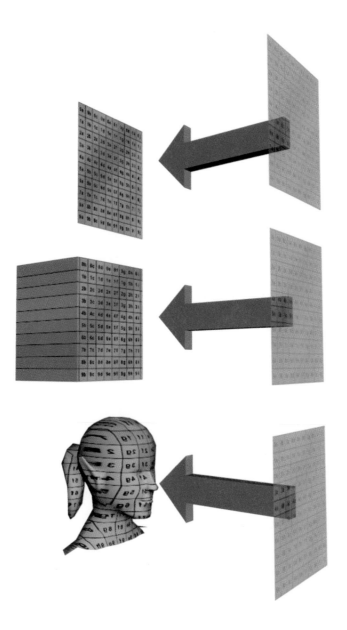

Figure 2-15
Planar mapping projects the texture onto the 3D mesh from one direction. This can be used on walls and other flat planar surfaces. However, it is limited and can't be used on complex objects. Projecting the texture in one direction creates smearing on the sides of a 3D model that don't face the planar projection directly.

Box

Box mapping projects the texture onto the model from six sides. This works great on boxes! This mapping scheme can be useful in some varying situations if you plan for it. Obviously, you can use it on more complex boxes, and if you design on the grid you can make things work to your benefit. In Figure 2-16 you can see how the box mapping type works in the upper left-hand corner of the image. At the top right is a rusted box texture and a close-up of the edge of the texture. I made the edge of the box exactly 16 units wide in the texture. Now look at the box model below that. It has an edge that is exactly 16 units wide as well. I can use box mapping here, and the fact that the texture is projected straight through the model causes that 16-unit edge of the texture to map perfectly on all the

Figure 2-16
Upper left, how the box mapping type works. **Top right,** a rusted box texture and a close-up of the edge of the texture. The edge of the box in the texture is exactly 16 units wide. The box model below has an edge that is exactly 16 units wide as well.

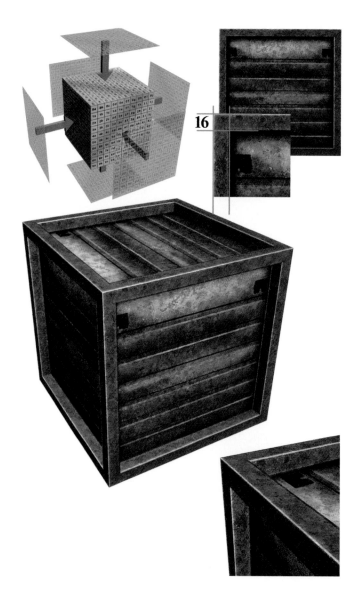

edges of the outer and inner rims of the box. The lower right-hand corner has a close-up of the box and you can see how the highlights and all the edges meet cleanly.

Spherical

Spherical mapping surrounds the object and projects the map from all sides in a spherical pattern. You will see along the edge where the texture meets unless you have created a texture that tiles correctly. Also, the texture gets gathered up, or pinched, at the top and bottom of the sphere. Spherical mapping is obviously great for planets and other spherical things. See Figure 2-17.

Cylindrical

Cylindrical mapping projects the map by wrapping it around in a cylindrical shape. Seams will show if you have not tiled the texture properly. Cylindrical mapping can be used on tree trunks, columns, etc. See Figure 2-18 for the visual of cylindrical mapping and some examples.

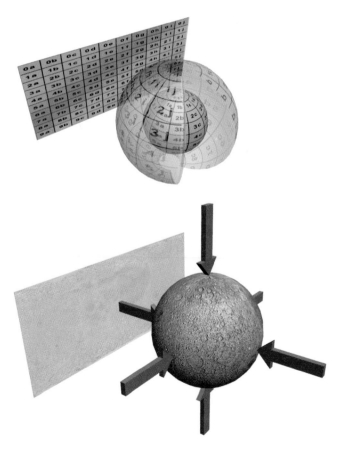

Figure 2-17
Spherical mapping surrounds the object and projects the map from all sides in a spherical pattern. You will see along the edge where the texture meets unless you have created a texture that tiles correctly. Spherical mapping is great for planets.

Figure 2-18
Cylindrical mapping projects
the map by wrapping it
around in a cylindrical shape.

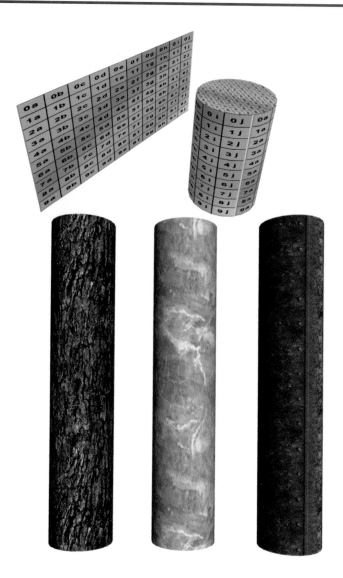

Those are the most basic UV mapping types and are the most
common ways that world textures will be applied. Actually, world
textures are mostly planar or box mapped onto the faces of the
world. Applying these standard UV mapping types is pretty
straightforward and usually automatic in the game editor and can be
easily changed by the level builder.

Shader Technology for Artists

No book that discusses computer art would be complete without at
least a mention of programmable shaders and shading. Shaders
allow a level of realism in games that is stunning and getting better
all the time. Very simply, a shader is a mini-program that processes
graphic effects in real time. There are two main types of shader on

modern graphics processors (GPUs): vertex and pixel shaders. Vertex shaders manipulate geometry (vertices and their attributes) in real time, while pixel shaders manipulate rendered pixels in real time. The ability to manipulate a pixel in real time is what makes the shader so powerful. Shaders can be used for many complex material appearances and image effects: hair, fire, shadows, water, reflections, and so forth. It is so flexible that the list is almost endless and a shader programmer can write almost any effect you can imagine.

Pixel Shader. A pixel shader is a program that can process a pixel in real time to create various graphical effects.

Shaders, from the artist's point of view, are often a bit of a black box. Our involvement usually requires that we generate input for a pre-existing shader—set parameters and/or assign textures, then look at the end result. Since the artist's role is mostly confined to creating input and judging the output of the shader, we often have nothing to do with the code. In some cases shader code is written or edited by an artist, but most newer shader-creation tools are more like the material systems in Max and Maya, requiring no programming knowledge. Figure 2-19 shows a diagram of how a material shader works from the artist's point of view.

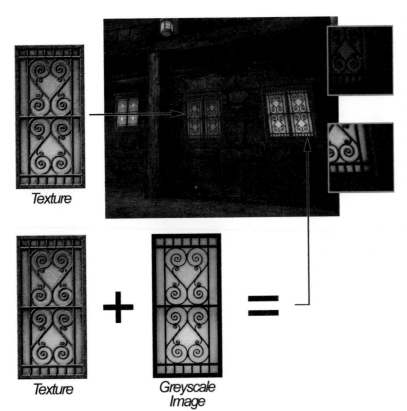

Texture

Texture + Greyscale Image =

Figure 2-19
Shaders typically require input from the artist, are processed in real time, and look stunning in a game. Here is a simple flow of how one shader works for the artist. The window texture by itself in the game world is dark. We can use a shader to tell the game engine what parts of the image to make bright and what parts to leave dark based on the grayscale image. You can see how the frame is unlit while the glass is bright. To the right of the image are close-ups of the dark and lit windows.

Although this book's sole focus is on the creation of 2D assets (textures), shaders often require the use of 2D assets as input, and the artist is usually the one tasked with not only creating those assets, but also understanding, creating, and implementing the shader to some degree. So, while shaders can replace much of the work an artist would do on an asset, they may also increase our workload. Already there are effects in games where the artist is no longer painting a texture as an isolated entity but is creating a series of textures that must all work together for a desired effect. Using shaders requires more planning, a different way of thinking about creating the art, and more organization. The artist needs to learn her shader tool, organize more assets (assets that may be linked to each other and are therefore more rigid in their mobility after a shader is in place), and learn the mental discipline of creating assets that are not the end result but component parts of the final result.

We will have to get used to painting textures devoid of certain properties that will later be processed in real time. One reason to understand the fundamentals of light and shadow, or develop the skill to see the base material of a scene behind all the dirt, reflections, and other surface properties, is that we may soon be building textures starting with a very plain surface (even a pattern) and building a complex organizational tree of maps and effects to create a final surface (much like we already do in 3D programs and how some texture generators work). For example, instead of painting a reflective highlight onto a chrome surface in Photoshop—trying desperately to make the highlight look good, but not too pronounced—you can now leave it out and assign a shader to the material that will simulate accurate chrome highlights in real time (Figure 2-20). While shaders can make our lives easier in some

Figure 2-20
Instead of painting a highlight onto a surface in Photoshop, you can now leave it out and assign a shader to the material that will simulate highlights in real time. It is hard to see in these stills, but the top row of images has a window with a fake, unmovable, highlight in the glass. The middle row of images has a highlight that moves as you do and looks like a real reflection as a result (look at the bright spot in the lower row of panes). The bottom row of images is a more pronounced chrome effect. You can see it move across the surface more easily as well as compare it to the same model next to it with a plain texture on it.

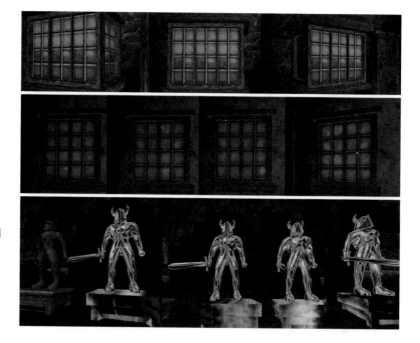

respects, and definitely can make our games look better, they can also be a bit complex to understand at first and require a greater degree of organization.

Common Shader Effects

Like most things dealing with computer game technology, shaders are a vast and complex topic riddled with new vocabulary, concepts, and technological requirements. In addition, each game engine and each game project will have its own vocabulary, process, and subtle nuances in dealing with shaders. But you will always deal with some basic shader effects, and here are some samples of them. You may notice that these shader effects are very similar to filter effects in Photoshop, materials in Max or Maya, and many post-video effects. Post-video effects are effects inserted into a film or video after the footage is shot, during the editing process.

The most common application of shading is to provide the artist with a rich variety of surface materials, including not only metals, plastics, and natural-material surfaces, but also animating surfaces like water, fog, lava, and others.

Bump Mapping

You know by now that a texture is a flat 2D image, but there are several techniques for adding depth to a texture that not only look better because of the depth but also due to the fact that the effect is processed in real time. One of those techniques is called bump mapping. A bump map is usually a separate image used to make the surface of an object appear to have an irregular surface—to look bumpy. The bump map, the image used to create this effect, is usually grayscale, and the lighter areas of the map appear raised and the darker areas appear to be lower. Bump mapping is an option that adds the type of subtle depth to a surface that does not require additional geometry. And, since bump mapping is processed in real time, the effect makes the world seem much more real as the light and shadow of the bump-mapped surface move with the player (Figure 2-21).

Normal Mapping

Normal mapping is the variation of bump mapping most commonly used in games, and artists will often use the terms interchangeably. In normal mapping, the artist still creates a grayscale map of the surface details but adds a final processing step (usually with a Photoshop plug-in, like the one on this book's DVD) that converts it to a red-green normal map before final delivery. Essentially, a normal map contains more information and, in turn, the game engine can render the pixels in a more accurate and dynamic fashion. A normal map can make a surface look far more complex,

Figure 2-21
Bump mapping uses a separate grayscale image to add subtle depth to a surface without adding additional geometry. The top image is actually two images. I flipped one horizontally so you can see the same part of the image together and compare them. The left side of the image has no bump mapping, while the right side does have bump mapping. The image on the lower right is a surface with the bump map applied and no texture.

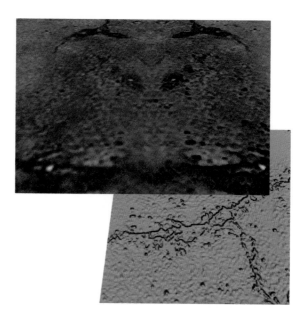

Figure 2-22
Top, just the color map; **middle,** typical "bump mapping" result based on normal maps; and **bottom** (it's hard to see in this image), new "relief mapping" from the same data. Note the offset as the grout is "dug into" the surface complete with shadows from the stones.

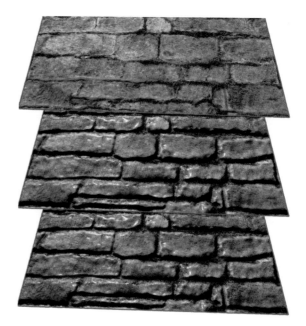

like actual geometry, as it is lighting the surface one pixel at a time as opposed to one polygon at a time (Figure 2-22).

Subsurface Scattering with Shadows

In this example in Figure 2-23, the red color in the shadowed area of the skin comes from the simulation of light scattering through the soft tissues of the skin itself. While a comprehensive scientific simulation would require a long computation, a simple shading trick

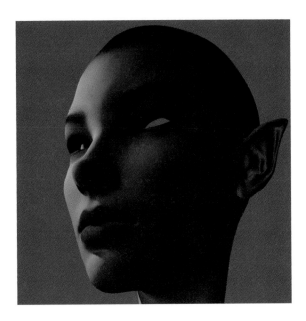

Figure 2-23
Subsurface scattering with shadows simulates light scattering through the soft tissues of skin.

or two is often enough to give the artistic feel—in this, case the shader runs about as quickly as any other simple shader, yet gives a soft feel to the face that lets the viewer get the sense of soft, living tissue. In addition to the usual color maps, the artist provides a color for the subcutaneous scattering, and a slider-based number telling the system how deeply light will penetrate into the face. The shader also provides convincing self-shadowing.

Thin Film

Materials with thin transparent layers, such as oil slicks or the glazed teapot shown in Figure 2-24, refract their highlights at grazing angles. This look is terribly difficult to achieve without programmable shading, but simple when shading is available. The artist can adjust the apparent thickness and reflective index of the film, which can be applied atop almost any other sort of material.

Wood

Some of the earliest material shaders were use to simulate "solid" textures, like those of granite, aggregate stone, and wood. The shader example in Figure 2-25 maps the colors of concentric wooden rings through the volume of the skull model, rather than along surface UV coordinates. See how the texture is consistent around complex shapes like the jaw connection and eye sockets. In this particular, quick-executing example, the artist can assign the position of the wood's "trunk" axis, the overall scale, how smooth or wobbly the rings will appear, and can select the range of wood colors—providing the means of simulating many different sorts of wood from a single, fast, shader.

Figure 2-24
Thin film simulates a thin
film or glaze like an oil slick.

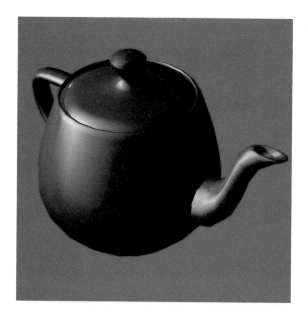

Figure 2-25
This wood shader creates
a wood grain that maps
perfectly to a surface. This
makes the artist's life much
easier.

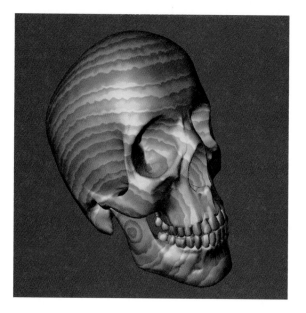

Ocean Waves

An aspect of programmable shaders often difficult to express on the
pages of a book is their dynamic nature. The shader in Figure 2-26
not only contains the complex coloring of ocean waves, but actually
drives their animation as well. The model, before the shader is
applied, is just a simple grid of triangles. The shader modifies the
vertices on the fly, creating wave shapes, and colors each pixel of
the final shape to create the appropriate colors depending upon
how we look into the water—bright along the horizon, and deeper
blues as we look into the deep. The artist can control the

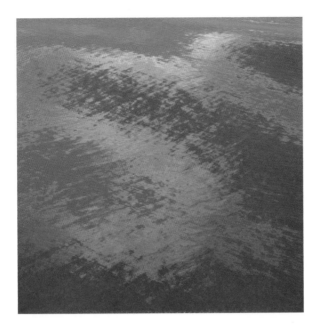

Figure 2-26
Ocean waves are actually a combination of complex pixel coloring, but the shader animates the geometric plane the water material is applied to.

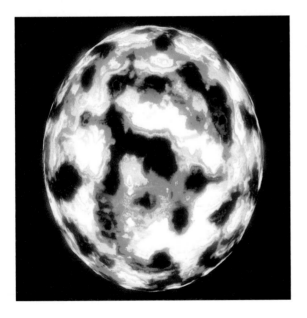

Figure 2-27
Lava animates the materials colors and allows the artists to set which parts of the lava are hot and cool, as well as other parameters.

surrounding environment maps and color gradients within the water, as well as the speed and depth of the wave animation.

Lava

Material colors can also be animated, as this example in Figure 2-27 shows. The artist-supplied inputs include some colors, a narrow map containing a set of color gradients for the cool-to-hot parts of the lava, and a broken crust map—which is actually in this case a

Figure 2-28
This fire effect is a combination of moving geometry with an animated flame texture mapped to it.

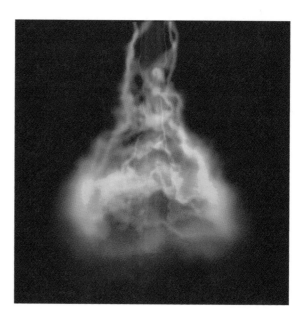

picture of tree bark!—along with some parameters to define just how far this lava should pulse and flow.

Fire

Yet another animated effect, the fire in Figure 2-28 is created by combining animated textures on multiple clear panels, stacked one in front of the other. The vertex portion of the shader keeps the panels aligned to the view, regardless of their view direction, while the pixel shader animates the flame pattern. The flame pattern itself is based on a whorl of fire shapes provided by the artist.

Raytracing

Complex raytracing (the simulation of real-world light properties) may consume large resources and long blocks of time, but today's graphics cards are quick enough to perform limited raytracing in real time. Simple spheres and places are straightforward to raytrace. While they may seem esoteric, raytraced planes are a great way to add convincing window or TV-monitor light to parts of a scene, particularly tiny reflective surfaces like characters' eyes (see Figure 2-29).

Image Processing in Shaders

A second use for pixel shaders is the application of complex imaging effects. Blurs, glows, color transformations, and other effects can be applied quickly and relatively easily. An especially appealing feature of shader-based image processing is that it can be applied

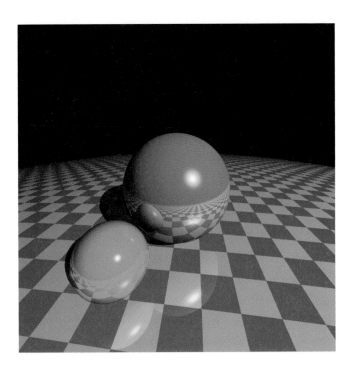

Figure 2-29
Complex raytracing is now
approachable in real time.

separately from the underlying 3D models and render pipeline, so
these effects can be added to existing art assets without having to
change the art pipeline or how the renderer handles assets.

Blooming

Glow effects are some of the most popular. In this effect, glow only
appears around the brightest highlights—as if these overbright
areas are "blooming" in the eye of the player's eye (or camera); see
Figure 2-30. This is an effect popular for both video processing and
games.

Glowing Trails

By combining different parts of the image and processing animation
across multiple frames, a number of "persistent" effects can be
created. In Figure 2-31, the images of two spinning models are
repeatedly combined with blurred and fading copies of the previous
frames, leaving a glowing trail.

Corona

Images may have more channels than simple RGB. In Figure 2-32, a
glowing trail is also left behind—not from the color image, but from
its alpha channel. The glow is further distorted by an animated
noise channel to create an animated burning corona effect, which

Figure 2-30
Bloom simulates a special
type of glow that is surreal
and only appears around
highlights in the image.

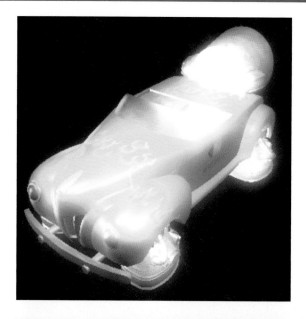

Figure 2-31
In this image two spinning
models are repeatedly
combined with blurred and
fading copies of the previous
frames, leaving a glowing
trail.

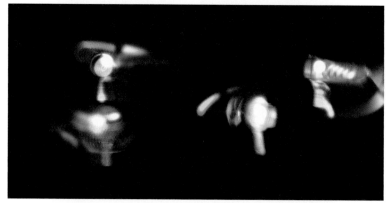

Figure 2-32
In this example, a glowing
trail is left behind.

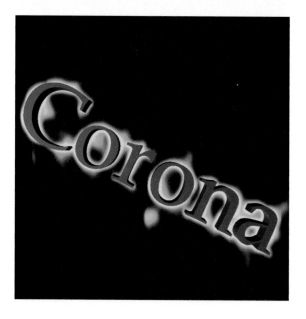

can be turned by the artist, who can specify (or even animate) glow colors and the fade, speed, and spread of the flame.

Mandelbrot Viewer

Normally reserved for technical theory demonstrations, modern GPUs actually have the horsepower to calculate complex fractal equations in real time. The image in Figure 2-33, for example, was smoothly scrollable at 30 fps, recalculated on every pixel for every frame. Comparative CPU-based algorithms would calculate a frame every several seconds.

Tiles

As a fanciful application, the image shader in Figure 2-34 converts any underlying image into a mosaic of 3D floor tiles. The image can be freely animated and re-rendered during the conversion, which is blindingly fast. Imaging-processing can give almost any game image or render a unique voice and feeling, whether it be floor tiles or complex night vision; if you can imagine a series of steps to alter the image, it can be expressed as a shader.

Shaders are allowing artists to mimic reality in exciting ways and require a different way of looking at texture handling, but they don't change the fundamentals of texture creation or remove the need to know them. These advancements, which are changing how game textures are created, actually make the focus on the basics of art in

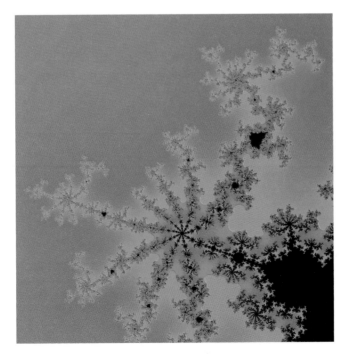

Figure 2-33
Modern GPUs actually have the horsepower to calculate complex fractal equations in real time.

Figure 2-34
This image shader converts any underlying image into a mosaic of 3D floor tiles.

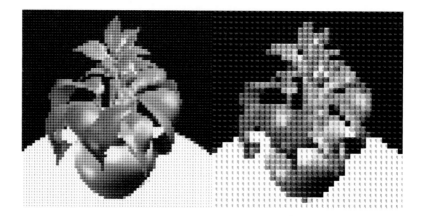

Chapter 1 of this book more relevant. The ability to break a scene down to its base textures is challenge enough, but to break a texture down into its base components is yet a deeper challenge. When in-game art becomes a complex marriage of textures, filters, and procedures, the artist will become more important (and more challenged), not less so. Some predict that the artist will be replaced by shaders, but I don't think that will ever happen. There will always be a need for an artist to make things look better and more unique (at least we can change the default settings of a shader). Shaders are but another tool for an artist to use.

Conclusion

That was a quick overview of some vast and complex topics. But the concepts presented here are enough to help you create textures that will work in a game world. Learning and mastering any one of these concepts will take time, but fear not, for a good basis will allow you to build up to mastering these topics quicker and easier.

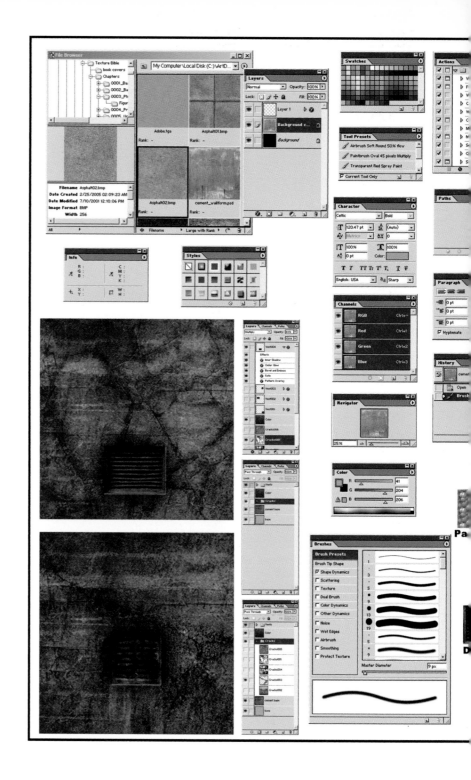

Chapter 3

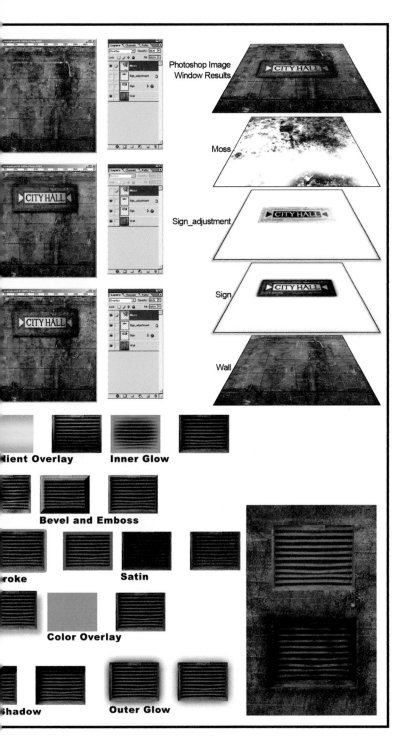

Photoshop Image Window Results

Moss

Sign_adjustment

Sign

Wall

ient Overlay

Inner Glow

Bevel and Emboss

roke

Satin

Color Overlay

hadow

Outer Glow

Introduction

Photoshop is the right hand of the game artist. While there are many 3D applications, Photoshop pretty much stands alone as the 2D application of choice for game developers.

A Quick Overview of Photoshop for Game Artists

"One machine can do the work of fifty ordinary men. No machine can do the work of one extraordinary man."

Elbert Hubbard
U.S. author (1856–1915)

This chapter is an "orientation" to the aspects of Photoshop that are most useful to the texture artist. This is not a tutorial chapter or a user's manual. While I mention some specifics about how certain aspects of Photoshop can be used in game development, they are simply mentioned in this chapter, and put into practice throughout the rest of the book. My goal is that the reader with a prior knowledge of Photoshop will gain the ability to move through the steps of the chapters quickly, staying focused on the creation of game art, and not hit the "Photoshop 101" speed bumps. I also wanted to give readers who don't have a basic knowledge of Photoshop an overview, and not subject them to disjointed bits and pieces of knowledge. For those readers this chapter will be particularly helpful. You don't need to memorize every aspect of Photoshop to use it; in fact, it is only by using Photoshop repeatedly that you will remember anything. However, this orientation will give you a feel for this complex application and the ability to perform the steps of the coming projects more easily.

Note: This chapter is written based on version 7 of Photoshop, with notes on the updates and differences that exist in Photoshop CS. I figured this approach would be most useful to the users of both versions of Photoshop.

Second Note: Some of the tools presented here will not be specifically mentioned in the project sections of the book, but are of great use to the game artists. The File Browser alone is worthy of mention and definitely worth learning to use to its fullest, but it plays no specific part in the texture creation process. You can open a file many ways in Photoshop; the File Browser is simply one of those ways but can be quicker and more useful in many circumstances. Photoshop is full of features that make things faster and less painful. There are always better and faster ways to do anything in Photoshop, so email me your tips and tricks.

I strongly encourage you to become familiar with every possible aspect of Photoshop. As you read this chapter, try the various tools I mention. No amount of instruction can replace experimentation. See for yourself what the tools do, use them, master them. This was a difficult chapter to write, only because I had to leave out a lot of stuff.

There are many books on Photoshop—thousands of them, I bet— that range from simple overviews to exhaustive user manual regurgitations. There are specific-to-topic books that look at Photoshop's abilities from the angle of digital photography, web site creation, scanning, text effects, and more. The Photoshop help files are also a great way to learn about Photoshop. They are comprehensive and well written, as well as presented in a traditional help file format that is easy to use. The help files allow for the viewing of Photoshop tools and features in several ways: contents, site map, index, and search. I find the "Related Subtopics" listed at the end of most topics very useful as I am trying to chase down a specific bit of information pertaining to some aspect of Photoshop. Even if you just skim over several topics and can't remember any specifics, if you are faced with a problem later pertaining to one of those topics, chances are you will remember reading about it and know right where to go to get the specific information you need to solve the problem.

So where do you start with Photoshop? We will start with the very basics, looking at the Work Area, but the hot keys and the right-click menus are the most important things you can learn about Photoshop. Together they allow you to create great art much quicker while being dangerously sedentary.

The Photoshop Work Area

The Photoshop Work Area (Figure 3-1) contains the following major elements:

- Menu Bar
- Options Bar
- Toolbar
- Palette Well
- Palettes
- Status Bar

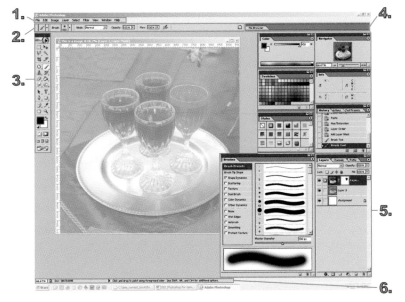

Figure 3-1
The main parts of the Photoshop Work Area are (1) menu bar, (2) options bar, (3) toolbar, (4) palette well, (5) palettes, and (6) the status bar.

The Menu Bar

The menu bar contains standard menu items you may recognize from other applications such as File; Open, Save, New, Export and Edit; Cut, Copy, and Paste, as well as other options that reflect the most common elements of Photoshop. The Layers menu contains commands for working with layers. The Image menu allows you to adjust, manipulate, and change the modes of an image. There are also menus for dealing with selections, filters, and the various view windows of Photoshop.

I will not detail the menus word by word because every feature contained in the menus is discussed in this chapter and the hot key/right mouse menu options are the way you should learn to work in Photoshop. Many people are taught the menus first, and then the "faster way" to do things. I think this is the wrong approach. I guess the logic is that you are learning a basis and adding to it, but you are not. What you are doing is learning a slow (very different) way of doing something (clicking three or four times through a menu system) and then being presented with an entirely different way to do things. Being presented with a shortcut later on, after entrenching yourself in the menus, will feel like you are taking three steps back and slowing way down to speed up in the future. Most people will resist learning a new shortcut when it is that much of a speed bump. They will also fall back into the "menu habit" when focusing on their work. So do yourself a favor and learn the fastest way to do something first. The menus aren't going anywhere and will be just as slow when you do need to use them.

The Options Bar

Almost all tools in Photoshop have several settings, or options, and they are displayed in the tool options bar instead of being hidden in a menu. The options bar brings up information and options based on the tool that is selected. When using the Zoom tool, you will see options like Resize to Fit, Fit on Screen, zoom in and out, etc. If you are using the Paintbrush tool, you will see options for Brush size, blending mode, opacity, and flow. If you set up a tool and want to save the state of that tool (all its settings), you can save it in the tool presets. In Figure 3-2, you can see the tool selected to the left and the various options available for that tool on the right; at the bottom is the menu of the options bar where you can load, save, and reset tools.

The Toolbar (Toolbox)

The toolbox holds all the tools you will use for creating and manipulating your images. In the section below, Toolbar Shortcuts, there is a more lengthy description of the toolbar.

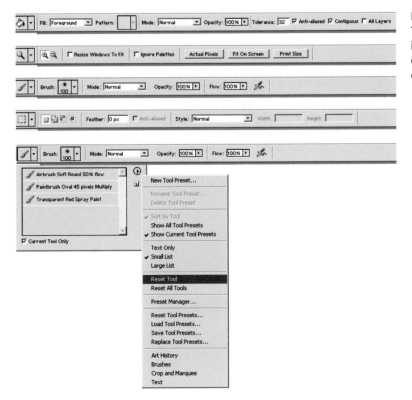

Figure 3-2
The icon for the tool selected is to the left and the various options available for that tool on the right.

Palette Well

The palette well allows you to drag any palette in the work area into the palette well and dock it there. Palettes are hidden when in the palette well, but you will see a tab with the palette name on it. Clicking on the Palette tab will bring the palette up. The palette will be available until you click outside the palette.

Palettes

Palettes are floating menus that contain information on layers, navigation, colors, styles, text, and almost any aspect of Photoshop can be displayed as a palette. Palettes can be resized, minimized, docked, and closed all together. You can even use the Tab key to hide all active palettes and display them again as you had them arranged before hiding them. Here is every palette in Photoshop for your viewing pleasure (Figure 3-3).

The Status Bar

The status bar (Window > Status Bar) is located at the bottom of the window and displays the magnification of the image, the file size, and even instructions for using the currently selected tool.

Figure 3-3
Here are all the palettes in Photoshop. Some we will talk about in depth, while a few we only mention.

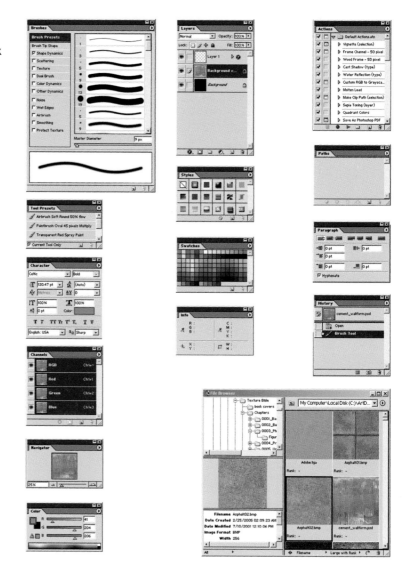

Hot Keys or Keyboard Shortcuts

Whatever you want to call them, the ability to press a key, or key combination, is much faster than clicking through numerous menus to get the tool you want. Many of us already know that Ctrl + C, V, or Z is Cut, Copy, and Paste. In Photoshop there are lots of keyboard shortcuts, so don't feel intimidated. I try to learn new ones every so often to keep adding to my knowledge, and I still don't know most of them—there are a lot! And you have the ability to create your own as well. Some of the basic ones I use most are:

F1—Help
F5—Brush style palette
F6—Color, Swatches, and Styles palette
F7—Layers, Channels, Paths palette

F8—Navigator, Info palette
F9—Actions, History, Presets palette
Tab—Toggles all the palettes on screen on and off
Shift + Tab—Toggles palettes on screen, excluding the toolbar.

The [and] keys make the brush size smaller or larger for the paintbrush, eraser, clone stamp, healing brush, doge/burn/sponge, blur,/sharpen/smudge tool, and others.

The numbers 1 through 0 on the keyboard will affect the opacity of the layer, going from 0 to 100% in 10% increments.

Toolbar Shortcuts

The toolbar (Figure 3-4) has shortcuts, too. Using them allows you not only to work faster but also will eventually help you eliminate the need to always have your toolbar open; as a result, you gain more screen real estate. This is true for the hot keys for palettes and other windows, too. Even if you don't know all the hot keys for a specific palette, just knowing what hot key brings it up and takes it away allows you to reclaim more of your workspace as you can quickly bring the palettes and tools you need up and down, rather than leaving them all about your work area. You can also double-click the header bar on top of any window to minimize and maximize it.

Since you can select and hold down on some of the tools in the toolbar to bring up other tools, here is the complete list of keys for those tools.

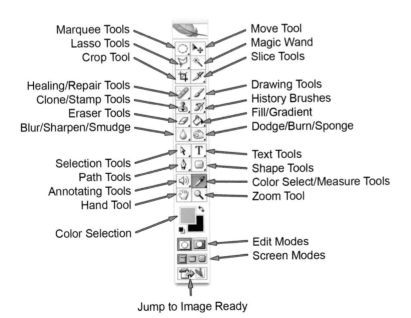

Figure 3-4
The Photoshop toolbar.

A—Direct Select Tool
B—Brush Tool
C—Crop Stamp Tool
E—Eraser Tool
G—Gradient Stamp Tool
H—Hand Tool
I—Measure Tool
J—Healing Stamp Tool
K—Slice Stamp Tool
L—Polygonal Lasso Tool
M—Rectangular Marquee Tool
N—Notes Tool
O—Sponge Tool
P—Pen Tool
R—Smudge Tool
S—Clone Stamp Tool
T—Horizontal Type Tool
U—Line Tool
V—Move Tool
W—Magic Wand Tool
Y—History Brush Tool
Z—Zoom Stamp Tool

Ctrl Shortcuts

Simply holding down the Ctrl key and pressing another key will give
you even more options.

1. Ctrl + N: Opens New Document dialog box
2. Ctrl + A: Selects the entire area of the current layer
3. Ctrl + D: Deselects a selection
4. Ctrl + J: Duplicates the selected layer
5. Ctrl + K: Opens Preferences dialog box
6. Ctrl + L: Opens Levels dialog box
7. Ctrl + F4: Closes current file
8. Ctrl + ' (single quote key): Displays gridlines
9. Ctrl + ;: Sets Toggle guides
10. Ctrl + R: Sets Toggles rulers
11. Ctrl + U: Opens Hue/Saturation dialog box
12. Ctrl + O: Opens File dialog box
13. Ctrl + P: Opens Print dialog box
14. Ctrl + Z: Undoes last action
15. Ctrl + Tab: Jumps between open documents
16. Ctrl + C: Copies
17. Ctrl + X: Cuts
18. Ctrl + Alt + Shift + X: Opens Pattern Maker
19. Ctrl + V: Pastes
20. Ctrl + T: Sets Transform tool

Logically, adding more keys to the combination allows for even more
options.

- Ctrl + Shift + S: Opens Save As dialog box
- Ctrl + Shift + F: Opens Fade dialog box
- Ctrl + Shift + X: Sets Liquify Filter tool
- Ctrl + Shift + N: Creates New Layer Preferences
- Ctrl + Shift + I: Selects Invert
- Ctrl + Shift + C: Copies all layers

Add even more keys to the equation.

- Ctrl + Shift + Alt + N: Creates a new empty layer
- Ctrl + Shift + Alt + S: Opens Save For The Web dialog box
- Ctrl + Shift + Alt + X: Opens Pattern Maker dialog box

Finally, there are navigation shortcuts. Holding the spacebar will turn the cursor into the Hand Tool and allow you to move around the image.

Note: Moving around the image is different than moving the image itself using the Arrow tool.

Other

- Using the Page Up and the Page Down keys when zoomed in will scroll the image one screen up and down.
- Holding the Ctrl key while using the Page Up and Page Down keys will scroll you from side to side.
- Holding the Shift key while using Page Up/Page Down scroll will move you in 10-pixel increments.
- Holding Shift while painting or erasing will make the line straight at 90- or 45-degree angles.

File Browser

The File Browser (Figure 3-5) allows you to view thumbnails of the images in a folder and drag them into Photoshop to open them. The fact is that no matter how descriptive your file names, you still have to see an image before you can decide if you want to use it or not. You can change the sizes of the thumbnail images from icon-sized to fairly large thumbnails. The navigation is easy, and the window is easily resized and moveable, making it even more useful. There is a View window that allows for the viewing of file information, too. You can sort and manage files to some degree using the File Browser. You can even process images; rename, move, and delete; and curious rotations are options. I find the "Reveal Location in Explorer" option useful. I am uncomfortable doing too much moving and deleting of files in the File Browser and like the fact that I can open a window to the folder the images I am viewing are in and process them there. The "Batch rename" feature is good and I do use that one. By default, the File Browser is displayed in the palette well (upper right-hand side of the Photoshop window). You should see a small file tab that says File Browser.

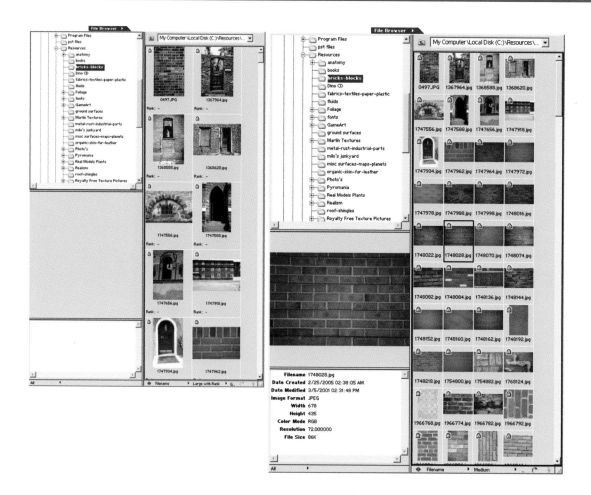

Figure 3-5
The File Browser allows you to view thumbnails of the images in a folder and drag them into Photoshop to open them.

History Palette

The History palette is like Undo on steroids (Figure 3-6). You can undo or redo multiple steps and even save a snapshot of the image. A snapshot is effectively a copy of the image you are working on. You can save the snapshot as a separate file. You can save multiple snapshots and save your work in steps. If you are working on a large and complex image, this can be very useful. Sometimes the size of a Photoshop file can get so large it starts to slow down your system. Say you are working on a complex wall image. Maybe you built up many layers to build the base wall and have many more layers on top of that. You can save a snapshot of the file (or use the Save As command, too) and flatten the layers that you consider final. This way the file is smaller and if you need to go back and alter the wall layers you can drag them over to the newer file you are working on and work on them again as layers. One of the options you will see associated with the History palette is Clear History. If Photoshop gives you a "low on memory" message, you can purge the history, which will free up some memory.

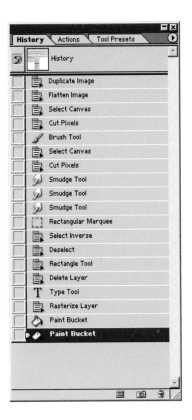

Figure 3-6
The History palette, Undo on steroids.

Right-Click Menus

Initially, the easiest speed trick to learn is to use the right mouse button to bring up the context-sensitive menus associated with each tool in Photoshop. All you have to do is remember to use them! If you are working with a selection, the menu that pops up when the right mouse button is clicked will pertain to selections; if you are working with the Zoom tool, the menu that pops up will contain the Zoom options. In fact, these little menus give you immediate access to options relevant to any active tool, palette, or selection you are using.

Guides, Grids, Rulers, and the Snap

Guides, grids, and rulers are very important in game art. We spent some time in the last chapter talking about working on the grid. Snapping to the grid is a very helpful feature, even a necessity, so we will talk about that first.

Snapping

Snapping allows you to place things exactly where you want them. When you drag an item within a certain distance of another item in

Figure 3-7
The options of the snap tool.

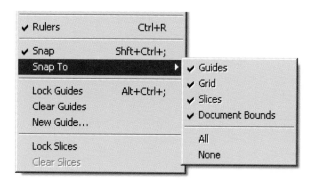

Photoshop, you can have those two items snap to each other like magnets. This means that you will either be enough pixels away from something so you can see that it is not lined up right, or the item will snap exactly to the item. This also means that you can't drag and place something only a few pixels away from something else because snap will catch it and snap it to the item. You can turn snap off, or use Nudge to position things, if you need to.

Things like selections, the crop tool, guidelines, painted lines, and images can be placed exactly where you want them using the snap tool. You can choose to turn snap off or choose what you snap to: guidelines, the grid, or the edge of the document. In Figure 3-7, you can see the options of the snap tool. Precise placement can be very important in game creation. Not only high end 3D game worlds, but user interfaces and menus require placement to the pixel. Mobile devices like cell phones are just as precise and more limiting. The screens are very small and every pixel counts and must be placed exactly in the right spot. If you open the options from the menu (lines, grid, etc.), and they are disabled, that is because the layer you want to snap on needs to be visible.

Note: Snapping guidelines to ruler units can be achieved by holding the Shift key when dragging a guideline.

Rulers

Rulers run up the left-hand side of the image window and across the top. You can turn them off and on with Ctrl + R or View > Rulers. You can set the ruler units to many different units of measure (right-click on the rulers), but in all likelihood you will be using *pixels*. Snapping to ruler units can be achieved by holding the Shift key when dragging out a guideline. Rulers will move and scale with your image, meaning that if you zoom into an image you will see the ruler units adjust in size and position. In Figure 3-8, you can see the rulers settings dialog on the upper left, on the upper right is an image that is zoomed out. Notice that the image is still anchored at 0,0 and that the numbers on the rulers preceding 0,0 are negative numbers. The lower left image is zoomed way in so you can see that the ruler units have gotten larger to reflect the zoom. On the lower

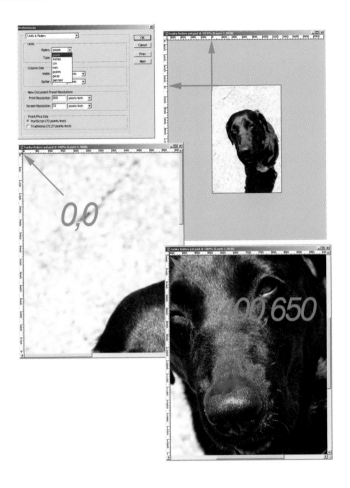

Figure 3-8
The rulers settings dialog is on the **upper left**, and on the **upper right** is an image that is zoomed out. Notice that the image is still anchored at 0,0 and that the numbers on the rulers preceding 0,0 are negative numbers. The **lower left** image is zoomed way in so you can see that the ruler units have gotten smaller to reflect the zoom. On the **lower right** you can see that the zoomed in image, when moved about, the rulers move with it.

right you can see that the zoomed in image, when moved about, the rulers move with it.

Edit > Preferences > Units and Rulers

Guides and Grids

The guidelines and grid in Photoshop behave the same, the difference being pretty evident (Figure 3-9). A guideline is one line (you can drag out as many as you like) and the grid is a grid. You can change the color and style of a guideline and the color, style, distance, and number of grid lines.

Guidelines are lines that you can drag out over your image and are not actually part of the art. They won't print or be in the images when you export it to another format. You can move and delete these lines as well as lock them in place. The grid also does not print or appear in your exported files.

To see your grid, use the hot keys in the above section, or choose View > Show Grids. To see a guideline, you have to create one.

Figure 3-9
The guidelines and grid in Photoshop behave the same. A guideline is one line (you can drag out as many as you like), and the grid is a grid.

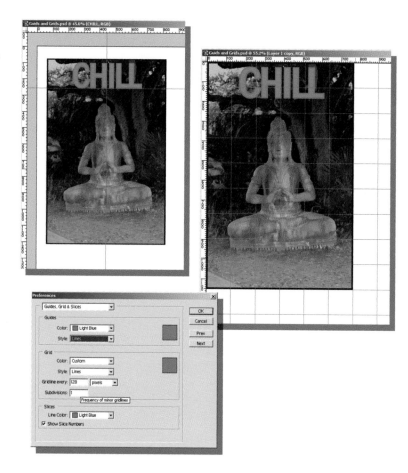

Simply place your cursor on a vertical or horizontal ruler and click and hold the left mouse button and drag. The line will stay where you let go of the mouse button. To move a guide, hold your cursor over the line and press and hold the Ctrl key. When the cursor turns into a double-headed arrow, you can move the line. You can remove one guideline by dragging it outside the image window and into a ruler, and you can remove all of them by choosing View > Clear Guides. Remember that hiding and clearing are different. Hiding means that the guides can be unhidden, while clearing them removes them entirely. You can use the History palette or the Undo feature to get them back, in most cases.

Layers

The concept of layers was introduced in the previous chapter. Here we will look at some of the specific features of Photoshop layers. Layers not only make life much easier for the texture artist, they are also critical to texture creation. Layers allow you to save your Photoshop file as many images on top of each other. You can control how each layer interacts with the one below it. In Figure 3-10, you can see an illustration of how layers work in

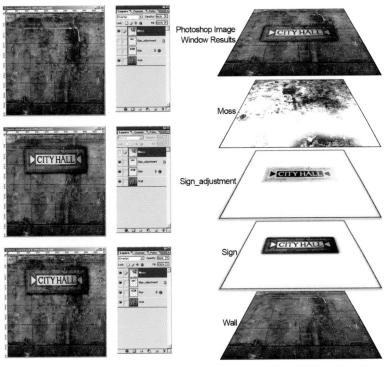

Figure 3-10
On the **left side** of this figure you can see three textures all created from one Photoshop file with various layers. To the **right** of the textures you can see the Layer palette for this file. Notice this is the same file with different layers turned on and off. To the **far right** is an illustration of how the layers in Photoshop are stacked on top of each other and how the final result is seen in the Photoshop Image Window. This illustration reflects the actual layers used in the image to the left.

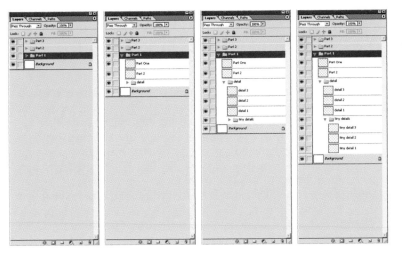

Figure 3-11
Photoshop CS introduces the concept of nested layers. You can put sets of layers into sets, into sets.

Photoshop. Photoshop CS introduces the concept of nested layers. You can put sets of layers into sets, into sets. See Figure 3-11.

The Layers Palette

Using the Layers palette, you can create, delete, hide, copy, and move layers as well as apply many effects and styles to them. You can also combine layers, link them, and add layer masks and

Figure 3-12
The parts of the Layers palette.

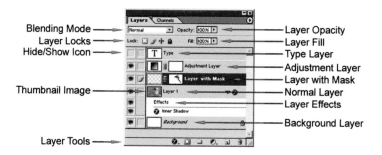

Blending Mode
Layer Locks
Hide/Show Icon
Thumbnail Image
Layer Tools

Layer Opacity
Layer Fill
Type Layer
Adjustment Layer
Layer with Mask
Normal Layer
Layer Effects
Background Layer

adjustment layers (we will discuss them too). You work with layers on the Layers palette. In Photoshop there are several types of layers and several options associated with layers. In Figure 3-12, you can see the parts of the Layers palette labeled. They are defined below.

- **Normal Layer**—This is a layer that is not modified or altered in any way.
- **Layer Effects**—These are special effects you can apply to the layer. We look at these in depth in the next section.
- **Type Layer**—This is a layer that contains type, or text. Text can be edited.
- **Background Layer**—The background is a bottom layer that is always locked and cannot be moved or have effects applied.
- **Adjustment Layer**—An adjustment layer is a non-permanent way to perform many adjustments to a layer that can be altered or discarded later, even after the file has been saved. We discuss these at length later in this chapter.
- **Layer with Mask**—The layer with a mask allows you to effectively erase parts of the layer by painting with black on the mask, but unlike erasing you have the ability to paint back parts of your layer using white. The original image remains unaltered. I almost never erase on a layer anymore, but use a mask instead. It is not only undoable, but easier to switch between black and white by hitting the 'X' key. There is no need to use Undo or mess with the History palette when you can effectively erase and un-erase your image.
- **Thumbnail Image**—This is a small picture of the layer.
- **Hide/Show Icon**—This icon indicates whether a layer is visible or not.
- **Blending Modes**—Blending Modes are discussed in detail a little later in this chapter.
- **Layer Opacity**—This adjusts how transparent a layer is; 0 is completely transparent while 100 is completely opaque.
- **Layer Fill**—Fill is similar to opacity except that Layer Opacity affects everything in the layer while Layer Fill only affects the layer contents, while Layer Effects remain 100% opaque.

Layer Locks

- Lock Transparent Pixels—This allows you to paint on the layer, but not on transparent pixels.

- Lock Pixels—You cannot paint on any part of the layer.
- Lock Position—You cannot move the layer, but you can make changes otherwise.
- Lock All—This completely locks the layer and allows no editing or changes at all.

Layer Tools

- Layer Effects—These are special effects you can apply to the layer. We look at these in depth in the next section.
- Layer Mask—This allows you to create a mask. With a mask you can effectively erase parts of the layer, but unlike erasing you have the ability to paint back parts of your layer. The original image remains unaltered.
- New Layer Set—This allows you to create a new layer set, a folder you can store many layers in. You can expand and collapse a layer set.
- New Adjustment Layer—This allows you to create an adjustment layer. We discuss these at length later in this chapter.
- New Layer—Click this to add a new layer. You can also drag a layer to this icon to duplicate it.
- Delete—This deletes the layer. You can click on this or drag the layer thumbnail to this icon.

Using Layers and Layer Sets

The Layers palette lets you move and manipulate each layer or group of layers. To move layers, you simply drag them. You can even drag layers into other Photoshop files. You can lock layers so they can't accidentally be changed. One of the most powerful aspects of layers is the ability to name them, color code them, and group them in sets. In some cases one element of a texture may have several layers associated with it. Maybe you have many variations of an element in a texture, or maybe you built an element from many separate layers. Instead of scrolling through many layers in the Layers palette, you can group the layers and collapse them. In Figure 3-13 is a texture with a layer set applied to it. In the Layers palette, on the upper right you can see that there are many layers that scroll off the bottom of the Layers palette. Add to that Layer Effects (we discuss them next) and you get one long Layers palette. In the middle Layers palette, you can see that the vents and cracks have all been put into their own Layer sets. On the bottom Layers palette you can see that the Cracks set has been opened while the other layer sets have been collapsed. You can see how much easier navigating a file like this can be using Layer sets.

In the coming sections I will introduce you to layer effects and styles, layer blending modes, adjustment layers, and their options. These are some of the most powerful tools for texture creation.

Figure 3-13
A texture with a layer set applied to it. In the Layers palette on the **upper right** you can see that there are many layers that scroll off the bottom of the Layers palette. In the **middle** palette you can see that the vents and cracks have all been put into their own Layer sets. On the **bottom** palette you can see that the Cracks set has been opened while the other layer sets have been collapsed.

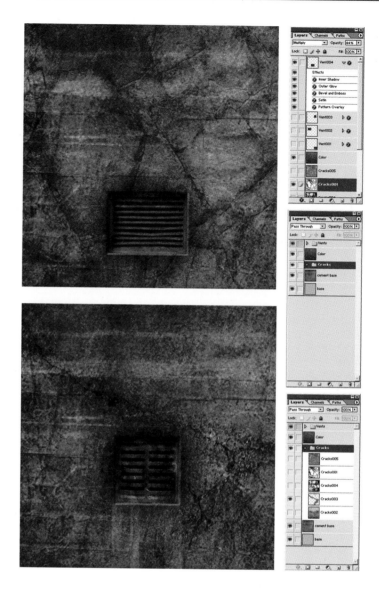

Layer Effects and Styles

Layer effects are a powerful tool. I use layer effects a lot in the creation of textures because not only do they make your work very flexible, if used correctly they can make great-looking textures quickly and easily. Layer effects can be changed, copied, and turned on and off. This is a primary way you can make a texture from a simple shape (remember Chapter 1?). By applying various effects such as drop shadows, inner and outer glows, bevels, overlays, gradients, strokes, and more, you can build up a texture.

Note: A layer style is a saved set of layer effects as well as a few other aspects of the layer such as the opacity and the selected blending mode. If you find yourself applying the same layer effects, with the same settings, repeatedly, then you can save a layer style and apply the effects in one click. You do this in the Layer Style window. Click New . . . to create the style based on the selected style, name it, and save it.

An important difference between layer effects and filters in that the filter permanently alters the pixels of the image and layer effects are real-time. If you put a drop shadow behind a square and then resize that square, the layer effects scale with it. A one-pixel stroke will always be exactly one pixel when you resize the object in the layer, whereas a one-pixel line that is part of the image will be subject to anti-aliasing and other resizing calculations and will get fuzzy, stretched, or disappear altogether. Figure 3-14 illustrates this. Layer effects stay the same even if you resize your entire image. So a one-pixel stroke that looks great on a 1024×1024 image will still be one pixel if you resize that image down to 512×512 and may look wrong. You can scale layer effects up or down by a percentage to match the scaling of the image, but it would be nice if there were an option to scale effects automatically.

Complaints about the use of layer effects stem from a lack of patience in applying and experimenting with the effects. Photoshop gives you so many options and so much control, you can get any result you want. Why paint a drop shadow when you can pop one in and tweak it to look just right? If you need to alter the shadow, or the element that it is under, you are not stuck having to repaint the shadow by hand. Figure 3-15 shows a vent that has each of the layer effects applied in two ways.

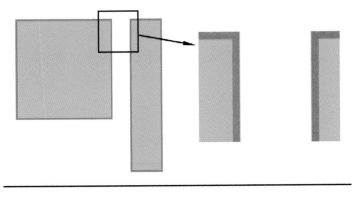

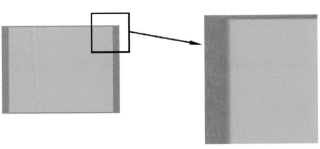

Figure 3-14
A one-pixel stroke will always be exactly one pixel when you resize the object in the layer, whereas a one-pixel line that is part of the image will be subject to anti-aliasing and other resizing calculations and will get fuzzy, stretched, or disappear altogether.

Figure 3-15
This vent image has each of the layer effects applied in two ways. The vent image on the **left** has the layer effect applied with default settings. The image on the **right** has had the settings of the effects adjusted. The larger example image on the **lower right** shows the vent (top) with no effects and the vent (bottom) with a variety of effects applied and adjusted.

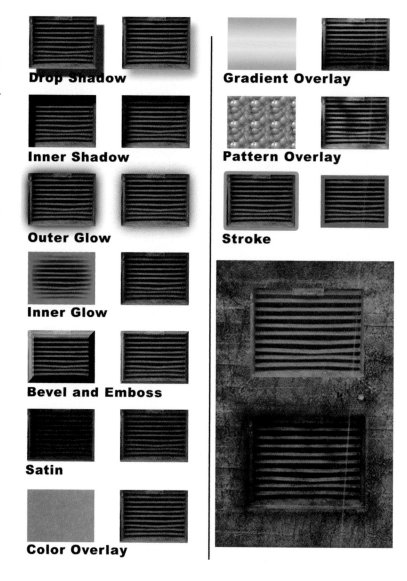

Drop Shadow

Inner Shadow

Outer Glow

Inner Glow

Bevel and Emboss

Satin

Color Overlay

Gradient Overlay

Pattern Overlay

Stroke

There are several layer effects and an almost unlimited way to apply them, given the many options each effect offers. Throughout the book we will be using layer effects and getting more specific with their application. Most effects contain the same basic parameters that can be applied in various ways. Color, size, distance, blending mode, contour, and opacity are most of the common effects.

Layer Blending Modes

Blending modes are among the most useful tools in Photoshop for the texture artist. Compositing is the term for building textures using multiple layers, and blending modes are critical to this process. Adding cracks to a wall, stains to a floor, or making almost any element look like it is part of the texture, and not just a separate image slapped on top, is largely accomplished with layer blending modes. Although blending modes function the same every time you use them, they will create different effects based on the contents of the layer and the layers below it. Blending modes are much simpler in their application than layer effects; you set the mode and adjust the opacity of the layer for the desired visual effect.

Blending modes work by affecting the layer below the layer to which the mode is assigned. The layer underneath is called the **base** and the layer on top, the one with the mode applied, is called the **blend**. Blending modes are grouped into six types:

- Normal and Dissolve
- Darken
- Lighten
- Contrast
- Invert/compare
- HSL

Note: You can cycle through the modes without having to use the drop-down menu by pressing Shift + Alt and the "+" or "−" keys. You can also use the mouse wheel to scroll through the modes.

Normal and Dissolve

There are six divisions of blending modes. The first set contains Normal and Dissolve. Normal is, well, normal. Nothing is done to the layer. Dissolve will look like nothing is happening until you start to decrease the opacity of the layer. Then you will see random pixels disappear.

The Darken Modes

The Darken modes are darken, multiply, linear burn, and color burn. With all of the Darken modes, white disappears and any pixel darker than white will darken the pixels in the base image. The various Darken modes darken the base image in different ways. Multiply looks at the pixels in the base and blend image and picks the darker one. Linear Burn does the same thing, but it results in a darker image; blacks really come out. Color Burn darkens and increases the saturation of the colors in the base image.

The Lighten Modes

The Lighten Modes are Lighten, Screen, Color Dodge, and Linear Dodge. These modes knock out the darker pixels in the blend image; black is knocked out completely. The Lighten modes lighten the base image in different ways. Lighten compares pixels in the base and blend image and uses the lighter one. Screen is the opposite of Multiply. Color Dodge and Screen always result in a lighter image than the base. Color Dodge lightens the base image and adds saturation to the underlying colors. Linear Light has a similar but stronger effect that can result in more whites.

The Contrast Modes

The Contrast modes are Overlay, Soft Light, Hard Light, Vivid Light, Linear Light, and Pin Light. Contrast modes are kind of a blend of the Darken and Lighten modes. Grays disappear and the lighter pixels brighten the image and darker pixels tend to darken the image. Soft Light makes the blend image act as if it were a soft light source. Hard Light looks at the brightness of the blend color and Screens lighter colors and Multiplies darker colors. Hard Light is meant to look like a spotlight using the blend as the light source cast on the base image.

The Difference and Exclusion Modes

Difference and Exclusion compare the blend layer to the base and pixels that are identical become black. Difference looks at the two pixels and subtracts the darker pixel from the lighter. Blending with white inverts the color and blending with black makes no change. Exclusion creates an image lower in contrast than Difference.

The HSL Modes

Hue, Saturation, Color, and Luminosity break up the color of the pixels in the blend layer and applies that information to the base. Hue applies the color of the blend without changing the Saturation or Brightness of the base, Saturation applies the amount of saturation of the Blend to the base, Color applies the color of the Blend to the Base, and Luminosity applies the brightness of the Blend to the Base.

Hard Mix Mode (CS)

Hard Mix posterizes the layers below based on the values of the layer this mode is applied to. Pixels brighter than 50% gray will brighten the layer and darker pixels will darken the layer.

Adjustment and Fill Layers

Adjustment and Fill Layers add a great deal of flexibility to texture creation. You can color, adjust tone, fill a layer with color, patterns, or a gradient. You can use masks with adjustment layers. The adjustment layer I tend to use the most is Brightness/Contrast.

Note: Before creating an adjustment layer, make a selection and a mask will be created for the adjustment layer.

Brushes

The brush is obviously an extremely important part of Photoshop. Brushes in Photoshop are very flexible and deep. The quick and simple use of a brush requires the selection of the Brush Tool and a right mouse click to select a specific brush. Here you can also load other brushes and change the size and hardness/softness of the brush. You can also create your own brushes.

The Brush palette adds a deep level of control over your brush. You can define the fade, randomness, spread, and other settings of your brush. You can even combine two brushes. As important as the brush is, I almost never use more than a standard hard/soft, large/small combination of the standard brush shapes, especially in the projects in this book.

Cloning/Healing

These brushes are extremely useful to the texture artist. Quite simply the Clone Tool allows you to sample one part of an image and paint on another part of the image. The sample point moves as your brush does. If you are careful you can be very accurate with the Clone Tool and rebuild hard edges, as well as remove defects from an image. The Healing Tool is similar to the Clone Tool in its use, but it "corrects" the sample to match the area of the image. The Healing Brush matches the texture, lighting, and shading of the sampled pixels to the source pixels. See Figure 3-16.

Filters

Last but not least we look at filters. When discussed, Photoshop filters are typically presented in the form of an example image with the effect of each filter shown on the sample image. While that approach has its uses, I will not do it here because, not only has this been done a million times in other books and publications, but this approach doesn't really convey the power of using filters. There are a number of variables that affect the result of using a filter(s). The image size, the foreground and background color, the settings of each filter, the combination of the filters you run, and of course the image you are running the filter(s) on. In this section I will discuss the major filter groups and how they affect your image. You can also fade the effect of most filters, and I find this particularly

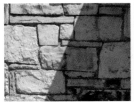 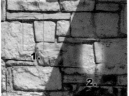 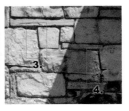

Figure 3-16
The Clone and Healing Tools. The image on the **left** is the original, the **middle** image (1) the Clone sample area, (2) the cloned area. **Right,** (3) the Heal sample area, (4) the healed area.

useful. The Fade command allows you to change the opacity and blending mode of the filter as well as several of the other Photoshop tools.

The Filter Gallery (CS)

New to Photoshop CS, the Filter Gallery allows you to see most of the filters as they are applied to the image. You can quickly click through the filters and see how they affect your image; see Figure 3-17. You can also add another filter to a stack and move, hide, and delete them. This is incredibly powerful, as you are no longer stuck running one filter at a time. Now you can go back and change the settings of an earlier filter and see the effects combined with the other filters in the stack.

Note: If you are working on a large image, or on a slower computer, you can make a selection and run the filter on the smaller section much faster. After you run the filter on the selection, you can Undo the filter using Ctrl + Z and deselect the selection, and then use Ctrl + F to run the filter on the entire image.

Artistic Filters

The first group of filters is the artistic filters, which can alter an image to make it look as if it has been painted by an artist in several styles.

Figure 3-17
New to Photoshop CS, the Filter Gallery allows you to see most of the filters as they are applied to the image.

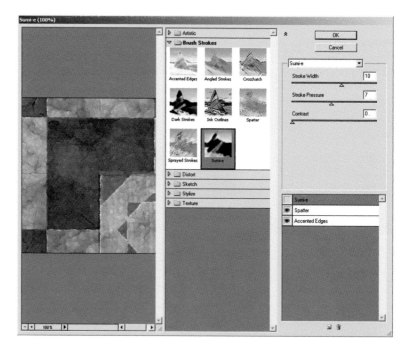

Blur Filters

The blur filters simply blur the image in various ways. You can use a blur to smooth an image you are overlaying, create a drippy stain, etc.

Brush Stroke Filters

The brush filters are similar to the artistic filters, only they focus on ink and brush effects rather than an artistic style.

Distort Filters

These filters distort your image in various ways. You can make the image look like glass, or twirl and zigzag it. These filters are not fully represented in the Filter Gallery in Photoshop CS.

Note: You can use the Liquefy Tool for precise distortions of an image.

Noise Filters

There are a few filters here that add or remove noise and artifacts from an image, but for texture creation Add Noise is the one you will use almost exclusively. Adding noise to a solid color gives the other filters something to work with. Running a filter on a solid color usually has little to no effect. Sometimes you even need to blur the noise a bit to get a better or different result.

Pixelate Filters

These filters basically clump pixels together in various ways. The effect, I find, is not useful for texture creation.

Render Filters

Render filters allow you to create 3D shapes, cloud patterns, and light effects among others. For texture creation the Clouds, Difference Clouds, and Lighting Effects filters are very useful. With Photoshop CS the Fibers filter was added. This filter creates a simple image of fibers that can be really useful for creating wood, bark, and other organic textures.

Sharpen Filters

The sharpen filters basically increase the contrast of an image for the most part. I find they create the conditions in an image you are trying to avoid as a texture artist.

Sketch Filters

These filters, for the most part, use the foreground and background color as they process your image, to make it look as if it were hand-drawn. These filters can be useful if you are creating a texture where you want that effect. The Halftone Pattern creates a line effect across the image, which can be useful when creating computer monitors.

Stylize Filters

These filters displace pixels for various height effects, for the most part. These filters are also underrepresented in the Filter Gallery.

Texture Filters

These filters can be useful to the texture artist, if used very sparingly. Actually, with the introduction of layer effects, I rarely use these filters. The stained glass filter can be useful, but not for stained glass, as you will see later in the book.

Other Filters

Under this last filter slot are the two filters most familiar to the texture artist, High Pass and the famous Offset filter. I mention the High Pass filter in the next chapter and discuss it. I also point you to a useful article on the High Pass filter. High Pass basically helps you remove hotspots. The Offset filter simply moves the image horizontally or vertically by an entered value. This filter is used a great deal to check for the seams in a texture. You can now use sliders to move the image back and forth, instead of only numbers. (Adobe! When will you let us drag the image around in real time? Is it that hard to do?)

Paths

Paths are great, wonderful, and essential to the creation of lines that are not only organic and curvy, but editable, too. This is not only useful for people who can't draw fancy lines. This can be useful for all, as it allows you to save, edit, and manipulate the paths in many ways. We use Paths later in the book, so you will be introduced to them then.

Conclusion

That was a quick look at the parts of Photoshop most useful to the texture artist. One of the best things you can do to become a great texture artist is to master Photoshop. It may take a while, but it is well worth it.

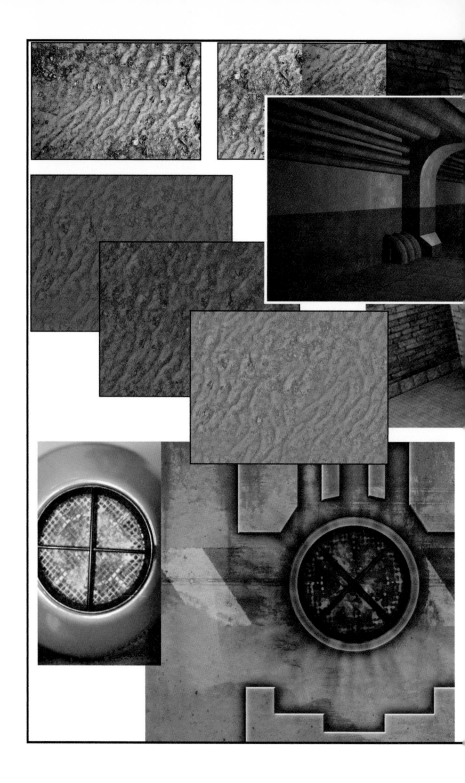

Chapter 4

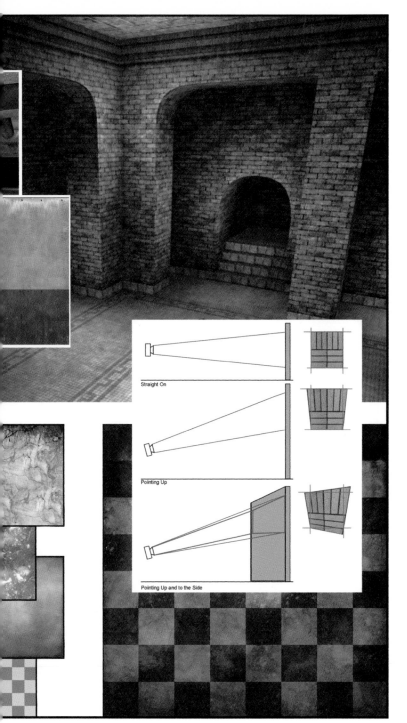

Introduction

In this chapter we will take the next step in creating the best game textures possible, which is to have the best texture resources possible. We will look at the various sources of digital resources for texture creation and each of the steps in the process of gathering, preparing, and storing your assets.

Prepping for Texture Creation

"Do, or do not. There is no try."

Yoda
Jedi Master

I love quoting Yoda.

While the focus of this book is the creation of textures using Photoshop so you develop strong Photoshop skills, in reality it is more common, easier, and more effective to use photo reference in texture creation. We will be using a little photo reference in this book, and the DVD contains a good collection of the kinds of images I find are the hardest to create in Photoshop without actually hand-painting them. Cracks, splats, drips, wood grains, and other organic random stuff, while they can be created in Photoshop, simply look more genuine when taken from a good source photo. Typically, a texture is built with layers containing various sources of imagery, and photo reference plays a big part in this process. Layers are "composited" together using the various tools in Photoshop such as layer blending modes. The concept of layers was introduced in Chapter 2, and Photoshop layers specifically were discussed in Chapter 3. Compositing layers was discussed in the context of layer blending modes in Chapter 3 as well. We will be using compositing throughout the book. Even if all the elements of a texture are created entirely in Photoshop, we will still be using layers and blending modes to composite the various parts together. No matter what source you get the image from, you always end up in Photoshop combining and manipulating the various sources to create the imagery that fits your needs. You will almost always use Photoshop in the creation and final output of the texture.

A resource, in the context of this book, is any digital image from any source that helps you create your art. Therefore, a small checkered pattern made in Photoshop that can be tiled across a canvas in Photoshop and used as the base of a tiled floor is a resource. A high-resolution digital photograph of a dirty surface that you might overlay to make the tiled pattern look dirty is a resource. And so is any other image that can be used in order to get the desired effect (Figure 4-1).

The examples are as endless as your imagination and limited only to the number of digital images you can collect. There are no cut-and-dried rules here. A resource that may seem useless to some may be exactly what you need. In general, you will want to avoid wasting space and dealing with the clutter of low-resolution, poor-quality, and just plain bad images. But if you come across an image that you have a specific use for, keep it! Keep in mind that while it is easy to make a texture like the above-mentioned plain-and-simple checkered texture, it takes time to create. Why not have one on hand that you can drop into an image when needed?

If possible, save everything you can. You never know when you will need a high-resolution image of a penny, a close-up of rotting meat, or 101 highway signs from South America. Naturally my first

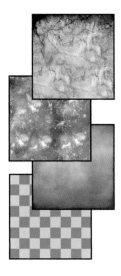

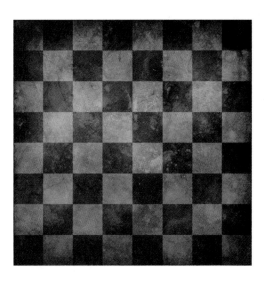

Figure 4-1
A resource is any image that can be used to create art, Here a simple checked pattern was used to create a tile floor by combining it with other images.

recommendation to you as a game artist is to buy a very large hard drive—the biggest you can afford. If you can buy a large external hard drive, do so. This makes the process of sharing, backing up, and switching to a new computer much easier. And in the event of a natural disaster you will be saved. "Honey you grab the kids, pets, silverware, and family pictures. I have to burn my 40 gigs of textures onto 67 DVDs!!! Meet you outside!" In addition to a large external hard drive I also have a RAID array in my system that mirrors several hard drives so if one crashes I don't lose any work, even the most recent work. It has also added peace of mind that when I leave town I can leave my external drive in safe location away from my house. If my computer got stolen, the house burned down, or my system got damaged in any way, I would still have my external drive. I could more easily replace the system than the data.

It is also a good idea to crop, resize, and otherwise manipulate your images to make them as size-efficient and user-ready as possible without degrading their quality. An image that tiles nicely and is already a power of two will not slow your inspired work flow as you can simply drop it into your work and not stop to crop, clean, tile, and otherwise make it useful.

In the process of greedily obtaining and hoarding digital images, you will discover that whatever time you spend upfront to make them easier to find and use in the long run will be worth every second. You need to categorize your assets by type (terrain, liquid, doors) as well as keep track of where you got them. Some texture collections have copyrights and "use restrictions" attached to them. Therefore, you might not be able to store all your images in one neat structure, but have them in various folders according to many criteria. We will look at that later in this chapter in some detail.

First, we will look at the process of gathering the raw images for your collection. There are many ways to collect images for your collection; all have their pros and cons.

Gathering Textures

There are many sources for textures and digital imagery, which include creating them in Photoshop, taking digital photographs, scanning them in, buying texture collections, surfing the Internet for useful images, and using 3D applications to model and render images.

Creating Textures in Photoshop

Although there are many ways to create a texture, I wanted to focus on using pure Photoshop as much as possible for this book. I believe that if you are able to create anything you want in Photoshop, then when you have the other resources at your disposal you will be much better and faster at creating textures. I will briefly introduce this method here and we will spend the rest of the book creating textures using Photoshop. Technically, every game texture you create will pass through Photoshop and become a Photoshopped image to some degree.

Many people get intimidated by the prospect of a blank slate in Photoshop when creating a texture, or they may be critical of this method based on low-quality work they have seen. Creating basic materials, and even objects, in Photoshop is not that hard and does not require special painting skills. In fact, you can create materials and objects with a greater degree of control, and thus create an image that may be better than a digital image of the same thing in some cases; see Figure 4-2.

Figure 4-2
The image on the **left** is a digital photograph and the one on the **right** was created entirely in Photoshop.

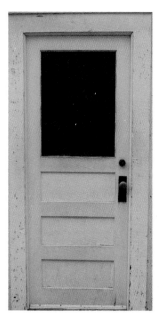 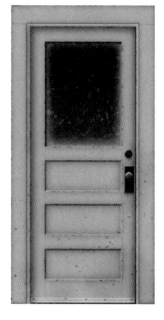

In the end, no matter what source you obtain your raw assets from, you will always use Photoshop (or a similar 2D image editor) to manipulate and assemble your textures in their final state. For example, you may create a frame for a window in Photoshop based on a photograph, create the glass panes from scratch, and use an actual image of a wood grain to add detail to the window frame and overlay a grime layer, too (see Figure 4-3).

There are some cons to this method. It does take some time to start from a blank slate and use all the proper filters and tools to create a realistic texture or material from scratch. If you are not patient and understand the methods, then textures will look "Photoshopped," which is not a negative term pertaining to Photoshop, but is a comment on a lack of quality in the image itself. Not adjusting any Photoshop default values or taking the time to tweak and test the texture will result in substandard work. One positive is that this method allows you to create an image that is uniquely yours. You will never be stuck without the texture you need. If you can imagine

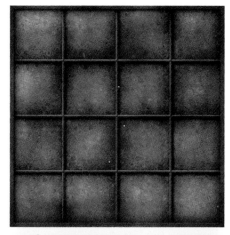

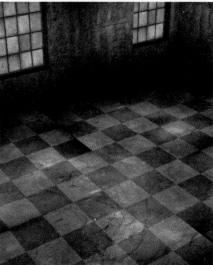

Figure 4-3
This window was created in Photoshop using a mixture of photographic and Photoshop elements.

it, you can create it in Photoshop. Just because you can't find a picture to manipulate, you don't have to stop working.

Even if you don't need to create from a blank slate in Photoshop, you will still need to use Photoshop to manipulate your images to make them useful to you. The better you know Photoshop and its many tools, the better your work will be no matter what method you use.

Finally, there is consistency. Knowing how to use Photoshop to its fullest will allow you to achieve consistency with your texture sets, and that is very important. No matter how great your textures look, if they don't visually mesh together in a game world it diminishes all the good you have accomplished in your texture work.

Digital Cameras

Using a digital camera to collect images is very common and becoming easier as the prices of digital cameras drop and their quality increases. The only real cons of this method are that people don't like it when you take pictures of their front doors and they will often call the police (true story). Art gallery owners don't like it when you take pictures of the paintings hanging on their walls (true again). And the government hates it when you take pictures of their secret alien storage facilities and will try to take your camera away from you (can't talk about this one).

In all seriousness, there are no drawbacks to this method other than the cost of the camera. Depending on what camera you purchase, you may be stuck with limited storage and resolution, odd formats, and slow data transfer times. But this should not be a problem with a fairly recent purchase. As of this writing, $300 will buy you a digital camera that should do the job well and make data transfer easy via flashcards or a direct connection to the computer from the camera. With a decent digital camera you can take pictures of anything and everything. The images will be yours (unless you are taking pictures of copyrighted artwork, people, etc.) and you can set up shoots for specific items. I have taken pictures of dirty dishes and fake blood smears on paper, and I have stood in the highway for the right angle on a sign—all for the sake of textures. Be warned that since 9/11, taking pictures of most places will be noticed and you need to be more careful. Before 9/11 no one would think much of you if you were taking a picture of the rusted door of a power station or warehouse, but now you may be watched or even reported. I have been pulled over and questioned by the police after taking pictures around a warehouse. Someone thought it suspicious and wrote my plate number down.

Digital images are versatile, too. Don't be limited to the original context or scale of the asset. Use the texture where it works. A rock can be the side of a mountain, a small crack in a sidewalk can be a large crack in a wall, the vent opening on a hairdryer can be a large sewer grate, etc. (Figure 4-4). This applies not just to scale, but to context as well. A really great source for some of the most

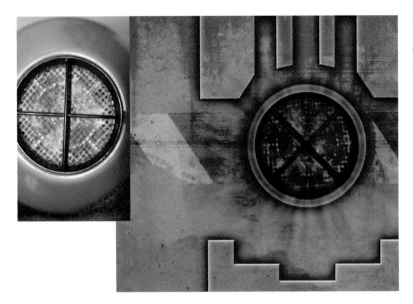

Figure 4-4
Don't be limited to the original context or scale of an asset. Use the texture where it works. A rock can be the side of a mountain, a small crack in a sidewalk can be a large crack in a wall, and in this case the vent opening on a hairdryer is a large sewer grate.

disgusting textures I have ever seen were simply close-ups of the pots and pans in the kitchen after dinner. Grease drippings from a roast, congealed butter after the vegetables have been removed, and dried ketchup can make for some great imagery. We have included some on the DVD of course. In Figure 4-5 are some of the sick images in my collection.

The possibilities are as endless as your imagination with a digital camera. Another benefit is the ease and extremely low cost of experimentation with a digital camera. You are not limited by factors such as the number of prints on a roll or the cost of film and developing. You can shoot and delete a thousand images for the price of ten.

Tips on Taking Digital Photographs

Taking digital photographs for use as texture resource takes a different mindset than traditional photography. Most likely, the first images you take will have aspects that will make them hard to use in a texture. You won't be able to see these problems right off and, in fact, you will have to go home and look at the images up close on your computer and try to work on them before the problems pop up. But there is no substitute for this, and going through this process a few times is the only way to develop an eye for spotting potential problems before taking the picture. Even so, here are some general tips for using a digital camera for capturing texture resource that will help speed up that process.

Image Resolution

This first one is an obvious one. The higher you set the resolution on your camera, the higher the detail will be in the image. This also eats up memory but makes for a better resource.

Figure 4-5
Guess what these are.

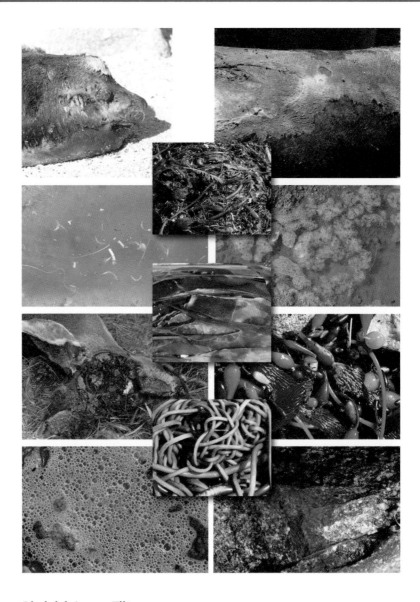

Diminish Image Tilt

This is a rather simple one. When you take a picture, look closely in the viewfinder. You will see some marks (Figure 4-6); whether they are lines, squares, or circles doesn't matter. These marks may be there for a number of reasons, but primarily they are there to help you line up your shot. These are very useful and easy to use when you are taking a picture of a surface with straight lines such as a brick wall or the frame of a window.

Watch the Auto Settings

Many digital cameras come with preprogrammed image control modes. These are various presets for the camera for taking various

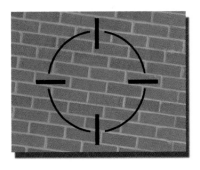 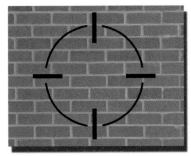

Figure 4-6
Save yourself some work; use the marks in the viewfinder to line up your shot. These are very useful and easy to use when you are taking a picture of a surface with straight lines such as a brick wall or the frame of a window.

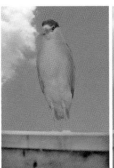 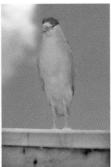 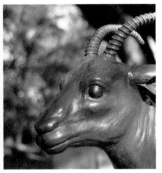

Figure 4-7
Many digital cameras come with preprogrammed image control modes. Be careful of the presets that have a shallow depth of field and other settings that can affect the image in an undesirable way. Depth of field is the area of the image that is in focus from the camera lens to infinity. You can have a shallow depth of field where items that are only with in a few feet or inches are in focus while objects that are closer are farther from the camera are blurry. To the **left** you can see that the bird and the background are both in focus; in the **middle** the bird is in focus, but the sky is not; and on the **right** is an image where the foreground object is in focus, but the background is not.

types of pictures: close-ups, portraits, sports, and nighttime pictures to name a few. The danger here is that some of the presets have a shallow depth of field and other settings that can distort or affect the image in an undesirable way. Depth of field is the area of the image that is in focus from the camera lens to infinity. You can have a shallow depth of field where items that are only within a few feet or inches are in focus, while objects that are closer or farther from the camera are blurry. In Figure 4-7, you can see a few examples of depth of field.

A shallow depth of field can be bad when it is so shallow that when you are photographing a surface, parts of the surface are out of focus and blurry and other parts are crisp. This can happen easily if you are taking a picture at an angle, looking up at a window, for example, and are using a shallow depth of field. The part of the window closest to you will be in focus and the farthest parts will be blurry.

Diminish Lens Distortion (Fisheye)

When purchasing a digital camera, make sure you get a decent lens. Cheaper lenses tend to give you a fisheye effect (Figure 4-8), spherically distorting the image, which can make it much harder to clean up your images for use. You can get a 5–mega-pixel camera the size of a pack of cigarettes, but the lens is the size of a drop of water and will give you bad distortion. There are cheaper cameras

Figure 4-8
When buying a digital camera, try to get a decent lens. Even high mega-pixel cameras often have cheap lenses that distort the image, creating a fisheye, or spherical, effect. This makes using the image as a texture more difficult as it takes more time to correct such errors and does more damage to the image when doing so. This image is very distorted due to the cheap lens on the camera and would be very hard to correct (not even worth it in my opinion). Notice the blue lines that are straight compared to the edges of the window frame.

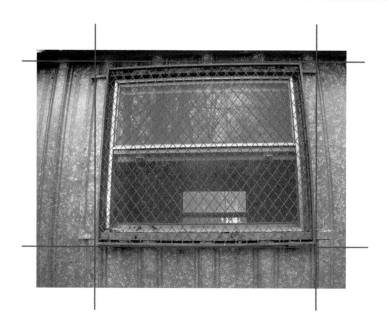

with lower pixel resolution and better lenses, and those are the ones I would buy over the ones with poor lenses.

If you have a camera with a lens prone to fisheye, you can counter the effect by getting as far back from the surface you are photographing and zooming in. See Figure 4-9 for an example of a surface that was photographed close up and zoomed all the way out and then farther away and zoomed in as far as possible. The effect is not very pronounced, but the bulge in the lines of the bricks will be very noticeable if you tried to tile this image.

Diminish Angle Distortion (Position)

Distortion also comes from the position of the camera in relation to the subject. This relates to perspective, which we discussed in Chapter 1. When you take a picture standing above, below, or to the left or right of whatever you are photographing, you are creating perspective in the image. You will not have straight lines and therefore have to make corrections in Photoshop. The Photoshop work is not too time-consuming when correcting straight lines that are at an angle using the Free Transform or Crop Tool (we look at that later in this chapter). Correcting a bulged out image may be harder, but what's bad about skewed angles as opposed to the bulge is that dramatically changing the perspective and angles in an image will cause it to fall apart visually. Even if the lines are perfectly straight, an object with any kind of depth, such as windows and doors that have protruding frames around them, retains visual information about the angle at which the object was captured (this relates to Chapter 1, too, particularly light and shadow). The human eye will detect those differences and the image will look off. There are ways to correct those errors that are

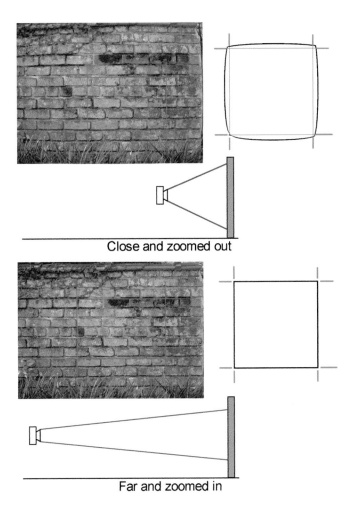

Close and zoomed out

Far and zoomed in

Figure 4-9
Distortion from a cheap lens can be countered somewhat by getting far back from the surface you are photographing and zooming in. This is an example of a surface that was photographed close up and zoomed all the way out and then farther away and zoomed in as much as possible. The effect may not look that pronounced but later, when you try to use this image to tile across a wall surface, it will be very noticeable.

time-consuming as you are basically rebuilding the image and this is best to avoid if possible. So, even if you get all the lines in the image straight in Photoshop, the shadows will just not look right. Things that are flat like signs can be more easily compensated for in Photoshop. You can see some examples of this in Figure 4-10 and an illustration on how to position yourself in Figure 4-11.

Diminish Lighting Problems

Lighting is a big concern, too. If you have studied photography or film, you may be familiar with the term the "Golden Hour." For photographers the best light for photography occurs one hour after sunrise and one hour before sunset. During this time the light is diffuse. For a texture hunter this is not always the best time to take pictures, because the light tends to be saturated with blues and oranges and is changing rapidly.

But during the day light is of very high contrast and harsh when the sun is overhead. When the sun is low in the sky, the shadows can be

Figure 4-10
Distortion also comes from the position of the camera in relation to the subject. When you take a picture standing above, below, or to the left or right of whatever you are photographing, you are creating perspective angles in the image that will have to be corrected in Photoshop. The windows on the **upper left** are okay, but the windows on the **upper right** are at too dramatic an angle. The **second row** shows some windows all taken at a good straight on angle. The **third row** shows a sign that was taken at a skewed angle but easily fixed as it is flat and lacks a lot of depth. These windows on the **bottom left** are at a very extreme angle. **Bottom right,** even after straightening the lines, the protruding frame retains visual information about the angle at which the window was captured and the image doesn't work.

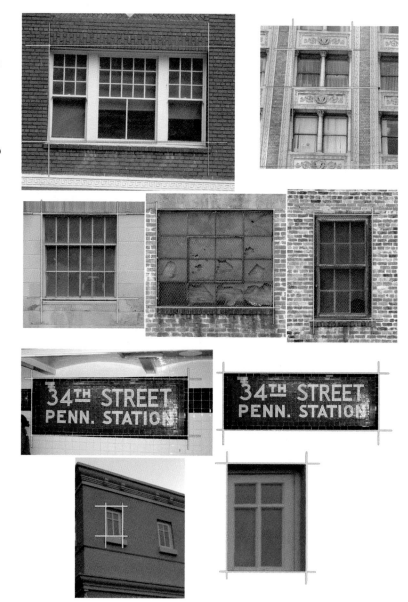

equally as harsh, but are longer. During these hours, when the sun is low in the sky, you are also faced with the problem that anything you are trying to photograph might be facing away from the sun and therefore silhouetted. These images generally come out really dark. This is not a good time to take texture source images either.

So what does that leave? If possible, wait for a cloudy or overcast day. While many photographers don't go out on overcast days, it is the best time for us to go out and shoot. Light is plentiful, it is just diffused by the clouds. There are no harsh shadows as the light is more evenly distributed. On overcast days, plants and trees in particular are more saturated. Although we have a lot of control

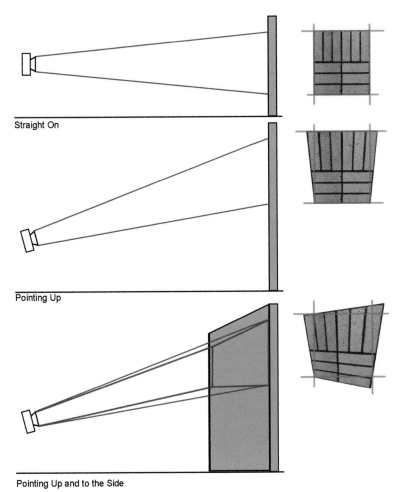

Straight On

Pointing Up

Pointing Up and to the Side

Figure 4-11
Ideally, you want to take a picture straight on to minimize angle distortion, but even if you can't get into an optimal position you can still minimize angle distortion by positioning yourself as straight vertically or horizontally as you can. **Top,** ideally the camera should be pointing straight at the subject. If this is possible, the image will be mostly square and easier to fix in Photoshop. The illustration in the **middle** is of the camera looking up, like at a window or sign high on a wall. In this scenario the image will come out wider at the top than the bottom. At the **bottom** you can see that taking a picture from an angle that is both horizontally and vertically off will create a very distorted image.

over our image in Photoshop, harsh shadows are almost impossible to remove. Figure 4-12 shows two wooden shutters, one shot on an overcast day and one on a sunny day.

Don't Use the Flash If At All Possible

Another problem is flash burn. Avoid the flash if possible. A professional photographer knows how to use a flash so that it casts just the right amount of controlled light, and maybe you can learn that, too, but in general if you take a picture using the flash, you will get harsh light and shadow and a large flash burn in the image. Even surfaces that don't seem highly reflective will be burned by a flash. In fact, even if you are photographing a very matte (nonreflective) surface, you will still get a large overlit area in the middle of the image and the edges will recede into darkness. This is just as bad as a burn for texture work. You can remove a mild flash burn in Photoshop, but usually that requires you to clone and paint the flashed part of the image to remove it. I would opt to take

Figure 4-12
Although we have a lot of
control over our image in
Photoshop, harsh shadows
are almost impossible
to remove. Here are two
wooden shutters, one shot
on an overcast day and one
on a sunny day.

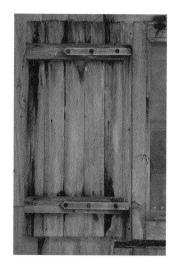
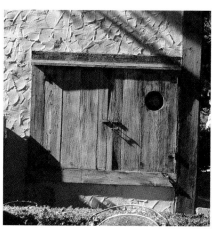

Figure 4-13
Avoid the flash if possible. In
general, if you take a picture
using the flash, you will get
harsh light and shadow and
a large flash burn in the
image. Even surfaces that
don't seem highly reflective
will be burned by a flash. The
top image shows a flash burn
and the **bottom** shows how
poorly it tiles.

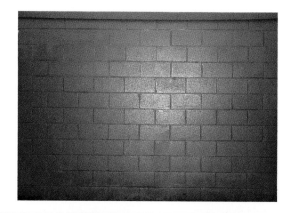

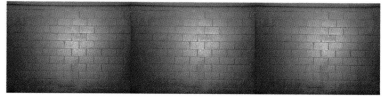

another path if possible. Figure 4-13 shows a flash burned image
and how poorly it tiles.

Plan for Alpha Channels

We talked about alpha channels in Chapter 2 (making parts of the
image transparent) and later we will look at various ways to create
alpha channels. Many of the techniques for removing backgrounds
to create alpha channels rely on the separation and deletion of the
background colors from the foreground objects. Knowing that, if at

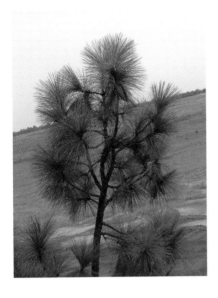 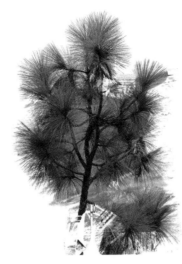

Figure 4-14
Plan for creating alpha channels if possible. If it is at all possible, try and make sure the objects you are capturing have a contrasting color behind them so the background is easier to remove. The figure shows an example of a plant that was photographed so the background could easily be removed and an alpha channel created.

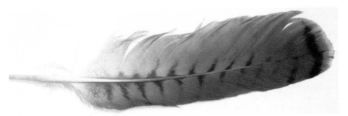

Figure 4-15
You can scan small 3D objects like knives, leaves, or feathers. Just be careful not to scratch the glass or spill damaging liquids into your scanner.

all possible, try and make sure the objects you are capturing have a contrasting color behind them. Figure 4-14 depicts a plant that was photographed so the background could easily be removed and an alpha channel created.

Plan for Tiling

If you know that you will be tiling the surface you are photographing, then try and capture all the edges and boundaries you will need to make the tiling easier. If you clip off part of the image, the tiling of that surface will be much harder. If you are photographing a surface, such as a brick or stone wall that you intend to tile, try and pick a section of the wall that has as few repeatable aspects if at all possible.

Scanners

Scanners are another way to capture digital images. Not only can you scan documents, you can scan small 3D objects like knives, leaves, or feathers (Figure 4-15). Just be careful not to scratch the glass or spill damaging liquids into your scanner. Keep in mind that even though scanners have dropped in price and increased in quality, it is often easier to just take a picture of an object with a digital camera rather than scan it. Keep in mind that many images you would like to scan may be copyrighted.

Scanners are great for artists who actually do their work on paper, but once again a digital camera might be better considering that artwork can easily be too big for a scanner and the paint or ink may rub off on the scanner glass.

Texture Collections

There are some terrific texture collections for sale that anyone can buy, and they fall into three general categories:

- The finished game texture
- The digital photograph collection
- The digital image of a surface or thing

The problem with the finished game texture is that anyone and everyone will recognize those purchased textures. They can almost never be used "as is" and will need to be modified so it is generally better to get a good set of base images and build your own textures. But if you can get your hands on these texture collections, they are very useful for learning. You can also use these in certain circumstances "as is." If you are prototyping or building a walkthrough that will not be sold on artistic merits, then these sets can be very useful and time-saving.

The digital photograph is the sort that features a kid holding balloons, a shot of the Chrysler building, the Statue of Liberty, or a sunset. These are artsy shots and while they may have their uses, they aren't generally as useful to the texture artist. Give me a good image of a rusted dumpster panel, cracked stucco, or a wall of wooden planks. The digital photograph is sold mostly as clip art for web sites and newsletters. Only a texture artist would love a high-resolution image of a pile of rotten meat swarming with maggots. Most people would prefer the kid holding the balloons.

Finally, we have the digital image of the rusted dumpster panel, the side of the dead seal, the close-up of pork drippings and dried vomit (see Figure 4-16). These are the images the texture artist lives for, the ones we find most useful. These are the images you will composite over other images in Photoshop using the layer blending modes to create some incredible textures. These images are best when you take them and swap them with your fellow artists. There is a good set of digital images on the DVD to help get you started or to add to your collection.

The Internet

The Internet is a great source of images. Of course, you will run into copyright restrictions and low-resolution images (among other

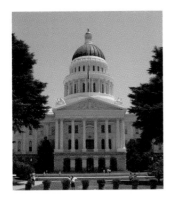
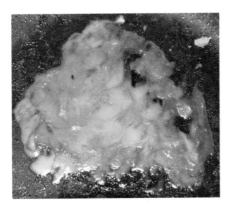

Figure 4-16
From left to right, an image of a digital photograph from a clip art type collection and a digital image of—ugh, that's sick. Which image would you prefer in your collection? (By the way, it's ketchup and bacon fat)

problems), but quite often the images you will find by going to the image search on Google will be surprisingly good (Figure 4-17). Even just for a source of reference, the Internet can be invaluable. Type in a few keywords and you can see pirate gold, maps, Persian rugs, almost anything you can imagine someone took a picture of and uploaded somewhere on the Internet. As of this writing, there are 1,187,630,000 images on the Google image search.

Using 3D Applications

Another method used for creating 2D textures is to model them in 3D. This method is great for modeling things that you can't get a picture of and that would lack the depth you need in Photoshop. This method also allows you to create a surface using all the lights, materials, and shaders the 3D package has to offer. You can render an image from a 3D application, process it in Photoshop, and then apply it to a lower poly-count game model. The big drawback to this method is that it relies on the facts that you (1) are a 3D modeler and that you (2) own the necessary software. That is the major drawback since you need to know how to 3D model, texture, and light as well as own the software. This method can also be time-consuming and must be weighed against other options.

Cleaning Your Textures

The process of cleaning up your textures is an important one. Time spent at this stage will save you much time later on. When an image is cropped, it saves space; when it is named and saved appropriately, it is much easier to find when you need it; and when an image tiles nicely, it can be used "as is"; you won't have to stop your creativity to clean up the image. Also, the process of working for a few minutes with each texture helps you become familiar with what images you have on your hard drive. This will speed you up and allow you to create better textures as you will be aware of the many options you have when building your texture. Of all the things you can do to manipulate an image when cleaning it up, the first thing you will most likely do is crop it.

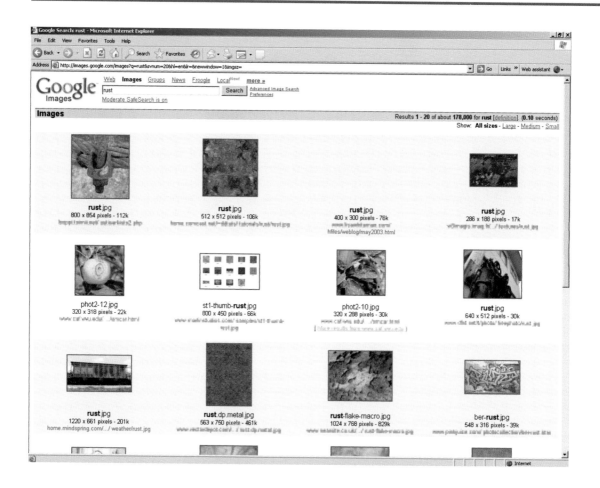

Figure 4-17
Type a few keywords into the Google image search and you can see pirate gold, maps, Persian rugs—almost anything you can imagine someone took a picture of and uploaded somewhere on the Internet. Searching for the word "rust" netted 178,000 images. *Google image search screen used with permission.*

Cropping

Cropping is simply the process of cutting off portions of an image. Cropping literally chops away the portions of the image outside the crop box (see Figure 4-18). The Crop Tool in Photoshop, however, can do much more than just cut your image down to size. Some of the features of the Crop Tool can be very useful and time-saving.

As you are cropping your images, keep in mind that while power of two textures (discussed in Chapter 2) are often your final goal, a perfect square of any size will be fine as long as you remember to start your texture work in the power of two, resizing the source to fit. Some resource images defy the perfect square rule, so don't stress. If the image is a panoramic scene of the horizon or to be used as an overlay for stains and weathering, then leave it as complete as you like.

Cropping an image can save file space, as well as resizing it, but I don't resize and I crop as little as possible. I like to keep the entire image and always use a copy of the image and never alter the original. Taking the image up in size doesn't buy you anything but a

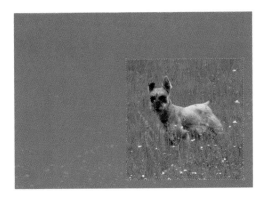 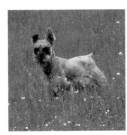

Figure 4-18
Cropping chops the image down to the size of the crop box and removes what's outside it.

larger file size and sizing it down or cropping it only degrades quality and/or removes portions of the image you can't get back later if you need it. I do crop a lot when I am working on windows, doors, and things like that as I straighten them, especially if all there is around it is a boring wall that looks like all the others I have.

Warning: Cropping is permanent unless you change the **Delete** option to **Hide** in the Option Bar in Photoshop. Once you do that the canvas size will be scaled down, but the image will still be the same size and is just hidden as it is outside the canvas area. If you use the Delete option and save and close your file, you can never get the cropped portion back. You cannot use the Hide option on an image that only has a background layer. You need to either convert the background to a layer, duplicate it, or create a new layer.

Note: You can make the canvas size larger using the Crop Tool. You can drag the crop box handles outside the canvas.

Here are some helpful tips when cropping an image in Photoshop. When using the Crop Tool you can:

- Hold down Shift and it will make the selection perfectly square.
- Hold down Alt and the crop box will drag and size from the center point of the crop box.
- Hold down the Shift and Alt keys and make the selection perfectly square as well as drag and size from the center point of the crop box.
- Press the Caps Lock key and your cursor will change to the small crosshairs instead of the thick Crop Icon that can get in the way of the image you are trying to crop.
- Enter a height and width in the options bar. After you drag out the crop box and hit Enter, the image crops and resizes. You will notice that you can size the crop box but not change the proportions. The height and width stay proportional to the values you entered.
- You can also hold down the Ctrl and Alt keys **after** you start dragging out the crop box to make the crop box selection the exact size of the dimensions you entered so the image will not resize after you press Enter.

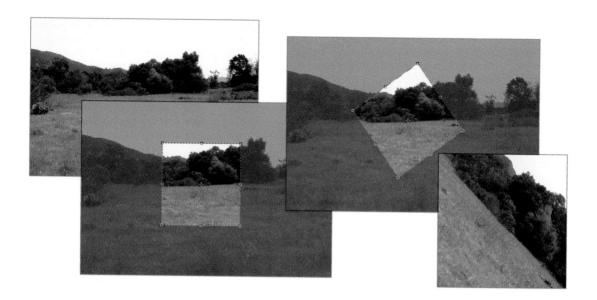

Figure 4-19
You can rotate the crop box and it will crop and rotate the image to match the selection. From left to right: the original image, the crop box dragged out, the crop box rotated, and the final result after pressing Enter.

• You can rotate the crop box and it will crop and rotate the image to match the selection. See Figure 4-19.

Fixing Perspective (Bad Angles) with the Crop Tool

Using the Crop Tool in Photoshop, you are also able to instantly fix perspective problems. I find this feature particularly useful. All you have to do is drag out a crop box on your canvas (doesn't matter how big it is as you adjust it later) and make sure the Perspective box is checked in the Options bar and then you can drag each individual handle to the corners of the thing you want to crop and fix. When you press Enter, BAM! The image is cropped and the perspective fixed. See Figure 4-20 for a visual of the crop tool fixing perspective in an image. This works best on images with straight lines. I mentioned earlier that a bulged out image is harder to work with than one with straight lines. This is one of the reasons. The lines connecting the crop box handles are straight, but if the area of the image you are trying to crop is bulged, the lines will be curved and you won't get a clean result when you crop.

Resampling an Image Using Crop

Resampling means to resize your image, to change the pixel height and width of the image. The crop tool allows you to crop your image based on the dimensions and resolution of another image. You must first open the image you want to take the information from and then select the crop tool. Click Front Image in the Options bar and then click on the image you want to crop. Drag the crop box out (it will maintain the proportions of the sampled image), and when you crop your image it will also resize it.

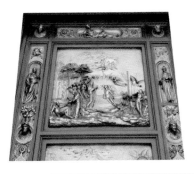
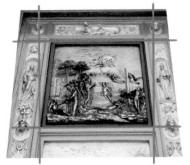
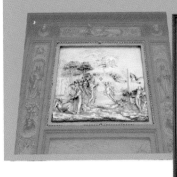
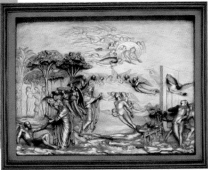

Figure 4-20
The crop tool allows you to instantly fix perspective problems. The image at the **upper left** is the source. The **upper right** shows the extent of the perspective problem with red lines. The lower **left image** is the crop box on the canvas after each handle has been dragged to the corners of the part of the image I want to retain and fix. **Lower right,** after you press Enter, the image is cropped and the perspective fixed.

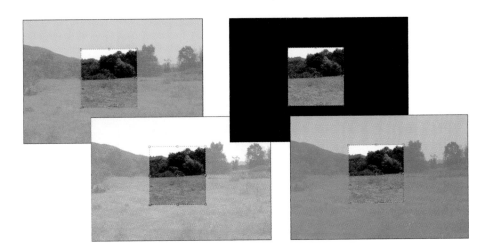

You can also change the color and opacity of the shading shield and turn it off and on (see Figure 4-21). The shading shield is the area outside the crop box that will be cropped.

Crop Using the Trim Command

The Trim command (Image > Trim) crops an image by cropping away the parts of the image that has transparent pixels; therefore, Trim will have no effect on a full layer (Figure 4-22).

Figure 4-21
You can change the color and opacity of the shading shield and turn it off and on. The shield is the area outside the crop box. Here you can see various settings applied to the shield.

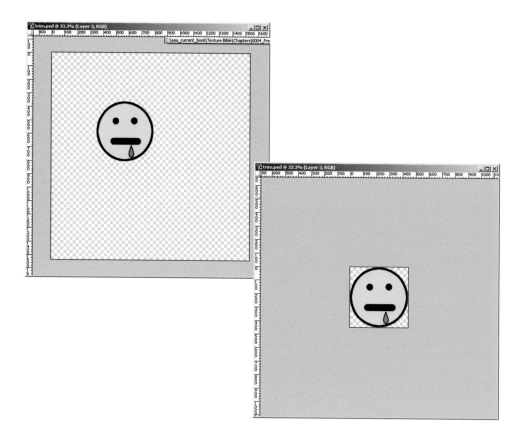

Figure 4-22
The Trim command crops an image by cropping away the parts of the image that has transparent pixels.

The Free Transform Tool

The Free Transform Tool allows you to size and distort the layer or selection in many ways. This tool is particularly useful in cleaning up textures and in texture creation. The Free Transform Tool allows you to scale, rotate, skew, distort, and change the perspective of an image as well as other options for quickly rotating or flipping of the image (see Figure 4-23). You can choose to flip the image horizontally or vertically or rotate the image exactly 90 degrees clockwise or counterclockwise as well as 180 degrees.

You will use the Free Transform Tool frequently in texture creation. As you are creating a texture, you will be bringing images together from various sources and they will be of various sizes. You may be working on an image that is one size, say 1024 × 1024, and paste in an image to use in the texture as an overlay or detail that is larger or smaller and will need to be fit into the texture.

Note: Once an image is in the computer, the maximum detail is set and cannot be increased. The Free Transform Tool is one way to make an image larger, but the amount of detail doesn't increase, only the number of pixels is increased by a mathematical process called *interpolation. This* does not increase the detail, it simply adds extra pixels to smooth the transition between the original pixels.

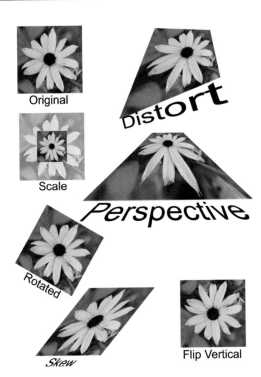

Figure 4-23
The Free Transform Tool
you to scale, rotate, skew,
distort, and change the
perspective of an image as
well as other options for
quickly rotating or flipping of
the image.

Warning: Be careful when doing any severe manipulation to an image, as you may degrade the image quality. Resizing, for example, does a lot of damage to an image. If you reduce a large image and later re-enlarge it, you will seriously degrade it. Once you shrink an image and save it, you lose the resolution of the original image.

Texture Tiling

A tiling texture is an image that can repeat over a surface and still look good. While it is easy to remove the seams in an image in most cases, it is more art than science to create a texture that can tile across a large surface, not have a pattern to it, and still look good (not being a blurry mess in order to tile). I purposely didn't discuss how to tile a texture until *after* I discussed the best way to collect and prepare your resources because some images are just not worth working with if you can help it. If the lighting is so bad, the resolution so low, or the image so distorted that you are looking at some serious reworking of the image, I would wager that it would probably be quicker to get a new base image than try and rebuild a bad one. There are so many sources of digital imagery it just doesn't make sense to perform major surgery on a bad base image. Some images are literally tiles—like floor tiles—and are easy to make repeat across a surface while others can be complex manmade or organic patterns that are more challenging to work with. With these types of images the challenge is to not only make them tile, but to create an interesting texture without high contrast or unique details that makes the tiling noticeable (Figure 4-24). These errors are often called banding and hot spots.

Figure 4-24
On the **top** we have an example of an organic and inorganic image that do not tile well. The organic water image has severe banding: you can see harsh dark stripes running vertically in the tiled image. The inorganic white bricks have a very severe hot spot; there is a clearly identifiable spot on the texture that you can see repeating. The **bottom** two examples are a set of organic and inorganic images that tile much more nicely.

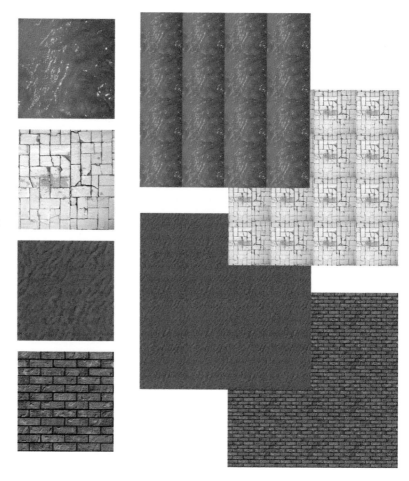

Tiling a texture is arguably the most discussed aspect of texture creation, but there is more to tiling than just using the Offset Filter and cloning away the seams. That method doesn't always work when tiling various surfaces. What approach you use to tile an image will depend on the image you start with, where the texture will be used, and even the technology used.

The Base Image

The condition of the base image and what the final outcome needs to be will determine what you will have do to the image to make it usable. At this point in the chapter you are well aware of the things you can do: cropping, fixing angles, smoothing the lighting, etc. If you are starting with an image that was shot dead on straight, you may not need to fix the angles. If it was perfectly lit, you will not need to spend time adjusting the lighting—you get the idea.

The Context of The Texture

Where will this texture be used? This has a lot to do with the tiling techniques discussed below. But context also has to do with how close the player gets to the image, how many times it will tile across a surface. You need to know this because you can spend a lot of time making a texture tile a thousand times across a large terrain and find out that not only will the image be used in a place where it will only tile four times, but you took too much detail out of the image trying to make it work where it was not intended to.

The Technology Used

If you are developing for a platform or technology that is limited to low-color 128×128 images, or a cutting-edge game engine using a high-end system that allows for high-color 1024×1024 images, you will obviously approach the processing and creation of the image differently. A larger image will allow for more detail and be a bit easier to tile due to the larger area covered. But image size is not the only technological consideration when determining the final appearance of your texture. What you can do with those textures in the game engine makes a huge difference in what the final form your texture will take.

Some game engines allow combining of multiple layers of textures on terrain (just like Photoshop layers), and this allows the texture artist to make a number of textures that are predominantly one material. Textures composed of one material are much simpler to tile. It used to be that terrain was covered in one texture and if you wanted something like a road or dirt patch, you had to create various versions of that one texture to place on the terrain polygons where you wanted the road to run or the dirt patch to appear. This was limiting to say the least; roads ran in straight lines and right angles, and you had to create a separate texture for any unique terrain detail. Now we can create a few versions of the terrain textures: packed dirt, grassy dirt, dried dirt, grass, dead grass, and other single-themed textures and paint them onto the terrain. We can make our base layer grass and paint on darker grass, dirt patches, a dirt road with a dirt to grass border. This is easier, and the results are far more pleasing. This approach also makes dealing with texture tiling much easier. See Figure 4-25 for an example of a terrain built using the layer system.

Some engines allow for random swapping of textures across a surface. You can create a texture and various versions of it and apply the main image to a surface and the game engine will randomly assign the textures to various polygons. This method usually relies on a naming convention so the engine will know that when **"Wall_Texture_001_a"** is present and there is also present **"Wall_Texture_001_b"** and more in the sequence, to use those other textures in the random tile.

Figure 4-25
(Top) Not too long ago terrain was textured by covering the terrain in one texture. Roads, dirt patches, and any unique area had to be created as a separate version of the base texture and placed on the terrain polygon where the detail appeared. Roads ran in straight lines and right angles. Nowadays **(bottom)** most commercial game engines allow for the layering of textures on terrain, like Photoshop layers. These textures can be composed of predominantly one material. Using a base dirt, grass, and other single-type textures, you can paint them onto the terrain. This method allows for a much more organic terrain with more variety using the same number of textures. The results are not only far more pleasing, but this approach also makes dealing with texture tiling much easier.

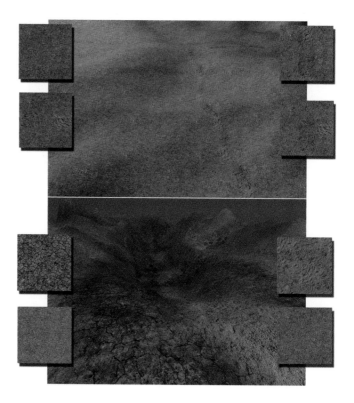

These random tiles are usually more subtle in their differences than the textures in a texture set as shown in Chapter 2. In a texture set you may have a very noticeable detail in the various textures: vents, large cracks, etc.,, but a random tile is meant to break up the pattern produced by a tiling texture and not add specific detail (Figure 4-26). Four vents showing up at random spots on a wall would look weird, whereas subtle variances in the pattern of a brick, and even gradual light shifts in this case, may work well. This is another technology that would allow for smaller textures. Four 128×128 versions of a texture randomly tiled would look better than one 256×256 texture tiled and would take up the same texture memory (if this doesn't make sense, look at Chapter 2 where we discussed the *power of two).*

But even this newer approach is being supplanted by an even newer technology. With shaders and projected textures, or decals, you can make the wall texture simple and add detail in other ways. Figure 4-27 shows an example of how a projected texture works. Shaders (discussed at length in Chapter 2 as well, with visual examples) can use even simpler textures and process varied detail in real time.

Fixing Light Variations Across an Image

You will notice that when you are tiling a digital image (right after you run the Offset Filter for the first time) there are often variations in the lighting across the surface. This is almost unavoidable and

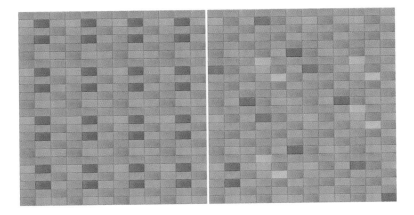

Figure 4-26
Some engines allow for random swapping of various textures across a
surface. This method usually relies on a naming convention so the engine
will know to include all textures of a certain naming pattern in the process.
These random tiles are usually more subtle in their differences than the
textures in a texture set. In a texture set you have noticeable detail, but a
random tile is meant to be subtle to break up the pattern produced by a
tiling texture and not add specific detail. In the **left** image you can see
a repeating pattern. On the **right** three versions of the tile have been
randomly applied to the surface. Some of the bricks are actually more
pronounced, lighter or darker, but work because of the random tiling.

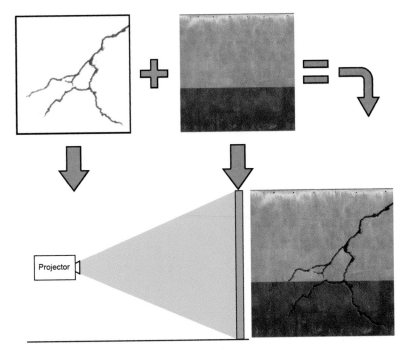

Figure 4-27
A projected texture works like it sounds. You can project a texture onto a
surface in the game world. Here you can see the image of a crack with an
alpha channel projected onto a wall texture, and the result is a wall with a
crack in it.

why I spent some time earlier saying, "Diffuse light good, flash bad." Probably the first thing you should correct in an image you plan to tile is the lighting. There are several ways to do this. Most commonly you can use the high pass filter or use the image itself to manually adjust the lighting (or a bit of both).

The high pass filter basically "reduces brightness differences, it also reduces the contrast of the image, paling the colors." The use of the high pass filter is detailed in an excellent article on Gamasutra, "The Power of the High Pass Filter," by Peter Hajba (www.gamasutra.com/features/20010523/hajba_01.htm).

I try many things in conjunction with the high pass filter. For one, I copy the image I am repairing on a new layer (Ctrl+A, Ctrl+C, Ctrl+N and Ctrl+V), blur the copy using the highest setting of Gaussian Blur (this makes the layer a solid color), or just use an adjustment layer (explained in the last chapter) and fill it with a desired color, and then I use the high pass filter on the original layer. Tweaking the high pass filter is a balancing act between the smaller radius (gray and flat) and a higher radius (little to no effect on the image) to even out the lighting. Then I play with the blending modes (also explained in the last chapter) and levels and other settings on the color layer. Sometimes I even use a copy of the high pass layer, invert it, blur it a little, and play with the blending modes and opacity to further adjust the lighting.

New to Photoshop CS is the **Shadow/Highlights** command (Image>Adjustments>Shadow/Highlights). This tool allows you to

Figure 4-28
On the **top left** is an image of dirt and to the **right** the image offset so you can see the lighting variance. **Below** are three versions of the image from the same PSD file. Playing with the blending modes and other variables will give you various results.

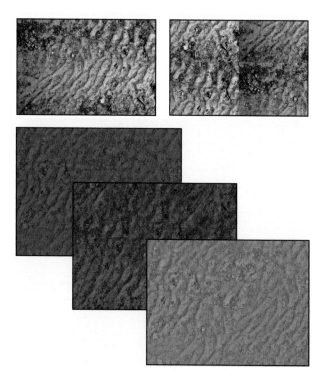

control the shadows and highlights in an image, especially silhouetted and flash burned images. The Shadow/Highlights command goes beyond levels and does not just darken or lighten the image. It treats the shadow and highlight areas separately from each other and enables independent control of the shadows and the highlights. Since the default settings are designed for images that have bad backlighting, you will have to play with the adjustments if your image doesn't look just right when you first open the tool.

Each image you process will be different from the last. There is no one perfect way to fix the lighting in an image. At first you may have to experiment with several ways, but after a while you will begin to have a sense for what the best approach may be more immediately for each particular image.

One-Way Tiling (Horizontal and Vertical)

Making an image tile on only one axis, horizontal or vertical, is much easier than making an image that must tile across a larger surface in all four directions. See Figure 4-29 for a visual of one-way tiling. One-way tiling is usually used on a wall where the texture only needs to tile across the wall, and not up and down it.

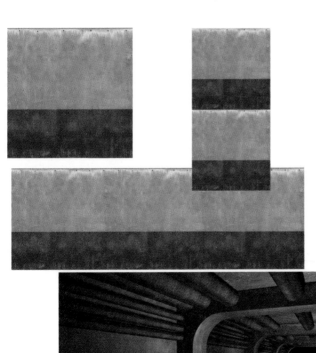

Figure 4-29
Upper left, the wall texture was designed to tile only one way, horizontally. **Right,** the vertically stacked textures show how the texture was not designed to tile and **below,** the texture horizontally tiled. At the **bottom,** the texture used in a scene where it is horizontally tiled.

Three- and Four-Way Tiling

Three-way tiling is used in the case of a wall set where the sides of the texture are designed to tile with each other and the top edge with another texture while the bottom edge doesn't tile at all. The top of the wall texture will tile with itself side to side and with another texture on the bottom (see Figures 4-30 and 4-31). The center tile must tile in all four directions (with itself) and the top of the bottom texture and the bottom of the top texture. This is easy to

Figure 4-30
Three- and four-way tiling is used in this wall texture set. The **top** texture only tiles in three directions; with itself, side to side, and with the base wall texture below it. The base wall texture in the **center** tiles in all four directions, while the **bottom** texture tiles in three directions, side to side and with the base above it.

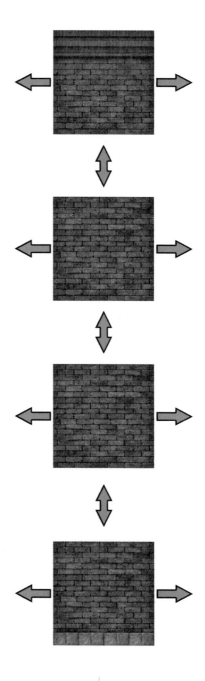

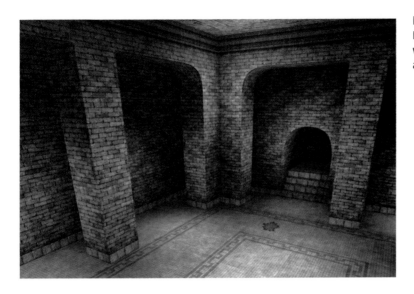

Figure 4-31
Here is the three- and four-way tiling texture set used in a scene.

understand when presented visually. Four-way can be easy if you are working with clean and simple textures like clean blocks and bricks. In the figures, the center of the brick wall tiles with itself, is clean, and is not a huge challenge. It gets a bit more challenging when you are working with stone walls and odd-sized bricks with dirt and weathering thrown in.

Organic vs. Inorganic Tiling

Inorganic surfaces are manmade and generally more easily tiled along seams. Things like walls, bricks, cut wooden planks, metal plates, windows, etc. are pretty easy to tile. Organic surfaces can be easy, too. Things like grass and dirt are fairly easy to tweak and blend into a seamless tile. The challenge comes when you try and tile things with obvious and complex patterns like cobblestones and other assembled stone surfaces that aren't on a grid. Organic surfaces with pronounced segments like pine bark, dirt, or rock with striations, or even certain grasses can be challenging to tile. Because of the randomness at which the objects or materials are laid out, they don't tile in the real world and are harder to capture and tile in the computer. This leads us into our next section on the various tiling techniques.

Tiling Textures

There are several ways to tile a texture, and like most other aspects of computer art, you will most likely use a bit of each technique to get the job done. Of course, most texture tiling starts with the classic Offset Filter. Everybody now!

- Copy the layer you want to tile.
- Run the Offset Filter.

- Enter half the height and width of your image (or with CS you can use the slider bars to move the image in real time).
- Erase the hard line in the texture that appears in the vertical and horizontal centers of the offset image with a soft brush.
- And you have removed the seams.

This is the first technique you will learn. If you are new to texture creation and have tried to find any information on the topic, you most likely didn't find much beyond the use of the Offset Filter. In four lines or less you can be taught to tile anything, right? Or maybe you need the deluxe version of the tutorial that tells you to use the Clone Tool to remove conspicuous detail that may be noticeable when the texture tiles. Unfortunately, making a texture tile usually involves more work than this. Even if the texture looks flawless by itself, when it is repeated over a surface several times it may be painfully obvious that your texture is tiling (Figure 4-32).

Figure 4-32
The Offset Filter is the first tiling technique you will learn, but making a texture tile usually involves more work than simply removing the noticeable seams. Even if the texture looks flawless by itself, when it is repeated over a surface several times it may be painfully obvious that your texture is tiling. The **top left** image is the original, the **top middle** is the offset image, and the **top right** is the image with no seams. But the large image **below** is the seamless tile tiling, but not very well. Notice the very repetitive patterns and the diagonal banding, too.

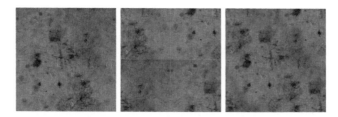

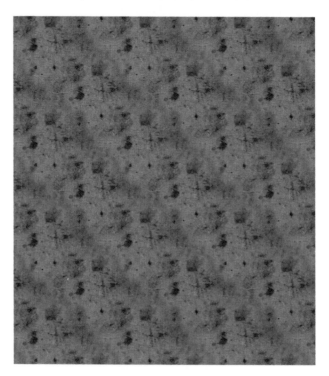

Edge Copy

Other than using the Offset Filter, you can also use a different technique. This method involves starting with an image larger than you intend the final texture to be and copying some of the outer portions of the image from one side and moving it over to the other side. You don't flip or rotate this piece. By selecting a piece of the image outside the portion of the image you want to tile and moving it over, you are creating a seamless transition between the left and right sides of the image. The seam you need to deal with now exists on the inside edge of the pasted portion and is easier to work with than an offset image. This process is detailed below.

You will still need to clean and clone, but I prefer this method when trying to tile an image with large irregular elements like stones. With this method you are working with one edge whereas with the Offset Filter you are trying to blend two edges at once.

Project: Tiling Stones Using Edge Copy

One problem with tiling stonework is that often there are wide variations of color, contrast, size, and even the positions of the stones. Unlike bricks, wooden planks, and other manmade materials, stones are not uniform in length and width and as a result don't fit together in a perfect pattern. There is another, simpler, way than this to make stones in Photoshop that are more uniform and easier to tile. I prefer that method and use it in the chapter on fantasy textures. But you should know this method in the event that you need to tile a specific image that fits these criteria. The following project illustrates edge tiling as well as a few tricks to make natural stones more uniform.

Setting Up the Image

1. Open the source image from the DVD for this project. Note that this image is larger than 1024 and not a power of two. That is preferred in this instance.
2. Set your grid to 128.
3. Choose a square portion of the image you want to tile. Use the grid and make sure your selection is a power of two. I selected the portion you can see in Figure 4-33 outlined in red. The square I chose is a 1024 × 1024 section with some of the image to the left and the bottom of the selection.
4. Drag out some guidelines to mark the four edges of your selection. These will help you later on. You may even want to zoom in and make sure your guides are snapped precisely on the edge of the selection.

Figure 4-33
Choosing the portion of the source image you want to tile.

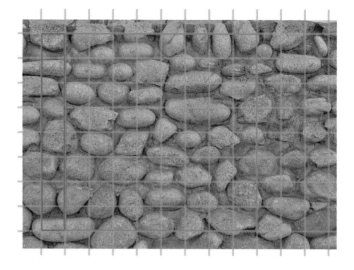

Figure 4-34
Making all the stones more consistent before working on the image makes tiling easier later on. The original image is on the **left** and the corrected image on the **right**. By cloning some stones over others, using various parts of several stones to create or fix another, the stone can be made to look more uniform.

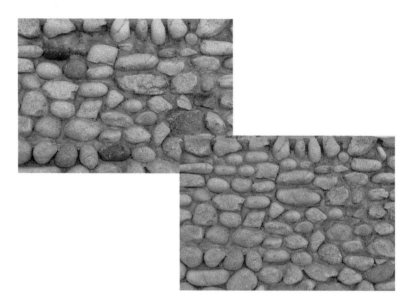

Cleaning Up the Image

The very first thing I do when working on an image like this is to make all the stones more uniform. I don't just mean adjusting the lighting, but actually resizing and moving stones just a bit to get them to be closer in size. I find it makes tiling easier later on. You can see the original image and the corrected image where the stones are more similar in Figure 4-34. I resized and moved stones by cloning some stones over others, using various parts of several stones to create, or fix, another. That technique is explained below. You can also play with the high pass filter, the Highlights and Shadows command, and other methods for adjusting the lighting and consistency at this point. In this case I simply used the high pass filter.

Copy and Crop Parts

1. Now select the left part of the image outside of your selection. This is the 128 × 1024 column marked in blue back in Figure 4-33.
2. Copy the section and paste it (creating a new layer) and move the selection over to the right side of your selection. Make sure you have snap turned on so it will snap in place and look like Figure 4-35. I turned everything off but the selection square so you could see the part of the image pasted over the right side and how obvious the seam is. You can see that the stones are far from blending together.
3. Repeat these steps for the horizontal portion of the image below your selection. Don't worry if this piece is not exactly 1024 × 128. This image was not a power of two to begin with, so the part at the bottom will not be 128 pixels high. Just make sure that the top of your selection is aligned with the bottom of the selected portion of the image we are going to tile.
4. Copy and paste this horizontal section into its own layer and drag it up to the top of the image and hide the layer for later.

Removing the Seams

To remove the seams I don't use the eraser. I find it so much easier, and faster, to create a layer mask and paint the edges away. If I make a mistake, I don't need to lose any work with the Undo command; I can just hit "X" and switch the brush color from black to white and paint back what I want.

1. Select the layer with the vertical portion of the image on it that we first created. Create a layer mask for this layer and start painting away the seams. You will find that some areas miraculously work and others simply will not. Just do your best

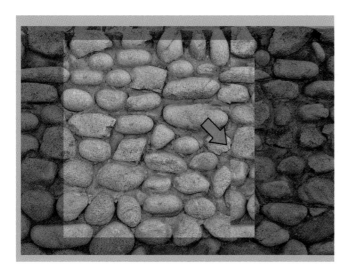

Fiugre 4-35
By selecting an area outside the part of the image you want to tile and moving it over, you are creating a seamless transition between the left and right sides of the image. The seam now exists on the inside edge of the pasted portion and is easier to work with than an offset image.

Figure 4-36
After you create a layer mask and paint away the seams, you will find that some areas work and others don't. Just do your best on this first pass and don't try for perfection just yet.

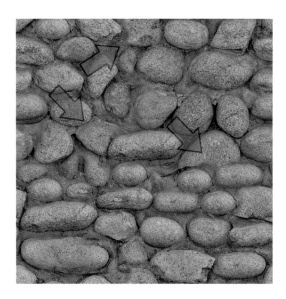

on this first pass and don't try for perfection just yet. Figure 4-36 shows what I ended up with, good and bad.

2. Unhide the vertical layer and do the same.
3. Flatten the image.
4. Use the Offset Filter. Since this is a 1024×1024 image, the offset values in both directions should be 512. You will see that while there are no hard seams we still have work to do.

Build/Rebuild Stones Using Clone

To get stones to tile involves a few tricks to make all the seams between the stones look good. Just copying the stones won't work because they are not all the same size, shape, or at the same angle. Usually, you will never get a copy of a stone from one part of an image to fit with the other stones in different parts of the image. Plus you want the stones to all look different (just not too different), and many copies of the same stone would stand out. The answer is to build and rebuild stones using parts of each other.

Where two stones have blurred over each other, you can find edges and corners from other stones to clone over these stones. Figure 4-37 shows the few steps it took to restore the space between the stones. You will also need to use the clone tool lightly in some cases to retouch the main surface of the stone, as in Figure 4-37.

This process may take some time so be patient and get those edges clean. I said earlier that you probably can't copy and paste a stone into your image and have it fit neatly, but you can copy small portions of a stone (a bottom edge or corner) and paste it in if it needs to be rotated to fit. You can also use parts from other images. If you took several pictures of the same stone wall, you can use stone parts from all the images to build one clean texture.

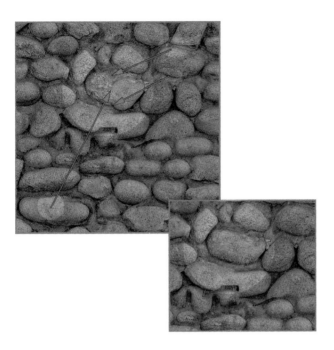

Figure 4-37
You can use edges and corners from other stones to restore or build the space between stones. You will also need to use the clone tool lightly in some cases to retouch the main surface of the stone. On the **upper left** are the blurred stone and the three places I determined I could take detail from using the clone tool. The **lower right** is the result of the repair.

Testing a Tiling Texture

After you have rebuilt and repaired the stones to your liking, you can test the tiling of the texture. This is easy to do using the define pattern option in Photoshop. Note that there is a difference between *defining a pattern* and the *Pattern Maker*. We are defining a pattern to later fill in an area; this does not alter the image. Pattern Maker attempts to create a tiling pattern using a selection. Pattern Maker gives me mixed results, sometimes good and sometimes bad. Even the good results will require some touchup.

1. In order to get the best result, you may want to first look at your image size. If you are working on a large image (and you should be), you might want to create a copy of the image and reduce it to 256 × 256 so you can tile it across a larger canvas without creating a super huge image.
2. Select your entire image (Ctrl + A). You can select an un-flattened Photoshop file, and this method will create a pattern using all layers that are visible.
3. Go to **Edit › Define Pattern**. These steps are illustrated in Figure 4-38.
4. The **Pattern Name** Dialog box will appear and you will see a small thumbnail image of your pattern and have the option to name it.
5. Say **OK**. Nothing will seem to happen, but your pattern is now in the Pattern Preset Library.
6. Create a new image (Ctrl + N) and make it at least four times the size of your texture. If your image is 256 × 256, then make the new image at least 1024 × 1024.
7. Select the entire surface of the new image (Ctrl + A).

Figure 4-38
The basic steps to define a
pattern to test the tiling of
your image. The **upper left** is
the beginning image and the
lower right the tiled result.

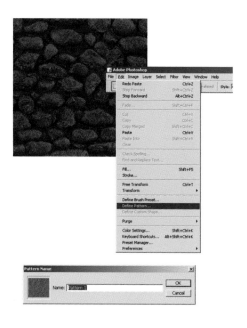

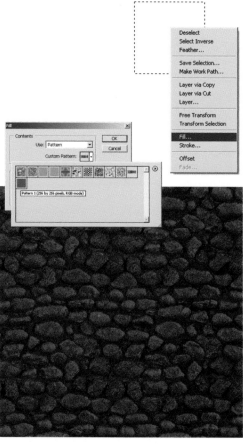

8. Right mouse click inside the selection and choose **Fill . . .**
9. When the **Fill** dialog box comes up, you will be able to choose what to **Use** to fill the selection with. You can also drop down the **Custom Pattern** list below that and your new pattern will be at the end of the list.
10. After you select the pattern, you have to click **OK** and the image will be filled with the pattern.

You can now get a much better idea of how your image will tile over a large surface. It is still preferable to put the image into the game engine it will be used in and see it tile there. The size of the pattern you create and the size of the test image you create to tile it in also depend on the final use of the texture. If you are creating a horizontally tiling wall texture, then you can make the pattern larger like 512×512 and make the new fill image 512 pixels high but 1024 pixels or more wide.

After a few times of doing this, your Pattern Preset Library will begin to get pretty full. You can delete patterns by going back to step 9 above, and when you have access to the pattern library, simply right mouse click and select Delete, or hold down Alt and the cursor turns into a cute little pair of scissors and you can left mouse click to delete the pattern.

Note: You can't undo or cancel the deletion of a pattern from the preset library!

Storing Your Textures

How you store your textures is important. The names you give your images, where you save them, the resolution and file format you save them as, and other decisions will directly affect how well you can work with them. As mentioned earlier in this chapter, you may need to store image assets according to several criteria in your personal collection based on ownership, image size, and usefulness. Here we will discuss how you name those images and save them in a directory structure so you can find and use them later on.

If you buy a texture set and want to save all those files on your hard drive so you have easy access to them, you should simply name a folder after the company and copy all the files into it. If you are surfing the Internet and you download a hundred images from various sources on a theme, name a folder "Internet Images of Dogs" or whatever you were researching and save them there so you know where they came from. When you start snapping your own digital images and creating your own textures, you will want to have a folder for raw assets and finished work, or by project.

When you name a folder or individual file, you will want to have a naming convention. This is a set of rules for naming the files in an organized fashion. Keep in mind that it is simple to create a naming convention and far harder to stick with it. One key to this is to create a text file or document with the legend to your naming convention and folder structure in it and place it in your art drive. Print it out and keep it nearby until you get used to the convention. Although we can use long file names now, it is always advisable to keep file names as short and consistent as possible. This makes it easier to skim them and sort them. In some cases computer applications still don't like long file names.

Tips for Good Naming Conventions

Use underscores "_" not dashes "-" as the computer will see the dash as a minus sign and that affects the sorting of file names, although some operating systems such as Unix don't like this.

Underscores are good separators for data: they make content easier to read. Consider "grndrtrghv2.tga" versus "grn_drt_rgh_v2.tga".

Using the above example, here is a sample naming convention for a set of images.

"grn_drt_rgh_v2.tga"

This might mean

Grn = Ground
Drt = Dirt
Rgh = Rough
V2 = Version 2

That might be for finished textures. For 150 raw images of pine cones, you may want to use numbering at the end like so.

"fol_pine_con_001.tga"
"fol_pine_con_002.tga"
and so on.

The naming convention for this raw asset is

fol = foliage
pine = pine trees
con = cone
= the number being the many images you took of pine cones.

Some artists like to include the size in the naming convention like "lrg" or "sml" for large or small. Or even the resolution like 256 or 512. Naming conventions, like so many other aspects of game development, are often dictated by the project, technology, and the company you are working for. A certain company might have strict naming conventions or they may leave you in charge of creating your own. A certain game technology may need certain naming conventions such as "_a" appearing at the end of a texture that uses an alpha channel. A large outdoor game might have a complex naming convention for foliage, while an indoor game with a few trees might simply have the trees stored as decorations or props.

No matter what, you need to be consistent and persistent with naming and organization. Writing the naming convention down and making sure everyone understands and uses it is a good idea.

Conclusion

This chapter looked at the important aspects of collecting, preparing, and storing of your textures and resources. Next we will start creating textures, and we will begin with the Sci-fi setting.

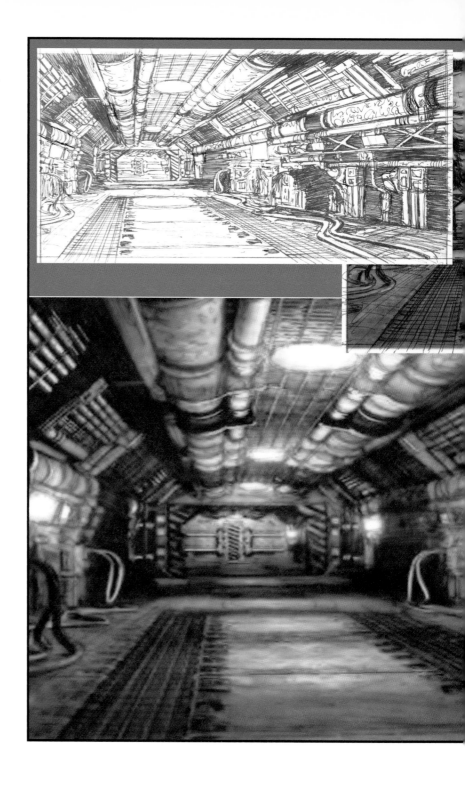

Chapter 5

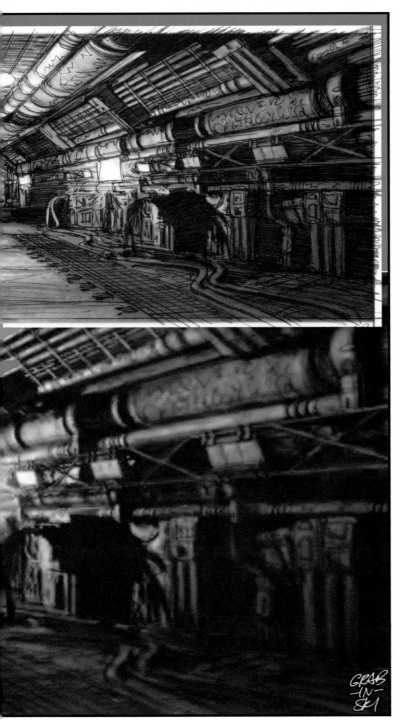

Introduction

For this first tutorial chapter I chose a scene that looks complex due to the geometry and effects, but in actuality the texture set is very simple. In this particular example, shown in Figure 5-1, we have some leeway to create a close approximation of the scene due to the fact that, while this concept art is beautiful, it lacks close-up hard detail that would dictate what we need to create for the scene. While some game companies will dump a load of concept art and textual descriptions on you, others might give you a loose image like this and let you fill in the gaps (because you are that good!).

Sci-fi Concept 2005 by Brian Grabinski

The Sci-fi Setting

Figure 5-1
This concept art is beautiful but lacks hard detail that would dictate exactly what textures we should create for the scene.

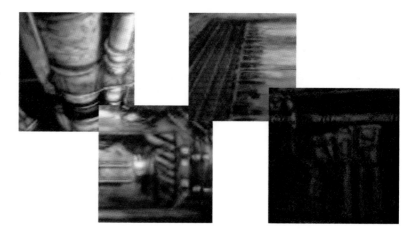

We will start by taking from the concept sketch ideas for the materials we want to create for this scene. As the texture artist we need to create a simple and versatile set of textures for the 3D modeler to use as they create/make up the finer details in the scene using geometry. In a real-life situation you would ask several questions about this, or any, scene before creating textures for it. How old is this structure? What is it made of? What is it used for? What is the atmosphere like here? For this exercise we will make assumptions about the exact materials the hall is made of and their condition.

Concept art and production issues aside, the method for creating these textures relies on a few smaller and simpler textures so it is a good place to start. It also requires some fudging on the specific details present in the concept art due to the limited set of textures we are working with, which is perfect for this example. While some texture creation demands a focus on high detail, those textures tend to have limited uses. This method produces textures that can be used in various ways and are designed to be used with the newer technology coming out (shaders like bump and normal mapping, etc.) There are ways to use a simple texture set with a high polygon scene that actually contribute to the visual diversity of the scene. These textures can be mapped in various ways, but since this method is designed for a more advanced game technology, we can also use lighting and other effects to help further contribute to the visual diversity of the scene.

This type of setting lends itself to this approach for texture creation. A structure such as this, that is industrial or military in nature, would really be built in such a logical and modular fashion. This method can also be used in more traditional settings where shaders will be adding more detail and the artist needs mostly to apply base materials and few detailed textures. I have built Gothic settings using this method and rather than corroded metal created various wood and iron trims and fills.

The Concept Sketch

The front plate shows the concept art for the space hallway. Like warehouses full of crates, the space station hallway full of pipes is a game staple. I figured I would stick to the archetypes of game environments so after you master these base settings you can expand outward to more unique and complex settings that stem from these roots.

Determining Texture Needs

Looking past the colored lights, glow effects, and the light suggestion of dirt and wear, we see metal—and lots of it. In fact, this place looks like it is composed entirely of the same type of metal with some specific detail in only a few places. The only textures that needs to be created that are not a metal variant are the black and yellow caution stripes and a few minor detail textures.

We will start with the base metal texture and build our set from that. Even the caution stripes are painted over this metal, so it is part of that texture as well. The trick to this method, where a few textures are used in many ways in a scene, is to build a set of textures that contain a selection of common parts the environmental modeler will repeatedly use on high poly-count geometry. Things like a grate with an alpha channel, a larger wall piece, a metal fill, and some textures with parts that can be used as trim that will all add rich detail to complex geometry.

Our set will contain

- Base Metal
- Metal Fill
- Wall Panel
- Floor Panel with (alpha channeled) Grate
- Detail Texture: Vent/Panel/Bracket/Hose
- Pipe
- Caution Stripes

Base Metal

The metal in this scene appears to be an industrial-type metal used for mass fabrication. It wasn't created to look pretty. I am sure the bureaucrats that had to handle this large job wanted something durable that met their specs but was cheap. No money wasted on fancy finishes or fresh lemon scent. This metal might have been loaded and unloaded many times before it reached its final destination. Then it was manhandled (or robot-handled) in the construction of this outpost. So we will start by creating a flat, mottled, and less than perfect tiling sheet of metal (with no lemon scent).

1. We work big to small so start with a 1024 × 1024 image. Name this image **sci_fi_metal_base** and create a new layer and name it **base**.
2. Filter > Render > Clouds.
3. Filter > Render > Difference Clouds—Use Ctrl + F and run this filter 5 times.
4. Filter > Noise > Add Noise—7.5%.
5. Image > Adjustments > Brightness/Contrast—Contrast—70.
6. Filter > Artistic > Colored Pencil—Pencil Width 6, Stroke Pressure 8, Paper Brightness 20.
7. Filter > Artistic > Fresco—Brush Size 2, Brush Detail 8, Texture 1.
8. Fade Fresco (Ctrl + Shift + F) 50%—Blending Mode—Multiply.
9. Filter > Render > Lighting Effects.
   Light Type—Spotlight
   Intensity—18
   Focus—63
   Gloss—68
   Material—25
   Exposure—16
   Ambience—32
   Texture Channel—Blue
   Height—71
10. Filter > Artistic > Plastic Wrap—Highlight Strength 4, Detail 7, Smoothness 3.
11. Filter > Sketch > Chrome—Detail 5, Smoothness 5.
12. Fade Chrome 50%—Blending Mode Exclusion.
13. Image > Adjustments > Brightness 10, Contrast –20.
14. Filter > Brush Strokes > Accent Edges—Edge Width 2, Edge Brightness 18, Smoothness 7.
15. Fade Accent Edges 60%.
16. Filter > Render > Lighting Effects—Use the same settings as before. They should still be set the same, but double-check.
17. Fade Lighting Effects 40%—Blending Mode Exclusion.
18. Copy the layer and offset it and erase the seams so you end up with a tileable image. Your image should look like Figure 5-2.

Metal Fill

The metal fill texture doesn't need to be as big as the base metal. The base metal is used to create the larger textures like wall and floor panels. The fill needs only to be a small texture created from the base that is much lower in contrast so it can tile over surfaces you want filled with metal. It is small for memory efficiency, too. I simply copied a 256 × 256 portion of the base metal into a new image and lowered the contrast a lot. You can make lighter and darker versions of the fill based on your needs. I only needed a darker one. You can see the metal fill in Figure 5-3 and how it would be used.

Figure 5-2
The base metal for our scene.

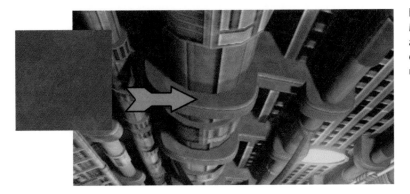

Figure 5-3
Metal fill is used to fill in areas that don't need a lot of detail. Here is the Metal fill used in the scene.

Wall Panel

Now that we have a base metal the rest is easy. Making this tiling wall panel will also be easy because (1) they are supposed to be modular and logically we can get away with repeating parts and (2) these wall panels can be pretty simple as they are hidden behind all the pipes.

1. Open a copy of the base metal and save it as **sci_fi_metal_wall**.
2. You will be applying a layer style to this image and you can't apply layer effects and layer styles to a background, locked layer, or layer set. You need to duplicate the layer so you can apply effects to it. Name this layer **base**.
3. Apply the **Inner Glow** layer style with the following settings:
   Structure
   Blend Mode—Vivid Light
   Opacity—65%

Noise—19%
Color—RGB: 216,216,216
Elements
Size—16 px
Quality
Range—50%

4. Apply the **Bevel Emboss** layer style with the following settings:
Structure
Style—Inner Bevel
Technique—Chisel Hard
Depth—81%
Direction—Up
Size—2
Shading
Highlight Mode—Screen
Opacity—51%
Shadow Mode—Multiply
Opacity—75%

5. Create a new Layer (Ctrl + Shift + N) and name it **Panel**.

6. Set your **Grid** to 32 units.

7. Using the **Polygonal Lasso**, outline the shape in Figure 5-4.
You can do what ever you like here, but the pattern I used was
designed so I could use it in a few places, specifically the
trimmed edges and crossbar.

8. Fill the selection with any color.

9. Set the **Fill** of this layer to 0.

10. Apply the **Drop Shadow** layer style with the following settings:
Structure
Blend Mode—Multiply

Figure 5-4
The pattern for the wall
panel.

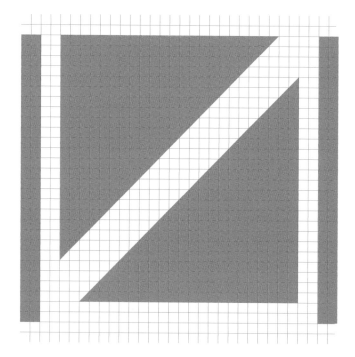

Opacity—23%
Distance—15 px
Size—73 px

11. Apply the **Outer Glow** layer style with the following settings:
    Structure
    Blend Mode—Color Burn
    Opacity—25%
    Noise—15%
    Elements
    Technique—Softer
    Size—46 px
    Quality
    Range—50%

12. A white inner glow with some noise and the right blending mode can make the edges of the metal look scratched and worn. Apply the **Inner Glow** layer style with the following settings:
    Structure
    Blend Mode—Vivid Light
    Opacity—92%
    Noise—19%
    Color—RGB: 190,190,190
    Elements
    Size—54 px
    Quality
    Range—40%

13. Apply the **Bevel Emboss** layer style with the following settings:
    Structure
    Style—Inner Bevel
    Technique—Smooth
    Depth—131%
    Direction—Up
    Size—6
    Shading
    Highlight Mode—Screen
    Opacity—75%
    Shadow Mode—Multiply
    Opacity—75%

14. At this point I turned my grid back on and used a very hard, small brush (3 pixels) and erased a small gap in the panel horizontally across the canvas. Your image should look like Figure 5-5. Take note of where the gaps are.

15. Create another layer and paste the layer style from the panel layer into it. You will have to go into the layer style and make the Bevel and Emboss depth deeper. On this layer you can add the little squares on the edges. They are 64 pixels wide and 22 pixels high. I offset the left and right columns of these shapes vertically by one shape so when the texture tiles the shapes look like they are interlocking.

I created another version of the wall panel, a simpler tiling panel reminiscent of sheet metal. All I did was to copy the wall panel layer and delete the contents of the layer using Ctrl + A and Ctrl + X. I was left with an empty layer with the same layer effects applied to

Figure 5-5
The wall panel with frame. Notice the gaps in the frames. This allows us to use this texture as trim in various places. The right-hand image is a variation of the wall panel.

 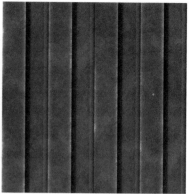

it and I added those simple panels using the grid and the selection marquee to fill them in. Then I tweaked the Bevel and Emboss style.

Floor Panel with Grate

The floor panel is very similar to the wall panel; in fact, you can use a copy of the wall panel to create it. Make sure you are using a copy!

The floor is more complex and involves creating an alpha channel for the grate and creating a diamond plate pattern. We will also put a little wear and tear on the floor.

1. Name your new image **sci_fi_metal_floor**.
2. Go to the **Panel** layer and Select All (Ctrl + A) and press Delete. The layer is still there with the layer styles, it is just now empty. Fill the Layer with any color.
3. Select the layer the **Base** metal is on (it should be below the panel).
4. Filter > Brush Strokes > Crosshatch—Stroke Length 33, Sharpness 12, Strength 1.
5. Fade 50%—Blending Mode Overlay. This makes the metal look duller and scratched.
6. Image > Adjustments > Brightness/Contrast—Brightness—5, Contrast—50.
7. Drag out a vertical guideline. Make sure you have **snap** on so this line will snap to the center of the image (View > Snap To > All).
8. Go back to the **Panel** layer and erase a line down the middle using a hard 9-pixel brush.
9. Select All and Select > Modify > Border—8 pixels.
10. Press the delete key to remove the very edges of the image. Deselect your image.
11. You can turn the Drop Shadow and Outer Glow effects off the Panel layer. Make sure the **Fill** is set to 0.

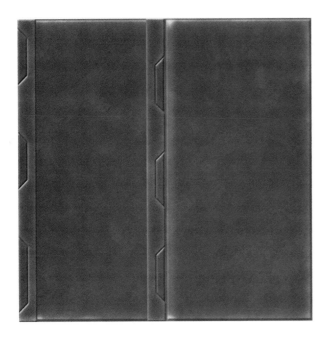

Figure 5-6
The floor panel more beat up.
The beginnings of the frame
in place.

12. On the base metal you can use the Dodge Tool and a soft
    45-pixel brush and subtly augment the Inner Glow, making the
    corners and a few random spots a bit more worn to the metal
    than the rest.
13. Duplicate the Panel Layer and delete the contents. Turn off the
    Inner Glow effect and using the Polygonal Lasso make a shape
    for a frame on the left side of the image that is only two grid
    units wide (64 pixels) and is only on the two vertical sides
    of the image. The inside edges of this frame needs to be
    straight. See Figure 5-6 for reference. I also made another layer
    that added some complexity to my frame. There are seams
    where parts fit tightly together on the frame and these are
    just another frame layer with fitting pieces. You could also
    accomplish this by using the eraser with a small hard brush on
    the same layer.
14. Duplicate the Layer Style of the Frame layer.
15. Copy the base metal layer and paste it, creating a new layer
    under the Frame Layer. Name this layer **Grid1**. We can't set the
    Fill to 0 for the grid because the parts of the grid overlap each
    other so we need to use some of the metal.
16. Use the Marquee Selection Tool on the grid to create one-unit-
    wide vertical bars that are one unit apart and fit between the
    frame. Invert the selection and delete the metal outside the
    selection.
17. Paste the layer style and make sure the Inner glow is not too
    big and that there is a subtle drop shadow and faint darkish
    Outer Glow. Even though we will be creating an alpha channel
    for the grid, you will still see the areas where the bars overlap
    and the shadows will be noticeable.
18. Create a horizontal version of these bars on a layer underneath
    the vertical bars. Your image should look like Figure 5-7.

Figure 5-7
The floor panel with the grid in place.

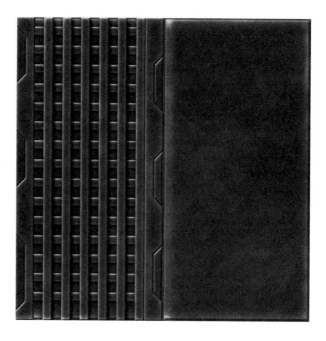

Now we will create diamond plate. You will recognize it when you see it if you aren't familiar with the term. It is a common texture, but like most things if I can make it in Photoshop and have it tile perfectly and be totally flexible, then I will do it. Spending the time upfront making an image or pattern that I can completely and quickly alter will considerably speed up my work in the long term.

Look at Figure 5-8. To make diamond plate, make the first diamond. This is nothing more than the space where two circles intersect. Fill a circular selection and move it over and invert it and use it to delete the portion of the circle outside the diamond.

Diamond plate is usually seen as a diagonal pattern, but I just tiled them straight up and down on a canvas larger than I needed, rotated it 45 degrees, and cropped the image down to 512. This pattern can be made into a diamond plate texture, or dropped into an image with Fill at 0 and Layer Styles applied. In this case the pattern was pasted into its own layer, the layer style copied from the Frame Layer, and the Fill set a 0. I also dropped the opacity down to 25%. See Figure 5-9.

To finish this texture off, I pasted a copy of the base metal at the very top of the layer stack and set the opacity to 50%, the blending mode to Overlay, and Colorized (Ctrl + U) the layer a desaturated orange-brown. This gives the metal a nice light swathe of rust, like it has been in place a while and is used enough to keep the rust worn away, but not cared for so much it shines. This also

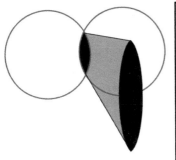
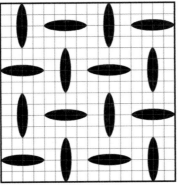
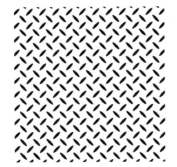
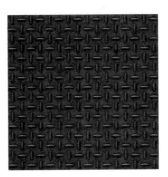

Figure 5-8
The diamond plate pattern
starts with one diamond
duplicated and rotated on
the grid.

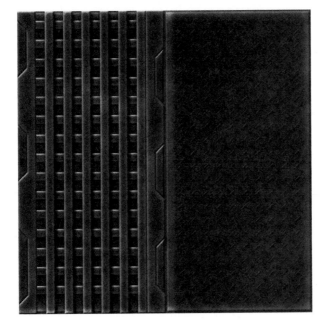

Figure 5-9
The floor panel with diamond
plate added. Don't want our
space marines to slip and
fall.

makes the entire texture look consistent and blends the elements together visually.

Finally, we must make the alpha channel for the grate. You can copy the image or create a layer set with all the layers in it and duplicate the layer set. Either way you have to:

- Turn off all the layers except the grate layers.
- Turn off the layer styles.
- Merge the layers.
- Select the areas outside of the frame and fill that with black.
- Use the color overlay style to make sure every pixel is black.
- Merge the layer with another empty layer so the pixels are really black (not just an applied effect).

The grate holes should be the only white you see. Figure 5-10 shows the alpha image for this texture.

Detail Texture: Vent/Panel/Bracket/Hose

Now we will create a texture that contains various areas of detail such as a vent, a panel, and two strips for a bracket and a hose that are able to tile horizontally. These small detail pieces can be mapped in various places to add a lot of visual variety.

1. Open a copy of the **sci_fi_metal_wall** and save it as **sci_fi_metal_details**.
2. Remove all but the Base and Panel layers. Delete the contents of the Panel layer and turn the Fill up to 100%.

Figure 5-10
The alpha image for the floor panel grate.

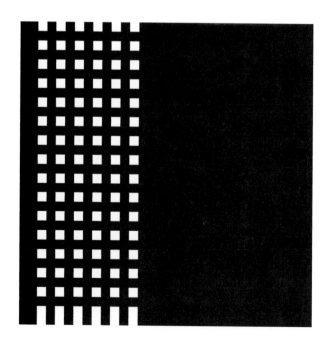

3. Use guidelines to divide this texture evenly in half vertically and horizontally. Make sure snap is on. The lines should be at the 512-pixel point on a 1024 image.
4. Create a New Layer Set and name it **Vent**. Put the Panel layer in this set and rename it **vent frame.**
5. Copy the base metal and paste it into the new Vent Frame layer.
6. Using the Marquee Selection Tool and the grid, delete the metal, leaving a square in the upper right-hand side of the image. Delete the center of the square leaving a one-unit (32-pixel) frame.
7. Change the following settings in the layers styles:
   Drop Shadow
   Distance 8
   Size 10
   Inner Glow
   Choke 10
   Size 18
   Bevel and Emboss
   Highlight Mode—Soft Light
8. Duplicate the Vent Frame layer and place it below the Frame layer. Name it **vent louvers** and delete all the frame. Lower the **Fill** to 0.
9. On the Frame layer select the empty space inside the frame. Go to the Louver layer and fill it with a color.
10. Use a small, hard eraser (3 pixels) and erase lines every 2 units on the grid.
11. On the Frame Layer you can play with the Outer Glow size and opacity to get the vent to look more dirty around the louvers underneath. Your image should look like Figure 5-11.

1. Duplicate the vent layer set and name it **panel.**
2. Delete the louver layer from the new layer set and delete the contents of the vent frame layer and rename it **panel.** Set the **Fill** to 0.
3. Fill this new layer with a color.
4. Using the Marquee Selection Tool and the grid and delete all but the upper left square of this image. I erased some lines down the center of this panel to create a few smaller panels.
5. Duplicate the layer again and place it above the panel layer. Name it **panel2.**
6. Change the Outer Glow settings. Take the Choke down to zero and lower the size to 29 px.
7. Add a Gradient Overlay. Set the Blending Mode to Color Dodge and the Opacity to 20%.
8. Using the grid and selection Marquee, create a few random shapes and invert the selection and delete the metal around your shapes. Your image should look like Figure 5-12.

Note: At this point you will notice that the layer styles from the various layer sets overlap each other. You can create a layer mask for an entire layer set and mask the section off.

1. Duplicate the panel layer set and name it **bracket.**
2. Delete the panel layer.

Figure 5-11
The vent on the detail texture.

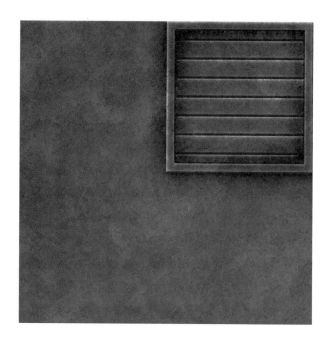

Figure 5-12
The panel details. The layer effects of each layer set have been masked.

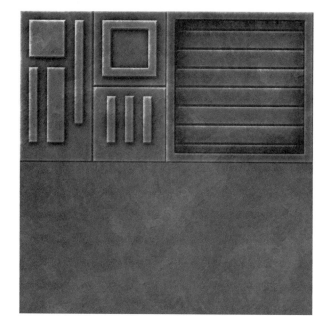

3. Delete the contents of the panel2 layer and rename it **bracket**.
4. Adjust your layer set mask so it only reveals the 1024 × 256 rectangle below the middle of the image.
5. Turn off the Gradient Overlay and apply a Color Overlay and set the Opacity to 25% and the color to RGB: 84,68,39.
6. Select the 1024 × 256 area of this layer and fill it with a color. Keep this region selected.
7. Since the Layer Fill is set to 0, we are seeing the layer style and effects of the bracket layer and the texture of metal is from the base layer. Go to the base layer.
8. Filter > Brush Strokes > Angled Strokes—Direction Balance 50, Stroke Length 23, Sharpness 4.
9. Fade Angled Strokes (Ctrl + Shift + F) to 70%.
10. Go back to the bracket layer and delete some sections of the rectangle to look like Figure 5-13.
11. I duplicated this image, cropped it, and made the bracket horizontally tileable and pasted a copy back into the bracket layer set.

1. Create a new layer set and name it **hose**.
2. Create a new layer and name it **hose**.
3. Adjust your layer set mask so it only reveals the 1024 × 256 rectangle at the very bottom of the image.
4. Copy a 1024 × 512 section of the base metal layer and paste it into the hose layer. Make sure it is snapped in place along the bottom.
5. Filter > Brush Strokes > Accent Edges—Edge Width 2, Edge Brightness 18, Smoothness 7.
6. Use the grid, the Dodge Tool, and a soft 65-pixel brush, and put vertical highlights evenly spaced along the hose. Do this again with a smaller brush (27 pixels).

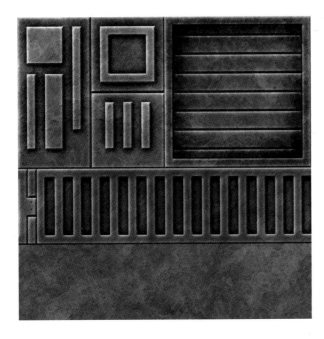

Figure 5-13
The horizontally tileable bracket.

7. Create shadows between the highlights with the Burn Tool.
8. Create a new layer and name it **ridges**. Set the **Fill** to 0.
9. Use a small hard brush, 13 pixels, and draw the vertical ridge lines on the light part of the hose. You can use the Offset Filter horizontally to make sure the ridges are consistent across the hose.
10. Apply the following layer effects:
    Drop shadow—Default settings.
    Outer Glow—Change the color to black, the Blending Mode to normal, and the size to 18.
    Bevel and Emboss—Change the Technique to Chisel Soft and the Size to 3 pixels.

Your image should look like Figure 5-14.

Pipe

We need to make a tileable strip of shiny metal for the hydraulic pipes on the door and we can also use this to make a few of the pipes in the hall shiny, as if they were just installed or repaired.

Open a copy of the Metal Fill and save it as **sci_fi_metal_pipes**. Crop this image down to a one-to-four ratio—512 × 128 or 256 × 64 depending on the file size you are working with. Lighten the metal using Levels (Ctrl + L) and lower the contrast. Run the Spatter filter on this. Use the Burn and Dodge Tools to put horizontal highlights down the center of the pipe and shadows below and slightly on the top of the pipe. Figure 5-15 shows the pipe texture and the texture in use.

Figure 5-14
The horizontally tileable hose and the final texture.

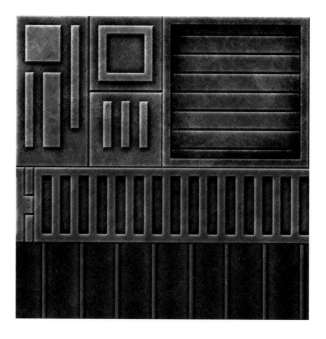

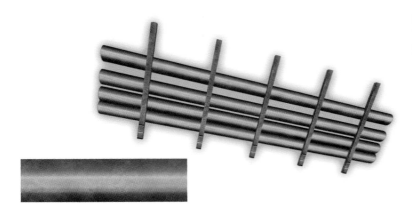

Figure 5-15
The pipe texture and the
texture in use.

Caution Stripes

The caution stripes start as nothing more than black and yellow
alternating strips. You can create them vertically, and the artists can
later rotate them 45 degrees on the model. The work is in making
the stripes look painted on the metal.

1. Open your base metal and save a copy as **sci_fi_caution**.
2. Create a new layer and name it **stripes** and fill the layer with
   dark gray RGB:66,66,66.
3. Turn on the grid and make the yellow stripes 3 units (96 pixels)
   wide. Use a yellow RGB:234,219,111.
4. Filter > Noise > Add Noise—6%.
5. Filter > Noise > Colored Pencil—Pencil Width 10, Stroke
   Pressure 6, Paper Brightness 21.
6. Filter > Blur > Gaussian Blur—3 pixels.
7. Filter > Sketch > Torn Edges—Image Balance 25, Smoothness
   12, Contrast 12.
8. Change the Layer Blending Mode to Overlay, Opacity 75%.
9. Use various erasers and make some subtle worn spots and
   scratches in the paint.
10. You will have to offset the stripes and remove a hard edge. See
    Figure 5-16.

Figure 5-16
The caution stripes.

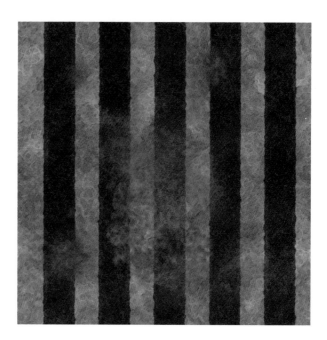

The Complete Scene/Overlay Variation

Here is the complete scene using the textures we just created. In this exercise I attempted to emulate the concept art as closely as possible, but I also did a variation that took me only a few minutes. I put a rust overlay on the textures and changed the lighting in the scene. Since the lights are no longer glowing so brightly in this darker scene, I made a little yellowish dirty texture for the glass. See Figure 5-17 for the rusted texture set. In reality, you would use various types of asset to create a texture. Even if you do everything in Photoshop, nothing replaces the look of adding an overlay of a quality digital image. Several overlays are often used in texture creation.

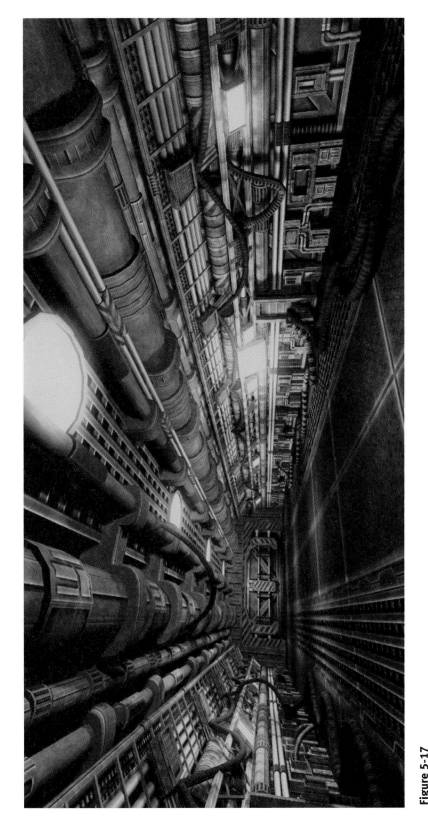

Figure 5-17
The final 3D scene with the textures we just created.

Figure 5-18
The texture set with a rusted overlay. A quick and simple step that changes the scene the textures are used in dramatically.

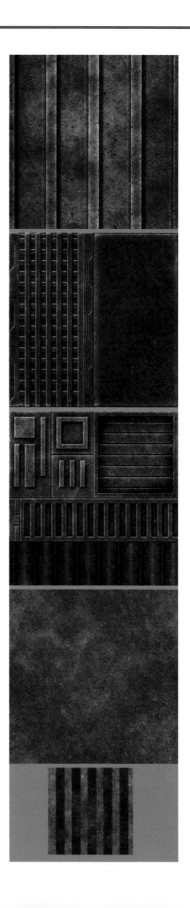

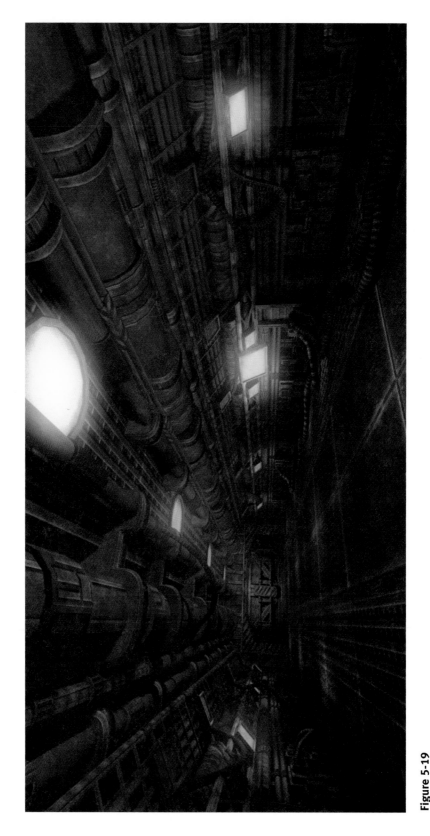

Figure 5-19
A variation with a simple rust overlay and lower lighting.

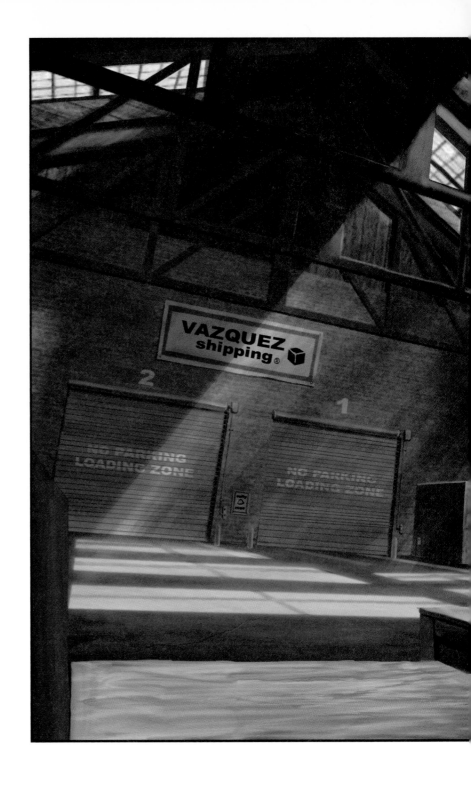

Chapter 6

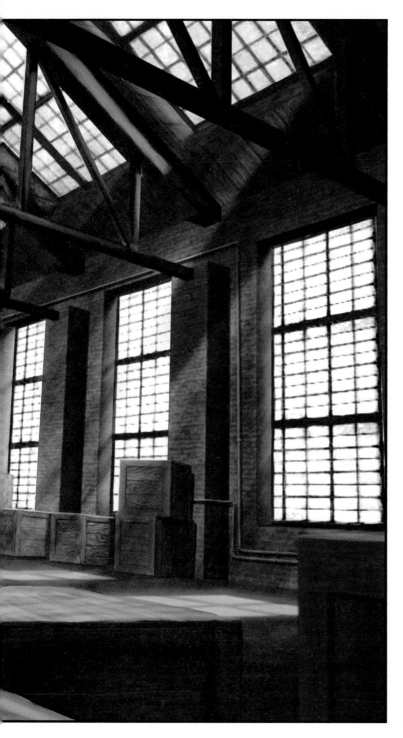

Introduction

In this chapter we will learn to work more faithfully to the detail in a concept sketch, or any reference material, that may be given to us. When you need to create textures for a game environment, you are usually creating them for a world that has been thought out, detailed, and developed to the point that showcasing your creativity is not the primary goal of your work. You are showcasing your talent and ability to recreate what you see in the materials in front of you.

Warehouse Concept 2005 by
Jose Vazquez

The Urban Setting

As we discussed earlier in the book, textures traditionally come in sets: base, wall, floor, and ceiling variants as well as fill, trim, etc. This chapter focuses on breaking out the materials that need to be created for a scene and then the details that also need textures created for them. Even though this approach is changing somewhat with technological advances, it is still an applicable skill to many games and applications and a good skill to have when you are required to work with more advanced technology. We always start with the basics to build a material (shape, color, texture) and build detail on top of that. What you end up with is a full texture set that is easily altered and built on. By the end of the chapter you will have created all the textures needed for the urban environment concept sketch on the facing page. We will use the standard urban environment so popular in many military, sci-fi, driving, and other game genres in this chapter as it offers a good variety of materials and objects.

Unlike the last chapter, where we used fewer and simpler textures on a high-polygon count scene, here we will be putting more detail into the textures and using fewer polygons. In the last chapter we mostly made simple variants of one texture as opposed to the full texture set composed of materials and images for specific uses (like signs or a door). In the fantasy chapter we will go all out on polygon and texture usage to create a high-detail world.

The Concept Sketch

The front plate of the chapter shows the concept sketch for our urban area, a warehouse interior. In order to create a set of textures for a scene, you need information that is often not yet known to you or even anyone on the project. If you are in the early stages of development and are helping to test and prototype, you will be creating many variations of the assets needed for a scene. This is one reason to work large to small and in an organized/modular fashion. Even if all the specifications are in place, you will still mostly likely be producing many variations of the textures you are creating.

Technical questions aside, as these were addressed in the earlier chapters, you will also have to ask some questions pertaining to the fiction of the game world and the space you are creating textures for in particular. Some concept sketches are fuzzy in nature and often don't come with accompanying verbal descriptions. Usually, you will be given a thorough briefing on the game and the world space, but something that looks like one material to you in the sketch might be something else. This scene is pretty straightforward. We can assume that the walls are bricks, the floor is concrete, etc. But look at the windows (not the skylights). They don't look right for windows in a warehouse (I had the artists draw them that way on purpose and promised I would say so in the book). The windows are also different than the skylight windows. As a texture artist you may see the opportunity to save on texture space (memory) by making one texture that is applied to both surfaces. You should probably check this out with your boss, but they will either tell you to go for it or explain why the windows are the way they are—in any case you can demonstrate that you are on the ball with this texture thing.

Breaking Out the Materials in the Scene

Look at the concept sketch again and let's start identifying the materials in the scene. We have to look beyond the details, decorations, light and shadow, effects, and determine what basic materials compose this scene. Look at Figure 6-1 and the subtle clues I left to help you identify the base materials.

Brick

Looking at the walls you can see that the structure is obviously made of bricks. We will make our own bricks in Photoshop. Bricks are a common texture that you can easily get on the Internet or simply photograph in the real world. But making your own bricks is not only faster in many cases, they often look better in a game as they are more visually consistent and easier to tile. Plus, if you build them up in layers, you have more control over the speed and variety of changes you can make to the texture.

Windows

I identify these next only because my eye is drawn to them. Looking closer I see that they will be easy to tile as they are made in

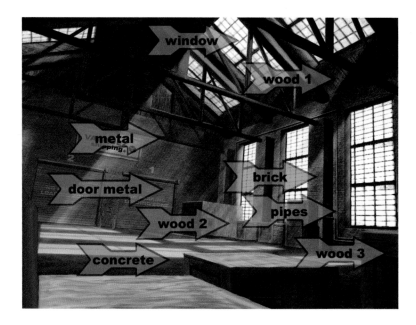

Figure 6-1
To determine what base materials compose a scene or environment, we have to look beyond the details, decorations, light and shadow, and effects.

sections (panes) that can be easily tiled, but how do you get them to glow like that? And what about those shafts of light?

Wood

I then notice that the ceiling is made of dark wooden planks. There are also other places wood is used: the crates and the wall of the little office. These are all variations of wood and can be made from a base woodgrain material.

Concrete

The floor is made of concrete. There are subtle cracks and details on this floor, but it is mainly a big gray plane. We will experiment with two versions: a smoothly poured floor with no seams and a floor with seams that looks as if it were poured in sections.

Metal

Finally, there is the metal. There are three types of metal in this scene that must tile. There are the beams, which are rusted, the grayish rolling garage doors, and the pipes on the wall. Unlike the wood, these textures are different enough that I will start with a different base texture to create two of them.

You will also notice that there are many other details that art will need to be created for and we will break those out after we create the base materials.

Creating Bricks

Creating bricks is easy. They are rectangles and are composed of two substances: bricks and mortar (mortar is the cement between the bricks). There are many styles of brick and many types of mortar, too. There are also variations of the patterns in which the bricks are laid out, their length and width, the space between them—even the mortar can be very different. An interior warehouse brick may have mortar that was put down sloppily and squishes from between the bricks, whereas the exterior of a house would have neat mortar that was scraped away to make the mortar indented and smooth.

Tiling bricks, when you first start doing it, can be a challenge. Bricks are various sizes and not always a neat fit for a power of two. In this exercise we will make our warehouse bricks, a standard red brick, and lay out the bricks using the grid so they tile perfectly. After this you will have a pretty flexible template for creating other types of bricks and even rough stones (as you will later in the fantasy chapter).

Way back in Chapter 1, we covered some of the basic elements of art. They were

- Shape (2D) and Form (3D)
- Light and Shadow
- Texture: tactile vs. visual
- Color
- Perspective

To create a texture from a blank slate in Photoshop, you start with shape, choose a color, start creating the visual texture, and work in the light and shadow toward the middle/end of things. You can approach the creation of a texture from many angles, but starting with shape seems to be the most logical progression to me. I like to lay the groundwork and make sure things all tile and line up properly. It is a terrible thing to have worked on a texture for a long time only to find that it doesn't tile. Bricks are especially tricky if you don't do some math and consider brick and mortar heights and widths as they relate to the grid.

Then I choose a color that is at least close to the object or surface I am creating (the great thing about Photoshop is that you can recolor things fairly easily later on). I start to tackle the visual texture of the object immediately; this takes the most time and experimentation. While this is a linear exercise, meaning I take you through the creation of the bricks in steps from beginning to end, in reality as you create your own textures you will go back and forth changing the color and light and shadow several times. You will need to tweak and change, even redo things until the texture is right.

Tiling Brick Pattern

Step one, shape. A brick is basically a rectangle. In order to make a brick pattern that tiles on the power of two, do the following:

1. Create a new image that is 1024 × 1024 and name it **brick_pattern**.
2. Set the grid at 32 and give it 2 subdivisions.
3. Create a new layer (Ctrl + Shift + N) and name it **Brick Shape**.
4. On this new layer we will create our first brick shape. Look at Figure 6-2 so you can see the shape and size of the brick. Notice how the selection is one unit away from each major gridline. The units are 16 pixels and the bricks 496 × 112.
5. You can copy and paste the brick until it looks like Figure 6-3. You will have to push some of the bricks off the canvas edge to make them fill the half brick spaces. Double-check your mortar spacing! Copying and pasting create a new layer each time you paste a brick, so alternately you can **Select All** (Ctrl + A) and hold down the **Ctrl** and **Alt** keys and click and drag a copy of the brick on the same layer. This is faster, but a little trickier. Every time you let up on the mouse the shape is pasted at that spot. You have to position exactly before placing a brick or you will be undoing a lot.

Figure 6-2
The brick shape close up as it is built on the grid.

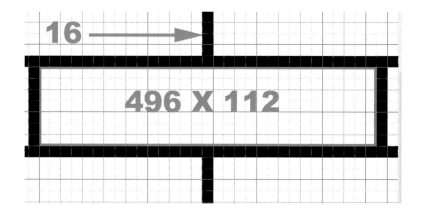

Figure 6-3
The brick pattern is the basis for the entire texture. Make sure it tiles right.

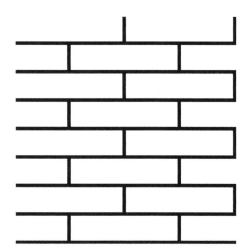

6. **Crop** the image. Make sure the **Delete** option is on and drag the Crop Tool over the canvas so it will not change the canvas size, but crop off the half bricks hanging out of the canvas space.

7. **Check** the Image Size to make sure it is still 1024 × 1024. I am including all these little steps to begin with because they are good habits to pick up. Checking things now and fixing them when you can still use *Undo* is much easier than discovering a mistake when the texture is complete.

8. Now use the **Offset Filter** and enter 512 for both the horizontal and vertical values. If you see any gaps or misalignments in the bricks, fix them now. Redo the exercise or, in the case of one brick being messed up, cut the brick out, copy another, and paste and position it in the empty spot. If you create a new layer, make sure you merge the two layers together. You can simply link the two layers and use Ctrl + E to merge linked.

Note: Merging layers creates a new layer that inherits the name from the layer that is selected when you merge. If you have the named layer selected when you merge layers, it will save you typing the name again.

Save your file. You now have a tiling brick pattern. Before you make a texture out of this, you may want to save a copy in your image collection.

Brick Texture

We will create the texture for the bricks and mortar separately.

1. We will start by selecting a color for the bricks. I used **RGB 131,85,67**. There are many ways to change the colors of the bricks; I simply used the Paint Bucket and filled them in.
2. Noise > Add Noise—8%.
3. Brush Strokes > Sumi-e—Stroke width 10, Stroke Pressure 4, Contrast 29.
4. Fade this filter (Ctrl + Shift + F) to about 10%.
5. Filter > Brush Strokes > Spatter—Spray Radius 20, Smoothness 5.
6. Filter > Artistic > Dry Brush—Brush size 4, Brush Detail 10, Texture 2.
7. Filter > Artistic > Paint Daubs—Brush Size 12, Sharpness 5, Brush Type Simple.
8. Fade by 50% and change the Blending Mode to lighten. Your image should look like Figure 6-4.
9. Here is where you have to do a little handy work. The edges of the bricks are still too uniform. We need to chisel them down, so hit the **E** key to activate the Eraser and right mouse click and select a hard brush, size 13 (see Figure 6-5).
10. You might want to copy the layer and hide it in case you want go back to this step later.
11. Start whittling down the edges and knocking some chips in the bricks. Take your time and be subtle. Remember that these bricks have to tile, and from far away subtlety doesn't pop, but

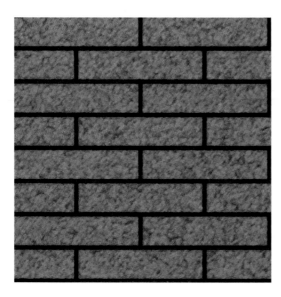

Figure 6-4
This is what the bricks should look like so far, after running a few filters.

Figure 6-5
Knocking the edges down
slightly with the eraser helps
make them look older and
more natural.

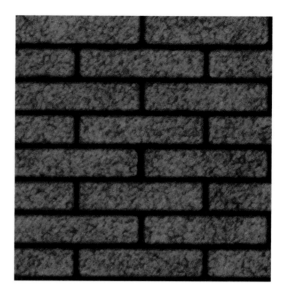

when the player gets close the subtle chips and imperfections
will look good. Work at 100% zoom or even 125% so you can
control your brush. I rounded off the corners to help the bricks
look older. When we put the mortar in it will have the same
interesting shape as it will follow the space between the bricks.

Mortar Texture

Creating mortar is easy since it is simply the space between the
bricks.

1. Create a new layer (Ctrl + Shift + N) and name it **Mortar.**
2. Select the layer with the bricks on it and use the **Magic Wand
   Tool** to select the empty space between the bricks.
3. Select the new **Mortar** layer and fill the selection with a very pale
   yellow. I used **RGB 200, 200, 175.**
4. Deselect the selection.
5. Filter > Noise > Add Noise—10%.
6. Filter > Artistic > Dry Brush—Brush Size 4 Brush Detail 7 Texture 1.

Your mortar should now look like Figure 6-6. The colors are still off,
but we will fix that toward the end, after we add some depth and
merge the two layers.

Brick and Mortar Depth

Giving the bricks depth simply requires the **Bevel Emboss** layer
style with the following settings:

> **Structure**
> Style—Inner Bevel
> Technique—Smooth

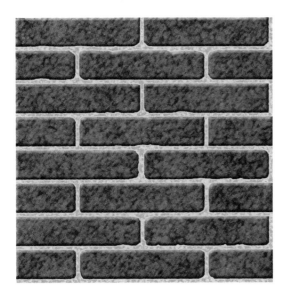

Figure 6-6
The bricks with the mortar added. The colors are off, but that will be fixed as we progress.

Depth—61%
Direction—Up
Size—13
Soften—5
Shading
Highlight Mode—Linear Light
Opacity—62%
Shadow Mode—Multiply
Opacity—63%

Adding depth to the mortar begins with an inner shadow. Note that as you apply filters you may notice they affect the edges of the image. Don't worry about that, we will fix it later.

Change the following **Inner Shadow** settings:

Opacity—57%
Distance—13 px
Size—13 px

Add an **Inner Glow**:

Structure
Blending Mode—Normal
Opacity—60%
Noise—20%
Color—Pure black
Elements
Size—22

Apply **Bevel and Emboss**:

Structure
Style—Inner Bevel

Figure 6-7
The bricks are starting to take shape as we add depth to them.

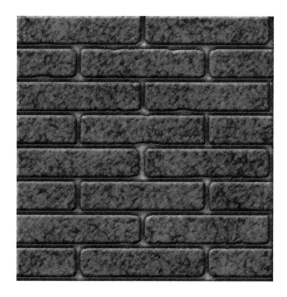

Technique—Chisel Soft
Depth—101%
Direction—Up
Size—10
Soften—6
Shading
Highlight Mode—Screen
Opacity—42%
Shadow Mode—Multiply
Opacity—35%

If your background layer is white, or a light color, you may notice that the bricks and mortar have some of the bright color showing through. To fix this, simply fill the background layer with black or a very dark color. Your image should now look like Figure 6-7.

Brick Completion

We are going to merge the bricks, mortar, and background together, so make a copy of the un-flattened Photoshop file so you can change things later if you like. You can also copy the layers and work in one file. Put the layers in their own layer set and hide the set.

1. Link the bricks, mortar, and background image together and merge them (Ctrl + E).
2. Filter > Artistic > Dry Brush—Brush Size 2—Brush Detail 10—Texture 2.
3. Fade this (Ctrl + Shift + F) and take the opacity down to 50%.
4. Filter > Brush Strokes > Spatter—Spray Radius 3—Smoothness 10.
5. Filter > Texture > Craquelure—Crack Spacing 52, Crack Depth 3, Crack Brightness 4.
6. Fade by 45% (Ctrl + Shift + F).

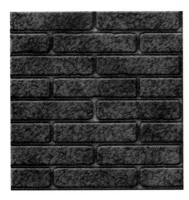 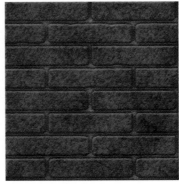 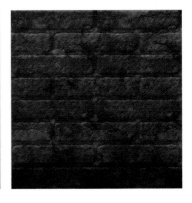

7. I found the bricks to be too saturated for the warehouse scene so I made a copy of the layer and adjusted the brightness up +16 and the contrast down −29. I could have gone back and changed the steps of this exercise to end up with the results I wanted, but I had you do what I did because that's how it really happens. Now we have two versions of the bricks instead of one.

8. Offset the image by 512 × 512 both ways and clone out the seams with a soft brush.

Figure 6-8
Now that we have a strong base that tiles well, we can make many variations of brick.

Top of the Wall

Having trim pieces, even subtle drip stains, around the top of a wall helps make the wall feel more real and the scene more solid. This is easy to do now that you have your base brick texture. You can experiment a lot, but always keep a few things in mind:

- Don't move or alter the base texture, and
- Keep a sharp eye on the edges that are supposed to tile.

Remember that the base texture must still tile with itself. If this is confusing, flip back to Chapter 2 and look at the figure that explains three-way tiling using this very example. I usually clean the tiling edge of my texture, the edge that needs to seamlessly tile with itself, just to be sure. Even a slight change in brightness from a glow or airbrush stroke on the tiling edge of the texture (that your eye can't even detect) will look like a hard line running around the room when you put the texture in the world. Simply use a hard eraser, or even the selection tool, to make sure no pixels are in the top few rows of your texture. You can even mask a few pixels at the top so if there is a slight line you can see it while you are still working on the texture.

We can add subtle drip stains, or we can add a general haze of dirt that may have accumulated in the corners in this old warehouse. Since we create drip stains on the windows in the next section, I will do the haze of dirt here.

1. Start by opening a copy of your base brick texture.
2. Our base brick texture has too few bricks on it to make a detailed tile set. I reduced the image to a 512 × 512 image and made the canvas size 1024 × 1024 and tiled it four times.

Figure 6-9
Trim pieces and subtle drip stains around the top of a wall help make the wall feel more real and the scene more solid. You may notice the trim at the top of the texture. After creating the bottom of the wall texture (which we will do after the top of the wall) I took that trim from the bottom of the wall and added it to this texture, scaling and darkening it.

3. Name the new image **Brick_Warehouse_Base**. Now you have a base brick texture and a new base texture for your warehouse. I further darkened, desaturated, and lowered the contrast to get an old brick feel.
4. Make a new layer and name it **Dirt**.
5. Make Black your foreground color and use the **Gradient Tool** with the **Foreground to Transparent** preset selected.
6. Drag from the top to the bottom of your image about halfway. Hold Shift so the gradient is straight.
7. Filter > Noise > Add Noise—50%.
8. Filter > Blur > Motion Blur—Angle 90, Distance 100.
9. Filter > Artistic > Dry Brush—Brush Size 2, Brush Detail 10, Texture 2.
10. Filter > Artistic > Fresco—Brush Size 2, Brush Detail 8, Texture 1.
11. Filter > Blur > Gaussian Blur—1.5 pixels.
12. Set the layers Blending Mode to Multiply and the Opacity at 67%. Your image should look like Figure 6-9.

Bottom of the Wall

This is a warehouse so we don't have to get too fancy with the trim that runs around the floor. Most likely it would just be a beat-up piece of wood or metal. We create wood and metal in more detail later in the chapter. For here we will make a plain and simple metal strip.

1. Create a new layer and name it **metal strip.**
2. Turn on the **grid** and set the grid size to 128 with 1 subdivision.
3. Drag out a selection that is 128 pixels high and 1024 high.
4. Fill this selection with a dark gray RGB: 105,105,105.
5. Lock the layer transparency.
6. Filter > Noise > Add Noise—7%.
7. Filter > Blur > Gaussian Blur—1.5 pixels.
8. Set your foreground color to black and use the gradient tool (while holding Shift) and start from the bottom and go halfway up the strip. You could also use a large, soft brush to paint this black strip on.
9. Fade the gradient (Ctrl + Shift + F) to 25% and set the Blending Mode to Color Burn.
10. Filter > Artistic > Fresco—Brush Size 2, Brush Detail 8, Texture 1.
11. Fade to 24% and set the Blending Mode to Overlay.
12. Apply the following layer styles.
    Outer Glow
    Structure
    Blending Mode—Normal
    Opacity—45%
    Noise—36%
    Color—Pure black
    Elements
    Spread—9
    Size—174
    Bevel and Emboss
    Structure
    Style—Inner Bevel
    Technique—Smooth
    Depth—150%
    Direction—Up
    Size—7
    Soften—0
    Shading
    Highlight Mode—Overlay
    Opacity—60%
    Shadow Mode—Normal
    Opacity—50%

Your image should look like Figure 6-10. You can take a few extra steps to add some detail and interest. I copied the dirt from the top image and flipped it vertically using the Free Transform tool and lowered the opacity of the dirt. I colorized the metal strip (Ctrl + U) a desaturated orange to make it look more rusted. Finally, I created a new layer, set the Fill to 0, and copied the Metal Strip layer style and pasted it to the new layer. I added those little vertical strips with a small, hard brush.

You are going to need to offset this image horizontally and fix the edges. In order to do that you will have to merge the layers so the layer styles are not editable anymore. You will want to copy all the layers in a layer set so you can change them later. Merge the copies of the layers.

Figure 6-10
Like the top, the bottom
looks better with trim and
some dirtying up.

Figure 6-11
Warehouse window
reference.

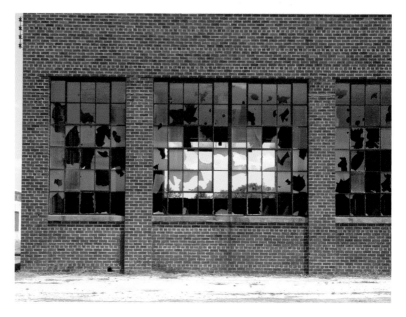

Windows

I mentioned earlier that the windows were purposely drawn wrong
in the concept sketch. They don't look like actual warehouse
windows. I went to a nearby warehouse and took the following
reference photo, Figure 6-11. You can see that these windows are

basically destroyed, but their construction can be seen in the reference photo and their color and texture taken from the actual concept sketch. In this section we will look at variations of these window panes and create a version with an alpha channel.

The Frame

Windows are easy just like bricks! They are a metal frame with panes of glass in them. We start with the metal frame and work down to the panes, in a similar fashion to the way we created bricks and created the mortar around them. Then we can control the amount of weathering on the windows to our liking.

1. Open a new file, make it 1024 × 1024. and name it **Windows_Warehouse_Base**. If your computer is having difficulties handling the larger files, you can work at 512 × 512 and simply adjust the effects and other parameters down by 50%.
2. Set your grid to **256** with **one** subdivision
3. Create a new **layer set** and name it **Frame**.
4. Create a new layer in the set and name it **Outer Frame**.
5. Set your foreground color to a very dark brown. I used RGB: 69,59,54.
6. Select the entire empty layer using **Ctrl A** and right mouse click and select **Stroke**. Set the **width** to 18 pixels and the **location** to inside.
7. I like to create the outer frame separate from the inner frame that holds the panes of glass as it adds more depth to the texture. Create a new layer and name it **Inner Frame**. Make sure this layer is underneath the outer frame layer.
8. Use the same color to draw lines along the grid. Use a **hard 13-pixel** brush.
9. Add the Layer Style **Drop Shadow** to the **Outer Frame** layer and change the following settings:
    Blend Mode—Normal
    Distance—8 px
    Size—16 px
10. Add noise. **Filter > Noise > Add Noise**—Amount—.75.
11. Copy and paste the layer style from the outer frame to the inner frame layer and change the size to **6**.
12. Apply the noise filter again. **Ctrl + F** will reapply the last filer you ran using the same settings. Your frame should look like Figure 6-12.

The Glass

Creating the glass panes is similar to how we created the brick mortar. We will make the glass and then delete the portions of the glass where the frame covers it. This gives us additional flexibility when using layer styles because many of them operate on the edge of an image.

Figure 6-12
The base window frame.

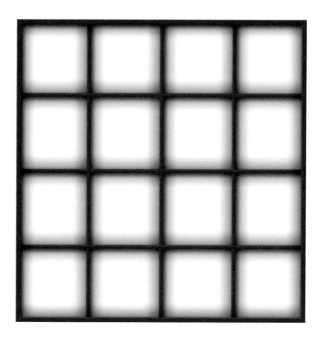

1. Create a new **layer set** and name it **Glass**. You can turn the **Frame** layer set off for this part of the exercise. It will be easier to see the canvas and speed up the computer's response time.
2. Select a muddy yellowish amber (I used RGB 127,106,48) and fill this layer using the paint bucket. Or **Ctrl A** to select all, right mouse click > Fill > foreground color.
3. Add noise. **Filter > Noise > Add Noise**—Amount 7%.
4. **Filter > Artistic > Dry Brush**—Brush Size 10, Brush Detail 4, Texture 1.
5. **Filter > Distort > Glass**—Distortion 8, Smoothness 3, Texture Frosted, Scaling 166%.
6. Hit the D key so your foreground and background colors are black and white. **Filter > Render > Clouds**—Fade this filter to 25%. (Ctrl + Shift + F).
7. **Filter > Blur > Gaussian Blur**—1.5 pixels.
8. **Filter > Artistic > Fresco**—Set all the settings to their max.
9. **Fade** the filter to 15% and set the Blending Mode to Multiply.
10. Cutting out the panes. Turn the **Inner Frame** layer on and select an empty pane. Right mouse click and **Select Similar**. Right mouse click again and **Select Invert**. Go to the **Glass** layer and press the Delete key to remove the portion of the glass behind the frame.
11. Do the same for the **Outer Frame**. Turn both frame layers off and your image should look like Figure 6-13.

Pane Variations

Creating multiple variations of the panes is easy and makes this texture very flexible. See Figure 6-13. Remember to create copies of

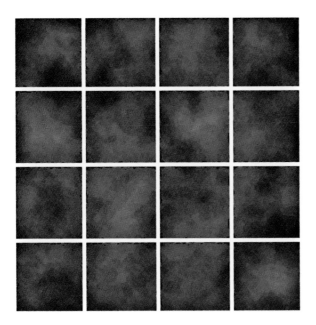

Figure 6-13
The glass panes without the frame.

the pane layer as you alter them. Some of the layer effects I applied to the panes that you might want to try are

- Subtle Dirt: Inner Glow, Color Black, play with the size, opacity, noise, and blending modes.
- Subtle Dust: Change the Inner Glow color to a very light gray, Blending Mode: Color Dodge, Opacity 65%, Noise 16%, Size 40 pixels.
- Subtle Highlight: Bevel and Emboss, try changing the settings to a large, low depth, highlight and soften it. This can give nice even highlights to the panes, just be careful they don't look bulged out.
- Inside Light Source: For a large tiling texture you want to keep things even, but in the case where this window might be used in one instance with no tiling you can add a subtle gradient using a layer style and experiment with the blending modes and gradient types to get the appearance that there is a stationary light source in the room beyond the window.

You can also play with colorization (Ctrl + U), desaturation, and other filters and effects for various looking panes. What you are trying to achieve may depend on the concept art, condition of the building around the window, and other environmental factors.

Weathering and Dirt

Various types of weathering and dirt can be applied to a surface depending on the location and the material the surface is made of. The concept sketch shows indoor windows that do not need any dirt or weathering (maybe a bit of rust on the frames and a hint of dirt

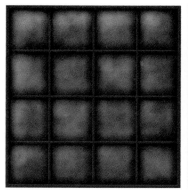
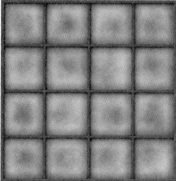
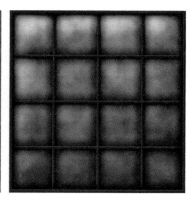

Figure 6-14
Window pane variations from **left** to **right** are subtle dirt, subtle dust, and subtle highlights/inner light source. They have also been colorized and the saturation and brightness adjusted.

on the glass). In fact, you may have noticed that the windows in the concept sketch are glowing a white-blue. That effect is a combination of making the texture the same color, using a shader to make the panes bright, and a special effect for the light beams. A more advanced shader called *bloom* can also be used for the glow to actually go outside the frames themselves. The light beams are easy, but we don't create them here. They are covered in the chapter on special effects.

But what if these windows were outside? The metal frame might be rusted. The panes might be streaked with rain and dirt. Depending on the location of the building and the condition it is in, this weathering could be mild to heavy. First, we can rust the frame.

1. Duplicate the layer set **Frame** and name it **Frame Overlay**.
2. Make sure the new Frame Overlay set is on top of the Frame set in the layer stack.
3. Open the new layers set and turn off the layer effects, link the two layers, and merge them together (Ctrl + E). You now have a solid copy of the entire frame.
4. Lock the **Transparency** on this layer.
5. **Filter > Noise > Add Noise**—10%.
6. **Filter > Artistic > Dry Brush**—Brush Size 2, Brush Detail 8, Texture 1.
7. **Colorize**. Ctrl + U, Hue 14, Saturation 30.
8. Change the Blending Mode to **Darken** and experiment with the opacity. Around 30% to 45% is light rust and 50% to 75% is heavy.
9. Changing the Blending Mode to Lighten will give you a brighter, drier-looking rust. Figure 6-15 shows a few variations of the rusted pane.

The panes can be weathered as well.

1. Start by duplicating the glass layer set and naming it **Outside Glass**.
2. **Desaturate** the glass layer (Ctrl + Shift + U).
3. Fade this by about 50% (Ctrl + Shift + F). Now the panes look faded as if they have been outside a long time.

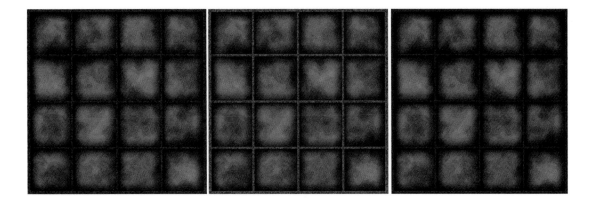

4. To create a general dirt layer, create a **new layer** on top of the stack and name it **smog**.
5. **Filter > Render > Clouds.**
6. Change the Blending Mode to **Multiply** and set the **Opacity** to 50%.
7. **Filter > Noise > Add Noise**—50%.
8. **Filter > Blur > Motion Blur**—90 degrees and about 30 pixels of blur.

Rain Streaks

1. To create rain streaks, turn off the smog layer (you can turn it on later if you like) and create a new layer named **Rain Streaks**.
2. Select a medium gray as your foreground color (RGB: 157,157,157).
3. Zoom way out so your image is pretty small and the canvas fills most of the work space; see Figure 6-16. This makes it easier to create various streak lengths.
4. Select a Brush of medium size and softness. Go to the **Brushes Palette** and under Shape Dynamic change the control to **Fade**. Set the pixel fade to 128. This is the window to the right of the fade selection.
5. Now drag a few lines down your window. Hold Shift to keep the lines straight. Vary the length by starting to draw higher above the canvas and vary the width using the [and] keys. Be subtle.
6. **Filter > Blur > Motion Blur**—90 degrees and about 30 pixels of blur.
7. Set the **Blending Mode** of this layer to Overlay and set the Opacity between 50% and 75%. I ended up at 63% in Figure 6-16. You can, of course, experiment with the color of the streaks, the blending modes, and opacity. You can even add some noise and run the Motion Blur filter again with a lower pixel blur for streaks with a little more body.

Window Alpha

An alpha channel is a grayscale image used in various ways to achieve many effects on a texture in a game engine. For more

Figure 6-15
Variations of the rusted pane, easily created because of the power of layers and blending modes.

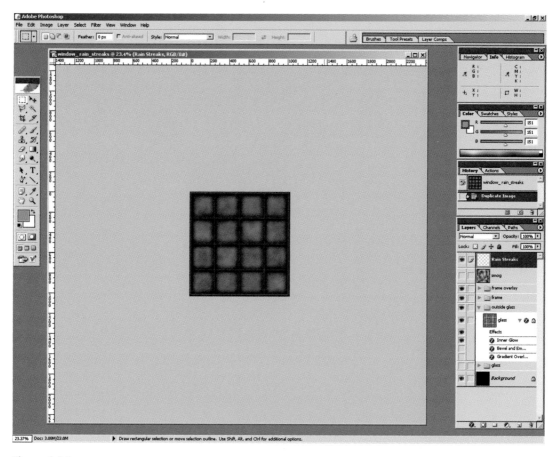

Figure 6-16
The image small and canvas large. This makes it easier to vary the length of brush strokes on the canvas without having to change brushes because you can start drawing anywhere you want outside the canvas.

Figure 6-17
Rain streaks on the window.

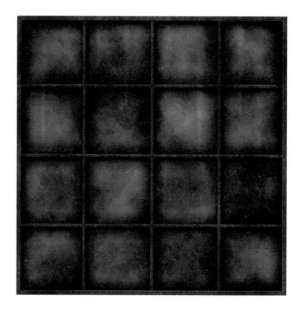

information, see Chapter 2. We will make an alpha image for this
window and use it in various ways.

1. Duplicate your window image. We will be merging layers and it
   is safer to work from a copy.
2. Duplicate the **Frame** layer set and name it **Alpha**. Make sure this
   new layer is on top of the layer stack.
3. Open the new set and turn off the layer effects, link the two
   layers, and merge them together (Ctrl + E). You now have a
   solid copy of the entire frame.
4. Use the D key to reset your colors.
5. Select an empty pane, right mouse click, and select **Similar,** and
   then **Invert** the selection and switch to the rectangular marquee
   and right mouse click and fill the selection with white. We want
   this frame solid white because in the alpha channel white is
   solid and no light will pass through the frame or reflect off it.
6. **Hide** the new Frame Alpha layer set.
7. The windows should already be the way you want them in the
   texture. If not, go back and change them before making the
   alpha so they match. When you are ready **Merge Visible**. The
   white frame should be a separate layer on top of your merged
   panes.
8. **Desaturate** the panes (Ctrl + Shift + U).
9. Using **Levels** drag the middle arrow a little to the right to
   darken this image.
10. Using **Brightness/Contrast** take the brightness down 20 and
    the contrast up 20.
11. Your image should look like Figure 6-18. If you keep the frame
    separate from the panes, you can adjust and alter the panes
    while keeping the frame solid white. With the panes this dark,

Figure 6-18
In most applications the
white in an alpha channel is
solid, so the frame is white
and kept as a separate layer.
It always stays solid white if
you adjust the panes.

they are almost completely see through so you will want to experiment with light/dark and contrast settings.

This alpha image can go into an alpha channel in Photoshop, or an image format that supports alpha, or can be used as a separate image. Some game engines use a separate grayscale image as the alpha while others will recognize the alpha channel of an image. Some can do both so you can use one grayscale image to define the opacity and illumination of the window and another to define the bump. In the case of a bump map for a window you would want the panes smooth, unless there were mud splatters that would stand off the glass, and the frame would protrude. In Figure 6-19 you can see the window texture with various effects on it that use the alpha channel. Notice that in the image with opacity there are broken panes. This was easily done by making the broken and missing portions solid black with hard edges.

Figure 6-19
The **top** image is simply the texture as it is. The **middle** image has an illumination shader on it. It is hard to see in this image, but if you were on a dark street these windows would be bright as if there were a light inside. The **bottom** image has an alpha channel used for opacity. White is solid, so black is clear. The broken panes are just solid black shapes on the alpha channel.

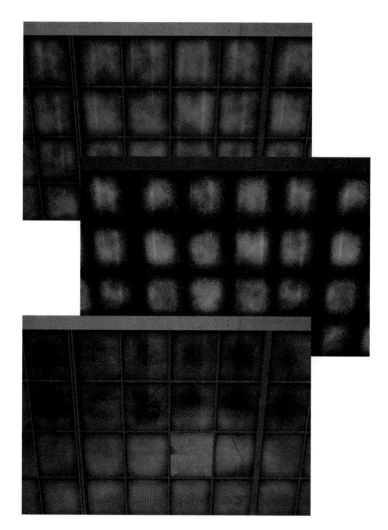

The size of the texture and the number of panes will fluctuate depending on your parameters. One approach is to make more panes in the same texture space; another is to make one pane if the panes are all the same. This would allow a smaller image size, but more detail per pane. You can even have a polygon for every pane in the window and make an image with several pane variations; normal and several broken in various ways. Then the environmental artists can cover most of the panes with the normal pane and randomly place the broken ones.

Note: Some game engines and 3D applications use black as solid and white as transparent, while some may use the opposite. If this is the case, you can simply **invert** your image using the invert command (Ctrl + I).

Wood

Our next material is wood. There are several places where wood is used in this warehouse, so we will start with a wood grain and create various versions of wood from there. One of the new features of Photoshop CS is the Fibers Filter and that comes in handy when making wood grain.

Basic Wood Fill

1. Open a new file and make it 512 × 512. Name it **Wood_Fill_001** (you may want to create more than one version so number helps).
2. Create a new layer and name it **Wood Grain**.
3. **Fill** the layer with a brownish color (RGB 85,80,70). I chose this washed out brown since this is older wood. Normally, I would have made a more saturated version and simply copied it to a new layer and desaturated it. This way I would begin building up different versions of the wood grain.
4. Make sure your foreground color is the brownish color and the **background** color is just a darker version of it (RGB: 61,58,50).
5. **Filter > Render > Fibers**—Variance 16, Strength 4.
6. This filter doesn't create a tiling image, so you need to copy this layer and **Offset** it by 256 in both directions.
7. Use a big, soft brush and erase most of the top layer except for the edges. Keep an eye open for any hotspots you may want to remove.
8. Use the **Offset Filter** again (Ctrl + F) and look for any seams or corners you may have missed and hit them with the **Clone Brush**. You should have an image like Figure 6-20.

This is a basic wood fill. As you use it in various places you may need to desaturate it, make it smaller and tile it, blur it—whatever works in the context you are using the texture. Our first variation of this basic wood grain will be to create the wooden panels that compose the ceiling of the warehouse.

Figure 6-20
Basic wood fill. Subtle, understated, and oh so useful.

Wooden Planks

The ceiling of this warehouse is composed of dark wooden planks. The steps to create planks are easy.

1. Open a copy of the wood fill and name it **Wood_Planks_001**. Create a new layer and name it **seams**.
2. Set your grid to **128**.
3. Use a small medium brush (5 pixels) and draw vertical lines along the gridlines using the darker background color from the last exercise. **Remember** to get the edges of the image too or you will have one wide plank when you tile this image.
4. Use the **Bevel and Emboss** layer style with the following settings changed:
   Style—Outer Bevel
   Depth—50%
   Size—6 px
   Highlight Mode—Vivid Light
   Opacity—100%
   Shadow Mode—Overlay
   Opacity—87%
5. Make a copy of the **Wood Grain** layer and link it to the seams layer. **Merge** them (Ctrl + E).
6. When you merge these layers, the formerly adjustable layer styles are now permanent and the image is fixed. As a result, there are pixels outside the canvas area so you need to use the **Crop Tool** to remove them. Simply drag the tool completely across the image and press Enter. Check your image size and make sure it is still 512 × 512.
7. Now you can use the **Offset Filter** and offset the image by 256 both ways. If you haven't used the Offset Filter since the last

Figure 6-21
Basic wood planks. I can't
think of anything else to say,
but they're cool.

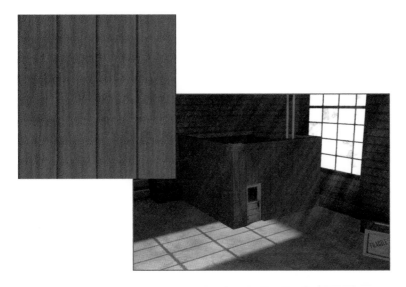

Figure 6-22
Some quick adjustments and
our wood planks are ready
for the office structure. Here
they are on the office
structure.

section, you can use **Ctrl + F**. You might have some small edge
imperfections so you can fix those now. Your image should look
like Figure 6-21.

Wooden Planks, Office

The small office is also made of wooden planks. These are nothing
more than a copy of your current planks altered.

1. Copy and paste the plank layer and name the new resulting layer
   Office Planks.

Figure 6-23
Wood grain made in minutes
with Liquefy and the Bloat
Tools.

2. **Desaturate** this layer.
3. Take both the **Brightness/Contrast** settings up +30.
4. Set your foreground color to RGB: 120,118,131. This is the washed out blue of the office boards.
5. Use **Hue/Saturation** (Ctrl + U) and check the **colorize** box. The saturation will be way too high, so take it all the way down to 3.

Wood, Crate

The crates are yet another variation, only this time we need to give the wood grain more detail, add knotholes, build the frame around the crate, and create seams.

1. Open and **duplicate** the **Wood Grain** image. Name it **Crates_Wood_001.**
2. We will first add knots and detail to the wood that would be undesirable for a tiling texture, but for the face of a crate will look great. Use the **Liquefy Tool** (Ctrl + Shift + X).
3. Start with the **Bloat Tool** with a large brush between 100 and 200 pixels and drag it a little in a few places to create the knots.
4. Then use the **Forward Nudge Tool** with a 200 brush and subtly push the grain around. You don't have to do too much here. You can maybe make the grain contour to the knotholes. Your image should look similar to Figure 6-23.
5. Set the **grid** to 128. Before we start making planks we are going to flip and rotate sections of the wood around so the planks look like they are cut from different boards. Turn on the grid, select the first and third columns of wood. Use the **Free Transform Tool** (Ctrl + T) and right mouse click and flip this

selection vertically and horizontally. You can select and flip or rotate the boards more later as well.

6. Add **seams** just as you did for the wooden planks by creating a new layer named **seams** and drawing lines down the gridlines. This time use a 3-pixel brush and change the following settings in the **Bevel and Emboss** layer style:
   Style—Outer Bevel
   Depth—97%
   Size—1 px
   Highlight Mode—Vivid Light
   Opacity—75%
   Shadow Mode—Overlay
   Opacity—75%

7. The wood needs to be colorized as well to match the crates. Set your **foreground** color to RGB: 167,140,82. Use the **Hue/Saturation** tool and (Ctrl + U) and move the saturation up to 37 and the brightness to +17.

8. Now we can make the frame. Set the **grid** to 64.

9. Use the **Polygonal Lasso Tool** and make a selection like the one in Figure 6-24. These sections are simply copied and pasted into their own layer and can be copied from any section of the wood grain. A vertical selection tends to work best.

10. Make **four different sections** and arrange them like a picture frame by flipping or rotating them.

11. Make sure the frame layer is **above** the seams layer. Turn the background wood layer off so you can see the four pieces. If there are small gaps, it's okay. Link the four layers and **merge** them together.

12. **Zoom** in with the grid on and use a 1-pixel brush to erase a small gap between the corners of the image and the inner

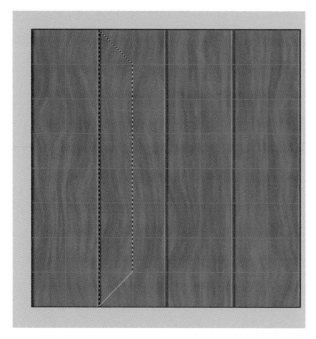

Figure 6-24
The shape you need to make with the Polygon Lasso for the crate edges.

Figure 6-25
The crate base is a starting
place for many variations.

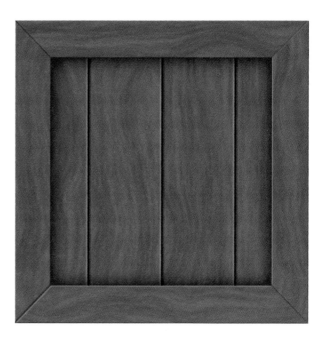

corner where the boards meet. Remember you can click once in
the corner to start a line and hold Shift and click where you
want the line to end. This will give a quick and perfectly straight
line.

13. Add the Layer Style **Outer Glow** with the following settings:
    Blend Mode—Normal
    Opacity—40%
    Size—35
14. Add the Layer Style **Bevel and Emboss** with the following
    settings:
    Style—Inner Bevel
    Technique—Chisel Soft
    Depth—90%
    Size—1 px

At this point your image should look like Figure 6-25.

You can add a lot of detail to crates in addition to variations of the
wood (Figure 6-26). You can weather them, add decals, and even a
stencil, like in the concept sketch. The stenciled letters FRAGILE
across some of the boxes are simply a text layer. Add a text layer,
size and position it using the Free Transform tool, rasterize it (right
mouse click), and add a little noise. Set your background color to
black and run the Spatter Filter. Zoom in and select the black
splotches on the edge of the letters (then right mouse click and
select similar) and delete them. Set the blending mode to color burn
and take the opacity down a bit. Now they look painted on.

These crate textures are the one texture in this scene that would
benefit the most from the use of a reference photo of real wood
either to build the texture with, or use as an overlay. Here are the

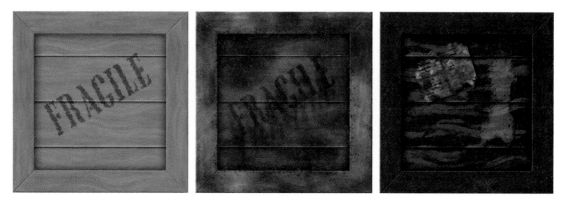

Figure 6-26
These crate variations were made quickly from the base.

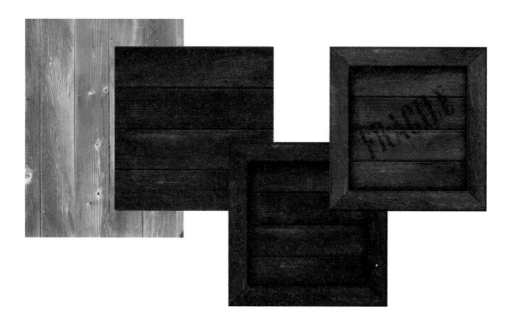

version of the crates I did using a real wood photo. The steps are the same as this exercise, only you don't spend your time making the wood grain; you spend your time cleaning and preparing the wood grain (using the techniques from Chapter 4).

Concrete

Concrete can be as simple as gray noise, but using a few tricks to make the concrete look splotchy and worn are worth the few extra minutes they take. The concrete in our scene is simple, but I will take you a bit further here so you are better able to create concrete for various uses. Subtle stains and weathering can be applied to the base concrete, but stronger details have to be added to a copy of

Figure 6-27
Sometimes there's nothing like the real thing. Wood-based textures like these crate textures often benefit the most from the use of a reference photo either to build the texture with or to use as an overlay.

the texture or created with an alpha channel so they can be projected.

Basic Concrete

1. Start with a new image—1024 × 1024. Name it **Concrete_Base_001.**
2. Create a new layer and name it **base.**
3. **Foreground** color RGB: 140,140,140. Fill the layer.
4. **Filter** > **Noise** > **Add Noise**—3%.
5. **Filter** > **Blur** > **Gaussian Blur**—.5 pixels.
6. **Filter** > **Brush Strokes** > **Spatter**—Spray Radius 15, Smoothness 8. Now we have a very basic and clean cement. The next step is to add subtle and varied stains.
7. Create a new layer and name it **Grime 1.**
8. **Filter** > **Render** > **Clouds.**
9. **Brightness/Contrast**—Brightness +10, Contrast +60.
10. Change the layer blending mode to **Multiply** and take the **opacity** down to 15%. Now you should have subtle dark stains on your concrete. Your image should look like Figure 6-28.

Rougher Concrete

To make the concrete a bit rougher, you can add some small pits, like the concrete was laid rough or just worn out.

1. Create a new layer and name it **Pits.**
2. Fill this new layer with black.
3. **Filter** > **Noise** > **Add Noise**—20%.

Figure 6-28
A basic concrete with subtle stains.

4. **Filter** > **Artistic** > **Cutout**—Number of Levels 8, Edge Simplicity 4, Edge Fidelity 3.
5. Take the **contrast** up +80 and the little clumps will pop out.
6. Select the black portion of the layer with the **Magic Wand** and delete it.
7. Change the blending mode to **Multiply** and the **Fill** to 0%.
8. Add the layer effect **Bevel and Emboss** and change the following settings.
   Depth—1%
   Direction—Down
   Size—1 px
   Soften—2 px
   Highlight Mode Opacity—36%
   Shadow Mode Opacity—36%

Stained Concrete

Not all stains are dark. Using orange as a base color, you can make rust stains similar to the way you make grime using black.

1. Create a new layer and name it **Rust Stains**.
2. Make your foreground color orange RGB: 167,98,10 and your background color white.
3. **Filter** > **Render** > **Clouds.**
4. You may want to run the Difference Clouds filter to get more variation in the pattern, but if you do run it twice so the colors return to orange and white.
5. Take the opacity down to 10%. You can play with the brightness and contrast to get stronger or weaker rust stains.

Figure 6-29
A rougher concrete made from the base.

Figure 6-30
Concrete with rust stains.

Grooved Concrete

Another effect you can add is the subtle grooves concrete retains from when it was smoothed out after it was poured.

1. Create a new layer and name it **grooves**.
2. Render black and white clouds on the layer and lower the **contrast**, −70.
3. Add some **noise**—9%.
4. **Filter** > **Texture** > **Grain**—Intensity 50, Contrast 50, Grain Type Horizontal.
5. Lower the **opacity** of the layer to 10%.

Sectioned Concrete

Sometimes concrete floors are poured in sections with a seam or wooden divider between the sections. For seams you can simply apply a bevel emboss filter to the base layer of concrete and you will get a neat seam around the concrete square. To make a wooden frame, do the following.

1. Create a new layer and call it **frame**.
2. **Fill** the layer with a dark brown.
3. Use the grid set at 16 units and 1 subdivision and select all of the image except for a 16-pixel-wide strip on all four sides. Delete the selected color in the middle.
4. Add a small amount of **noise** to the frame.
5. Set the background color to black and run the **Spatter Filter**.
6. **Fade** the filter by 50%.

Figure 6-31
Concrete with grooves in it from where it was smoothed after laying.

7. Apply the **outer glow** layer style and make it black. This should be a faint outer glow.
8. Apply the **Bevel and Emboss** layer style and make the depth and size very small.
9. **Merge** everything. **Duplicate** the layer and use the Free Transform Tool to make the image 8 pixels larger on all sides.
10. Crop the image and flatten it.
11. When you offset this image, the wooden frame should need little to no work on the seams.

By splitting the wood frame in half, we removed the problem of there being a double frame on all sides. If we were to only put the frame on two sides that would work until the texture hit a wall and the frame ended unnaturally. This way the frame will tile perfectly and we will see half a frame where the texture hits a wall. It just looks neater. See Figure 6-32.

For the most part, creating concrete in Photoshop is a process of experimenting with various filters on clouds and noise and then choosing a blending mode. Building a concrete texture involves several very subtle layers as concrete is generally covered in a variety of subtle stains and discolorations. Concrete is such a subtle texture that the best way to create concrete is to create a consistent base like we did here and overlay actual imagery of cracks and concrete textures. Figure 6-33 shows a few variations of concrete made from this base.

Figure 6-32
When putting a frame around the concrete, we split it in half so we see half a frame where the texture hits a wall. It just looks neater.

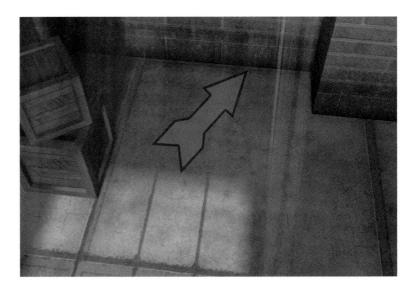

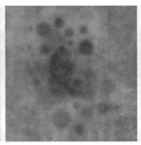

Figure 6-33
With one simple concrete base you can make many variations.

Details Using an Alpha Channel

You can add details like oils stains (where a vehicle may have been parked) signs, cracks, blast marks, and more either directly on the texture or by creating an image with an alpha channel to be projected on the texture. The oil stains in this exercise are nothing more than various-sized soft black brushes with the opacity set very low. To create the alpha:

1. Create a new layer named **oils stains** and paint some oil stains on it using various-sized soft, black, round brushes with the opacity set very low.
2. Go to **Select** > **Load Selection**—Choose the layer name. In this case it will say "Oil Stain Transparency" and it will make a perfect selection of the oil stains on the layer.
3. Go to the **Channels** tab and add a new alpha layer. It should appear solid black with the lines of your selection on it.
4. Select the rectangular marquee and right mouse click in your selection and fill it with white.
5. You can copy and paste this alpha channel into a separate image if you need to. Figure 6-34 shows you the texture with oil stains, the oil stains alone, and the alpha created for the stains.

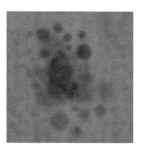
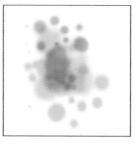
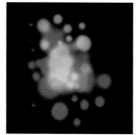

Figure 6-34
Detail that would tile if part of a texture can be projected in a few places to add interest. The detail texture can be masked with an alpha channel so you can achieve subtle effects like these oil stains.

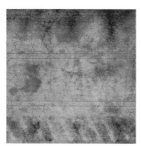
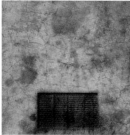
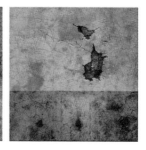

We focused on concrete used as a floor here, but concrete is also used on walls. Concrete walls can have paint on them, a layer of dirt at the bottom, trim pieces, and even a wood grain. Concrete walls are poured into a wooden form that is removed when the concrete hardens. The concrete often retains the grain of the wood from the form.

Figure 6-35
Concrete wall variations made with one base.

Metal

Metal is similar to concrete in how it is made in Photoshop, but we are of course going for a different look when we are creating metal. In this concept sketch there are three types of metal, lightly rusted on the beams, a dull galvanized sheet metal on the garage doors, and the metal pipes on the wall. Technically we already made metal when we made the frames of the windows, and the techniques are similar.

Rusted Metal

Creating the rusted metal for the beams.

1. Create a new image 1024 × 1024 and name it **Metal_Rust_001**.
2. Create a new layer and name it **base**. Fill the layer with a dark brown RGB: 81,65,54.
3. **Filter** > **Noise** > **Add Noise**—40%.

Figure 6-36
Our base rusted metal.

4. **Filter** > **Blur** > **Motion Blur**—Angle 45, Distance 45.
5. **Filter** > **Distort** > **Ocean Ripple**—Size 10, Magnitude 10.

This is a base rust. I used levels to darken it a bit for this scene. I made the image really big so it can be used in other places. For tiling on the beams I reduced this image quite a bit. I cropped it so I could make a smaller texture without losing much detail (Figure 6-36).

Garage Door Metal

The garage door metal is very similar to the wood paneling in that there is the same type of seams running across the texture. The metal itself is a grayish mottled pattern.

1. Create a new image 512 × 512 and name it **Metal_GarageDoor_001.**
2. Create a new layer and name it **base**.
3. Fill this layer with a medium gray.
4. Add Noise—5%.
5. Gaussian Blur—2 pixels.
6. **Filter** > **Pixelate** > **Crystallize**—Cell Size 33.
7. Add Noise—1%.
8. Create a new layer and name it **seams.**
9. Set the **Fill** to 0%.
10. Use a hard, small brush and draw line horizontally across the texture every 64 pixels.
11. Apply the following layer effects:
    Outer Glow
    Structure

Blending Mode—Normal
Opacity—51%
Noise—13%
Color—Pure black
Elements
Size—32
Bevel and Emboss
Structure
Style—Outer Bevel
Depth—111%
Direction—Down
Size—27
Shading
Highlight Mode—Linear Dodge
Opacity—46%
Shadow Mode—Multiply
Opacity—68%

12. Make a new layer and name it **hinge pins**.
13. Select a dark gray color and use a 5-pixel hard brush to draw lines across the image on the inside the bends in the metal. Use Shift to get them straight.
14. Apply the following layer effects:
    Outer Glow
    Structure
    Blending Mode—Normal
    Opacity—75%
    Noise—8%
    Color—Pure black
    Elements
    Size—10
    Bevel and Emboss
    Structure
    Style—Inner Bevel
    Depth—100%
    Direction—Up
    Size—5
    Shading
    Highlight Mode—Screen
    Opacity—42%
    Shadow Mode—Multiply
    Opacity—75%
15. Copy the layers and flatten the image.
16. Offset the image by 256 × 256.
17. Check you tiling and clean up the seams (Figure 6-37).

Pipes

The pipes on the walls are made from one simple texture. In this context we need to add the highlight, but in other cases this may be a situation where a shader is used.

1. Copy a vertical strip off the base metal of the garage door. Make this strip 128 wide and 512 high.

Figure 6-37
Garage door metal with hinge pins.

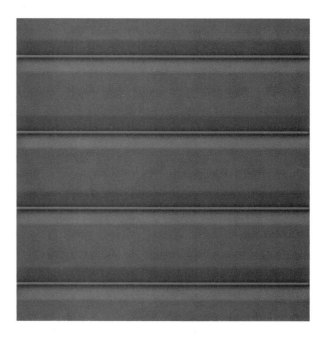

Figure 6-38
Pipe metal made from part of the garage door metal and a version with rust on it.

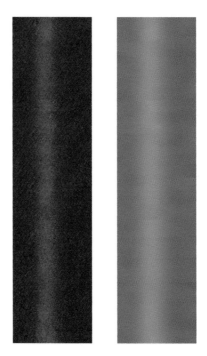

2. Paste it into a new file. Ctrl + N will create a new image the size of the image you copied. Name it **Metal_Pipes_001.**
3. Lighten the image a bit using levels.
4. Blur > Motion Blur—angle 0, Distance 22.
5. Use the Dodge Tool and a soft 65-pixel brush and lighten the vertical center of the pipe (Figure 6-38).

If you want dirty pipes, you can go back and grab a copy of your rust texture and slap it on. Play with the opacity and blending modes.

Like virtually every other surface, metal has a wide variety of appearances depending on the type of metal, the way in which the metal is used, and the environment it is in. Our window frames had a spattering of light dry rust on them while the beams are evenly covered in a heavier rust. In other contexts metal may have paint chipping and wearing off it or it may be shiny and new. The list is endless and we will tackle some of those other metal types and conditions in coming chapters.

Breaking Out the Details

Now that you have built the base materials of the scene you can start looking for the details you will need to create using the base texture, or as a new image entirely. Look at the concept sketch again and let's start to identify the details. The numbers and the stenciled sign are the easiest; the small sign and banner require a few more steps. The door is fairly complex and involves several steps. We will tackle that last.

Numbers

You will quickly learn that making signs, banners, and the like are easy with fonts, filters, and some patience. The numbers above the two garage doors are nothing more than a font that is either laid

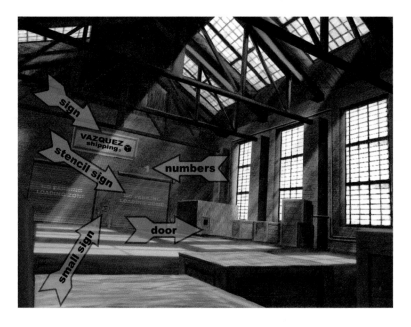

Figure 6-39
Now that you have built the base materials of the scene you can start looking for the details you will need to create using the base texture, or as a new image entirely.

onto a copy of the base brick texture or is an image with alpha channeling. Since the alpha version of this is more challenging, we will take that approach.

1. Create a new image and name it **Detail_Number1_001.**
2. **Fill** the background with black.
3. Snap one guide at the horizontal center of the background and one at the vertical center.
4. Use the **Text Tool** and put a number one down; the Arial Black font seems to match the closest.
5. Use the **Free Transform Tool** and make the font fill most of the image. Keep it centered and proportional.
6. Right mouse click on the text layer and rasterize it.
7. Make sure your background color is black and run **Filter** > **Brush Strokes** > **Spatter**—Spray Radius 16, Smoothness—8.
8. Use the **Magic Wand Tool** to select a black splotch on the edge and then right mouse click and choose **Similar.** Press the Delete key to remove the black parts of the number. You may want to turn the background layer off so you can see.
9. **Noise** > **Add Noise**—9%.
10. Take the **opacity** of this layer down to 60%.
11. **Blur** > **Gaussian Blur**—.5 pixels. If you want to see how the number will look in context, you can drop a copy of the brick texture on a layer behind the number.
12. To create the alpha for this, you do it just like we did the oil stains earlier. Go to **Select** > **Load Selection**—Choose the layer name. In this case it will say, "1 Transparency."
13. Go to the **Channels** tab and add a new alpha layer. It should appear solid black with the lines of your selection on it.
14. Select the rectangular marquee and right mouse click in your selection and fill it with white.
15. You can copy and paste this alpha channel into a separate image if you need to. Figure 6-40 shows you the texture with the number, the number alone, and the alpha channel created for the number.

Figure 6-40

Painted on numbers and signs are easy with fonts, filters, and patience. This number is using an alpha channel. **Left** is the number projected on a wall, **middle** is the number image, and **right** is the alpha channel for the number.

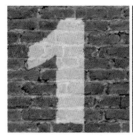
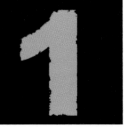
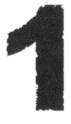

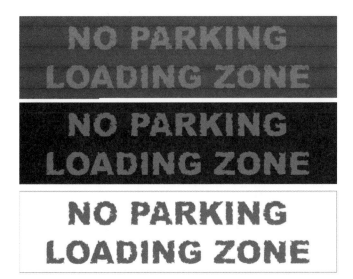

Figure 6-41
The stencil sign is done the
same way as the numbers.
Top is the sign projected on
the garage door, **middle** is
the image, and the alpha is
at the **bottom**.

Stencil Sign

The stenciled sign is done in the exact same way as the numbers,
only you need to make the image size larger. In this case I made it
1024 × 256. I also took the opacity down further to 40%.

Small Sign

Between the garage doors is a small caution sign. Signs are easy to
make and weather.

1. Start with an image that is 512 × 512 and name it
   Signs_Caution_001.
2. Create a new layer and name it **base**.
3. Fill this layer with a safety sign yellow RGB: 164,145,87.
4. Add Noise—3.5%.
5. **Blur** > **Gaussian Blur**—2 pixels.
6. The sign is not the same proportions as the square image we
   have to work with (power of two) so we need to use the
   rectangular marquee to trim it down to the general size of the
   sign. In actual development we would find some other texture
   to fill in that dead space since this doesn't need to tile, but for
   now we will leave it blank.
7. Now drag out a vertical and horizontal line to the center of the
   sign, **not** the image.
8. To make the red border, create a new layer and name it **red
   border**.
9. Set the foreground color to a dark red, RGB: 160,35,38.
10. Drag out the rectangular marquee on the red border layer until
    it is generally the right size. Use the guidelines to center it
    vertically and horizontally.
11. Select the Rectangular Marquee tool and right mouse click in
    the selection. Choose **Stroke**—Inside—16 pixels.

Figure 6-42
Once you set up a template for a sign, you can crank out a wide assortment of variations quickly.

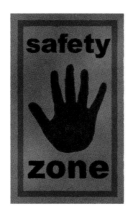 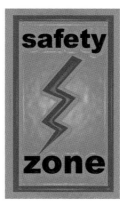 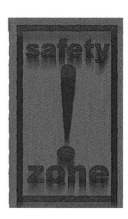

12. Create two text layers. One says "safety" and one says "zone"; the font is Arial Black and the color black.
13. The hard hat is the one thing that if you can't draw it you can use the custom shape tool or Wingdings and add a lightning bolt, exclamation point, a hand, etc.
14. Figure 6-42 shows variations of the sign. Just a filter or two and it takes on a drastically different appearance.

Banner

The big banner over the garage doors is created the same way as the small sign. Start with an image that is 1024 × 256. Create a base layer. Fill this layer with a very light gray, add a small amount of noise, and Gaussian Blur it slightly. You can use the same settings as you did for the small sign. You make the red border the same way as well as the letters. There is even a Registration mark under the Custom Shape Tool. You may have to load all your shapes to find it. I used the rectangular marquee on a new layer to make the box shape and used the eraser to make the lines on the box. The sign ends up being very bright and clean. I took the contrast, saturation, and brightness down and added a little more noise.

The last thing you can do that would add a lot to this banner would be to draw some folds on it. This is easier than it sounds. Select the **Burn Tool** and a large, soft brush. Drag out a few long lines that darken the banner where a fold shadow may be. Just drag from one of the upper corners diagonally to the center. Use the **Dodge Tool** and do the same, only do this on top of the darker parts (light and shadow). The effect is great looking and easy to do. I did a few more areas and even zoomed in and made some tight folds at the corners of the banner (see Figure 6-43).

Door

The last detail we have to create is the office door. This is not hard, but it does have many steps.

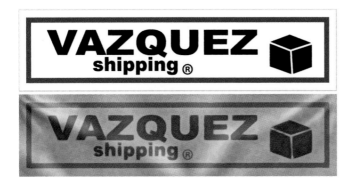

Figure 6-43
This banner was as easy to make as the little sign, and the folds in the cloth were just an extra simple step.

1. Create a new image 512 wide by 1024 high. Name it **Door_Office_001.**
2. Create a new layer and name it **Material.**
3. Fill this layer with a light blue/gray RGB: 155, 158, 164.
4. Filter > Noise > Add Noise—3%.
5. Filter > Blur Gaussian Blur—.5 pixels.
6. Set your grid to 64 with 1 subdivision and turn it on.
7. Duplicate the Material layer and name it **Frame.**
8. Use the rectangular marquee and select the space where the door will fit into the frame. This should be a 64-pixel frame on the top, right, and left with the bottom cut out.
9. Make sure the Material layer is turned off.
10. Press Delete and you will see your doorframe.
11. I am having you apply effects you won't see until after the door is more complete. So you won't see much change as you enter the parameters. Apply the following layer styles:
    Drop Shadow
    Structure
    Blending Mode—Multiply
    Opacity—24%
    Distance—5 px
    Size—7
    Outer Glow
    Structure
    Blending Mode—Multiply
    Opacity—21%
    Color—Pure black
    Elements
    Technique—Softer
    Size—10
    Bevel and Emboss
    Structure
    Size—4
    Shadow Mode Opacity—50%
12. Make sure your background color is black.
13. Filter > Brush Strokes > Spatter—Spray Radius 12, Smoothness 8.
14. Fade this (Ctrl + Shift + F) to 25%.
15. Duplicate this layer and name in **Inner Frame.**

Figure 6-44
Your frame and inner frame
should look like this.

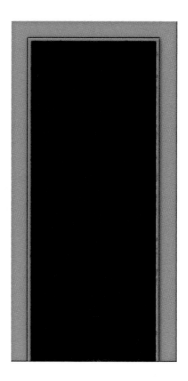

16. Turn on your **grid** and set the subdivisions to 6. Keep the grid at 64.
17. Use the rectangular marquee and select a one-unit border around the inside of your frame.
18. On the **Frame** layer, press Delete.
19. Activate the **Inner Frame** layer and right mouse click and Invert the selection. Press Delete.
20. Run the Spatter filter on the **Frame** layer again. If it was the last filter you used you can hit (Ctrl + F) to run it again with the same settings. I used the burn tool with a 5-pixel soft brush to put a subtle frame line at the top of the door. Your image should now look like Figure 6-44.
21. Now we will make the door itself. Select the empty space on the inside the **Inner Frame.**
22. Duplicate the **Material** layer and name it **Door.**
23. Invert the selection and delete the portion of the door behind the frame.
24. Copy and Paste the layer style from the **Frame** layer. You only need to change the **Bevel and Emboss** style to **Emboss.**
25. Turn your 64 grid on and change the subdivisions to 3.
26. Look at Figure 6-45 for visual reference. Use the rectangular marquee and select the upper window and the three panel spaces in the door. Aside from good proportions, keeping the width of all the frames in the door the same is important. The bottom panel of the door can be a bit larger, like a real door. I made the thickness two units all the way around. Make sure your panel spaces are the same size, too. I made the window 18 units high and each panel 5. Press **Delete.**

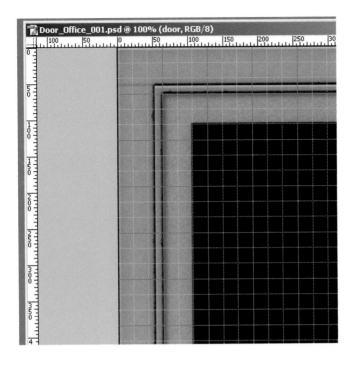

Figure 6-45
Cutting out the window and panels is easy, but pay attention to the grid and the placement of the elements.

27. Run the Spatter Filter again and fade it to 25%.
28. You can use the Burn Tool with a very small, soft brush to put the seams on the door where the boards meet, but were painted over.
29. Select the Magic Wand Tool and select one of the three empty panel spots in the door and hold Shift and select the other two. Duplicate the Material layer and name it **Panels**. Paste the layer style and make the following changes.
    Outer Glow
    Turn it off
    Inner Glow
    Opacity—25%
    Noise—12%
    Size—38 px
    Bevel and Emboss
    Technique—Chisel Hard
    Direction—Down
    Size—6 px
    Highlight Mode—Screen
    Opacity—47%
    Shadow Mode—Multiply
    Opacity—18%
30. Run the Spatter filter again (Ctrl + F) and fade it to 25% (Ctrl + Shift + F).
31. Select the empty place for the window and create a new layer and name it **Window.**
32. **Fill** the selection with black.
33. Filter > Noise > Add Noise—50%.
34. Filter > Artistic > Sponge—Brush Size 5, Definition 10,

Figure 6-46
Your door with the window in
it should look like this.

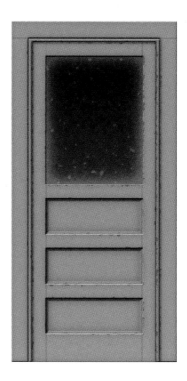

Smoothness 8. I took the brightness up 50 and the contrast
down 10.

35. Add the following layer styles:
    Inner Shadow
    Blend—Multiply
    Opacity—75%
    Distance—2
    Size—2
    Inner Glow
    Blend Mode—Screen
    Opacity—38%
    Noise—22%
    Color—RGB: 194,212,235
    Size—59 px
    Gradient Overlay
    Blend Mode—Lighten
    Opacity—18%
    Your image should now look like Figure 6-46.

Now we will add the details to the door like the knob, lock, and
weather striping at the bottom.

1. Create a new layer and name it **Knob_Plate_Lock**. Use the
   rectangular marquee and eyeball the knob plate. See Figure
   6-47 for where I put it.
2. Fill the selection with a light brown RGB: 74, 67, 62.
3. Snap a vertical guideline to the center of the selection. Use the
   Circular Marquee and hold Shift to keep the circle perfect. Make

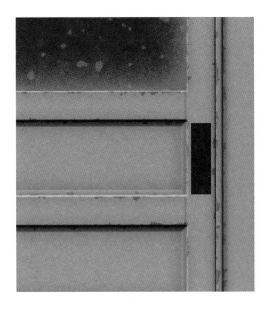

Figure 6-47
The placement of the knob plate.

the circle approximately the same width as the door plate and snap it to the guideline and place it above the plate and roughly centered where the three boards of the door meet.

4. Fill the selection with a light brown RGB: 74, 67, 62.
5. Filter > Noise > Add Noise—2%.
6. Filter > Artistic > Palette Knife—default settings.
7. Copy and paste the layer style from the **Inner Frame** layer and change the size in the **Bevel and Emboss** style to 3.
8. I used the same soft 5-pixel brush and the burn tool to paint a small black line to look like a key slot. I also copied the layer and merged it with an empty layer and used Motion Blur to make it blur up and down. Make sure this blurred layer is under the Knob_Plate_Lock. I moved it down 10 pixels and changed the blending mode to Overlay and the opacity to 50%. Finally, I used the Smudge brush to smear the pixels down so it looks rust stained.
9. Create a new layer and name it **Knob**. Use the same guideline you used for the lock and the circular marquee and place a selection for the knob. Make it the same width as the plate, maybe even a pixel or two larger.
10. Fill that selection with a brassy color RGB: 107, 92, 57.
11. Paste the layer style from the Knob_Plate_Lock layer and change the following settings (see Figure 6-48):
    Bevel and Emboss
    Depth—101%
    Size—6 px
    Soften—3 px
    Highlight Mode—Linear Dodge
    Opacity—53%

The weather stripping at the bottom of the door starts with a rectangular piece of the **Material** layer about 22 pixels high and the width of the door, maybe slightly smaller.

Figure 6-48
The stages of the knob and plate.

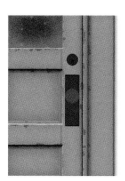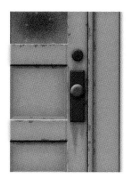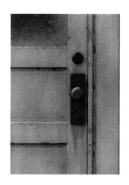

1. Create a new layer and name it **Weather_Stripping**. Make sure it is under the inner and outer frames, but on top of the door layer.
2. Paste the strip of material at the bottom of the door and centered. Nudge it up three or four pixels.
3. Brighten this strip. Ctrl + U — +20 Brightness.
4. Filter > Noise > Add Noise—2%.
5. Use the Burn Tool and a 13-pixel soft brush to darken the bottom half of this.
6. Use the Burn Tool and a 9-pixel soft brush to further darken the very bottom of the strip.
7. Use the Burn Tool and a 5-pixel soft brush to make a dark line roughly in the middle, leaving a gap between the darkened bottom.
8. Use the Dodge Tool and a 9-pixel soft brush to lighten the gap between the darkened bottom and the line you just made. Also, lighten the very few top pixels of the strip.
9. Add a drop shadow with the default settings and a slight outer glow. You will have to change the mode to Multiply, the opacity to 35%, and the size to 8.
10. Finally, I used the 5-pixel hard brush and a medium-dark gray and placed those five dots that look like nails holding the strip on when the texture is reduced and placed in a game. Even though most weather stripping has guide holes, I purposely eyeballed the placement of the nails and staggered them so it would look like someone hammered that on real quick.

All we have left to do is beat this door up some more. I can make it look weathered, dirty, and chipped.

1. Create a new layer on top of everything else and name it **Weathering**.
2. Fill this layer with black.
3. Filter > Render > Fibers—defaults.
4. Filter > Artistic > Colored Pencil—defaults.
5. Set the layer mode to Overlay and play with the Opacity; I liked 15%.
6. You can leave it this way, or clean off the window since glass and wood would weather differently. Go to the **Door** layer and select the window hole with the magic wand and go back to the weathering layer and delete it.

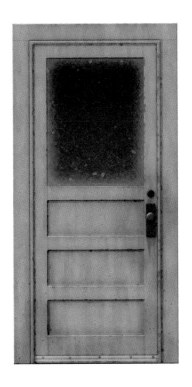

Figure 6-49
Final door.

7. Create a new layer and name it **Chips**.
8. Use the Gradient Tool with black as the foreground. Use the Foreground to Transparent preset. Drag the gradient up from the bottom a little over half the way. Hold Shift!
9. Filter > Noise >—jack it all the way up!
10. Filter > Artistic > Paint Daubs—Brush Size 5, Sharpness 22, Brush Type: Dark Rough.
11. Change the **Layer Blending Mode** to Multiply and the opacity to 27%.
12. Create a new layer and name it **Dirt**. This will be just a general darkening of the areas people come into contact with the door the most.
13. Change the **Layer Blending Mode** to Soft Light and the opacity to 35%.
14. Use a big, soft black brush (100 pixels) and hit the areas around the knob and near the bottom, especially by the inner part of the door where it opens.

Sometimes when I am all done with a texture, after I flattened the file, I like to run a filter over the whole thing (usually Dry Brush) and then fade it way down. This can give a texture a more cohesive feeling. Here is the final door, Figure 6-49.

The Complete Scene/Overlay Variation

Congratulations! You made all the textures for the urban environment. Here they all are in the warehouse scene (Figure 6-50). You may notice things I didn't address in the scene like the pipes for the rollup door, the switch, and the yellow stripes and pylons by the door. I left these out because to create them would be redundant. The pipe texture we made. The yellow stripes and pylons are based on the same techniques you learned in the sci-fi chapter creating caution stripes and the button and switch are created in the same manner as the detail textures from the sci-fi chapter. In Figure 6-51, you can see a variation made with some overlays and a lowering of light.

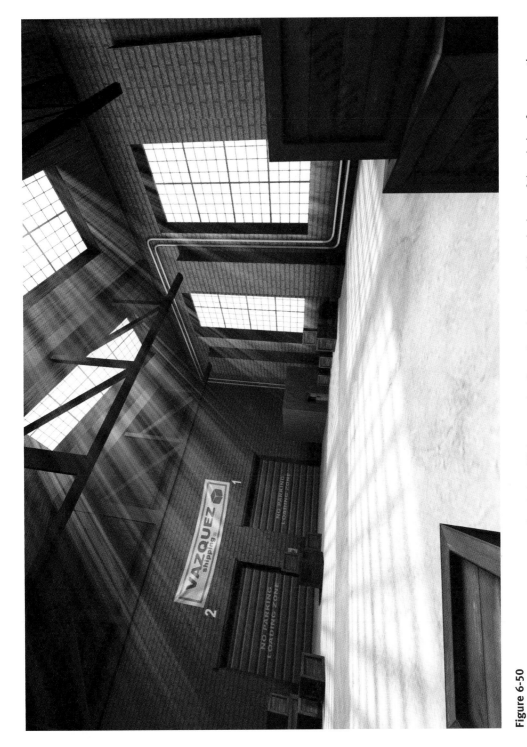

Figure 6-50
Here is the final scene. You may notice the shafts of light streaming from the windows and the shadows of the window frames on the ground. The light shafts are super easy and we will make those in the chapter on effects. The frame shadows are simply the alpha channel of the windows projected onto the floor.

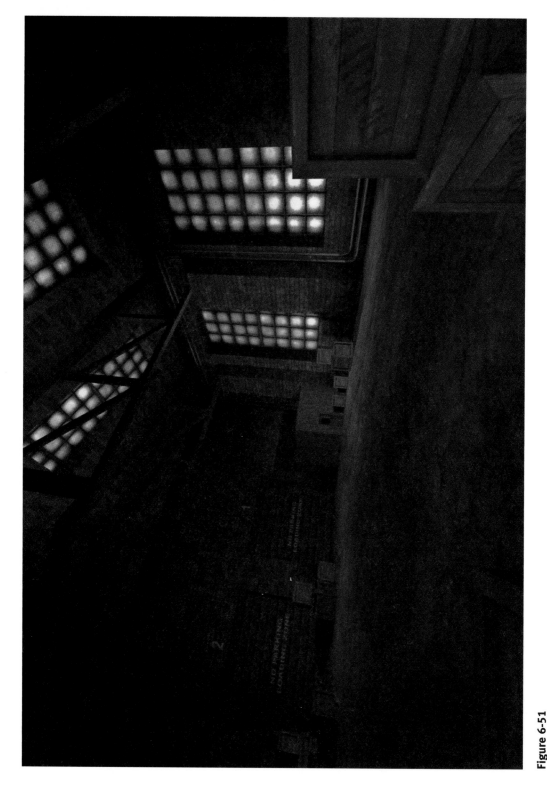

Figure 6-51
Here is a variation of the final scene using overlays and lowering the light levels. I also took the light shafts out of the scene.

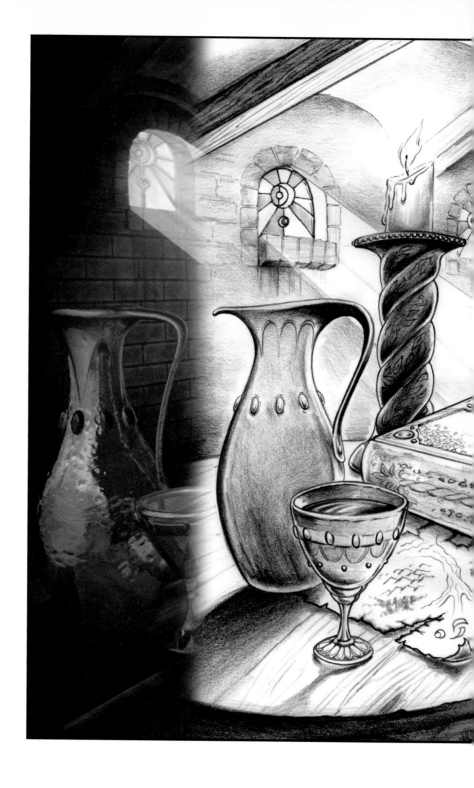

Chapter 7

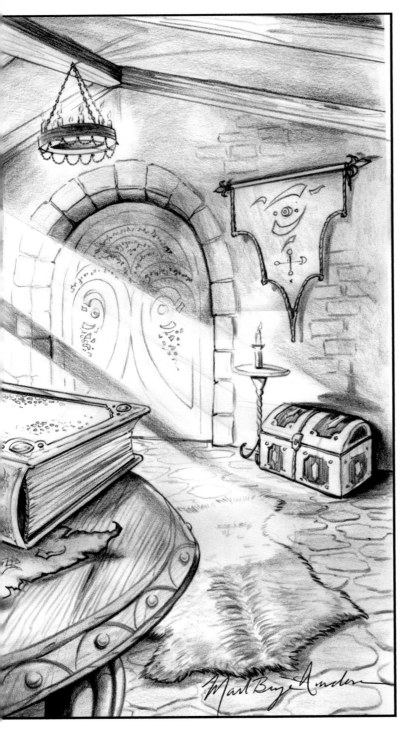

Introduction

This is the chapter where we go all out. We will make our base materials and several highly detailed textures for a high-polygon-count scene. We will also use the Path Tool to create the fancy curves you see in some textures of the scene. Finally, we will create the textures needed for a simple shader.

Fantasy Concept 2005 by
Mark Birge-Anderson

The Fantasy Setting

Figure 7-1
This setting can also be
medieval.

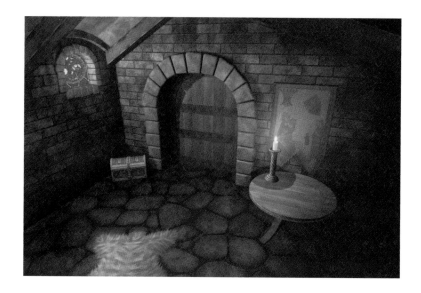

While we will be creating the art for the typical fantasy setting,
this setting can also be a medieval castle. Take away the
fantastic elements and you are left with a room in a castle.
See Figure 7-1.

The Concept Sketch

This concept sketch has a great level of detail. Aside from creating
all that detail, the challenge with this sketch is that it is in black and
white. This is a great exercise because sometimes you might have to
pick the colors of the textures you need to create. We will start with
the colors of the familiar materials that we can easily guess, things
like wood and stone. But what about the other items? The pitcher,
for example, what is that made of, ceramic or silver? Should the
color scheme reflect an evil or good inhabitant? And the door—is
that metal or wood? This place looks pretty nicely furnished and
well kept, so we can imagine that the colors will be fairly saturated
and the materials not as basic as ceramic. Judging by the spell book
and map this is a magician's room and the goblet appears to be
ornate and have gems in it. The pitcher looks like part of a set so it
is most likely not ceramic but of the same material as the goblet.
The chest seems well constructed and locked. I am assuming there
are some valuables in there. The windows are made of fine stained
glass. There is a thick and plush-looking animal fur on the floor. If I
had to guess I would say this was a good magician only based on
the fact that the symbols in the window seem to be of the sun and
moon with the earth in front of it. That doesn't look evil to me. The
fact that symbols on the banner, the book, and the door are the
same or similar to each other indicates an order or school of magic.
The banner also looks like the type held on a pole when rushing
into battle, so at the very least this person is well traveled, if not
actually an adventurer.

Breaking Out the Materials in the Scene

The materials common in the fantasy settings are rough stone for
the walls, stone flooring, rough hewn wood, and coarse metals; the
ceiling in this setting seems to be made of a light stucco or plaster.
We will add some weathering and wear, because even though
this is a very posh-looking room, wear makes things look much
more convincing and interesting. The good news is that we are
not starting from zero this time. We have already created several
textures that we can use as bases for these textures. If you skipped
straight to this chapter, don't worry, you can go back to those
sections. I will reference them in the text. The list of base materials
we need to create is

- Stone Flooring
- Rough Stone Wall
- Rough Wood Beams
- Plaster or Light Stucco
- Base Metals—Dark Iron, Pewter or Dull Silver, Gold

Breaking Out the Details

Aside from the common base materials, like wood and stone, we
need to break out the details—and there are a lot more of them in
this scene. I also included my assumptions about each item because
the sketch is in black and white and we need to know, before we
create textures, the colors and make up of the materials as well as
other information about the scene.

- Animal Fur Rug: Thick and plush bear skin.
- Chest: Wood bound in heavy metal, well worn too.
- Candlestick: Dark silver-like pewter. We also must create the
  flame and the candle itself.
- Spell Book: Metal bound with a hide cover and inset gems. The
  symbols on the cover and the spine are embossed.
- Map: Old and worn and is dark parchment with burnt edges and
  faded ink.
- Windows: Bright based on the light shafts and the glass looks
  clean and unbroken. The colors are yellow and blue based on the
  sun and moon.
- Banner: Cloth and the colors are the same as the window, but
  these colors will be more desaturated based on the material, the
  location of the banner, and its' assumed adventuring history.
- Door: Metal intricately carved with symbols and writing. The
  symbols and the writing have a magical glow.
- Pitcher and goblet: Gold with red gems.

After I did this exercise I emailed my assumptions to the artist who
drew this scene and I was on target. He told me that he envisioned
this to be the room of a member of an order of magic, only he
didn't think of it as good or evil, rather "a more druid-like order."
Technically that's good to me, being in line with nature and all, but
he didn't think of it that way as he drew it.

He added that what is most important to him, more than seeing detail, is to feel the room as if he were in it. "Do you smell mold and mildew or strong incense? Is it cold or warm? Do you feel tension or are you at peace in the room? Is the light cold or warm? As I draw, I put myself into the environment. It is how the detail becomes so, well, detailed and 'real'." These are the same questions texture artists need to ask themselves as they work. He was successful as a concept artist as his art conveyed all that information to me, and more. I think my assumption about the nature of this inhabitant being good was correct, but not conscious on his part, as he later emailed me with, "If I had done an evil environment I would have to have been thinking about it. I think I gravitate to light or good naturally without thinking about it." And "the rug IS bear skin."

Base Materials

We will start, as always, by creating the base materials for our scene. Several of these textures are created using images already created in this book.

Stone Flooring

We will start with our floor. We are creating a texture for the floor that is different than the wall (which we will create next) because a floor is exposed to different treatment than a wall. A floor has been laid down for a different purpose—walking on it—and therefore needs to be smoother. It will have different light and shadow than a wall. And last but not least, the same stone on the floors and walls would look bad. There would be no division, no distinction, between the wall and floor.

The way we will be creating the stone floor is very versatile. You can adjust the space between the stones, the size of the stones and the color and texture of the stones and mortar all by changing a few variables.

1. Create a new 1024 × 1024 image and name it **fantasy_stone_floor**.
2. Fill the background with a dark gray RGB: 68,68,68.
3. Filter > Noise > Add Noise—10%.
4. Filter > Artistic > Cutout—Number of Levels 8, Edge Simplicity 2, Edge Fidelity 2.
5. Filter > Brush Strokes > Accented Edges—Edge Width 4, Edge Brightness 23, Smoothness 3.
6. Create a new layer and name it **stones**.
7. Fill this layer with white.
8. Make sure your foreground color is black.
9. Filter > Texture > Stained Glass—Cell Size 45, Border Thickness 10, Light Intensity 0.
   I found these settings were best for this application, but these are some of the variables you can change to make a different type of stone. Smaller cells mean more and smaller

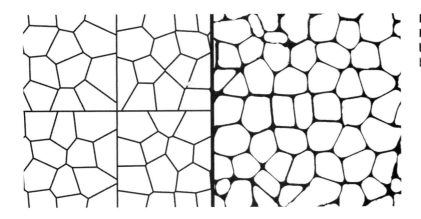

Figure 7-2
Right, the cells offset, and
left the cells ready to
become stones.

stones. Border thickness helps determine the space between
stones.

10. Filter > Other > Offset 512 × 512.
    You will notice a hard line running in both directions down the
    center of the image. Use a hard brush and the X key to toggle
    between black and white to fix the tiling problems now. It is
    much easier than trying to tile the stones later. See Figure 7-2.
    I also used this opportunity to make the cells/stones a bit less
    uniform. As you are doing this, zoom in to work and zoom out to
    look at your stones. You will have to do more than just smooth
    the lines. Even after the lines are smoothed, you will probably
    notice the spaces between the stones still run too straight and
    will need to be tweaked.
11. Filter > Blur > Gaussian Blur—10 pixels.
12. Filter > Artistic > Cutout—Number of Levels 8, Edge Simplicity
    4, Edge Fidelity 1.
13. Run this filter at least three more times using the hot keys Ctrl
    + F.
14. Use the Magic Wand to select the center of a stone. Right
    mouse click and select Similar.
15. Look at your selection. If you find that the spaces between the
    stones are too far apart, you can use Select > Modify >
    Expand—# pixels to close the gap. Contracting the selection will
    widen the gap between stones.
16. Fill with the selection with white (the stones should be white).
    Make sure the tolerance of the Fill tool is set to 255.
17. Select Inverse. Fill the spaces with black.
18. Offset this image again and clean it up. Sometimes there are
    gaps or artifacts to fix and they are so much easier to deal with
    now. Remember to use black and white, not the eraser. This is
    also an opportunity to remove any edges that may be too pointy
    or straight. You can even run the Ripple Filter on this, but don't
    make the lines too wavy.
    Tip 1: I find it easier to not try and paint the black lines
        perfectly, rather use one large brush (about 45 to 65 pixels)
        and cover the general area with black, overlapping the stones
        on either side of the lines, hit your X key and paint the white

stone back in. I find this is not only easier, but looks better because the larger brush makes for a smoother stone edge.

Tip 2: Offset the image again to check your tiling, only this time don't enter exactly 512 for a 1024 image, try 256. The reason for this is that an exact offset often covers a mistake in tiling that you won't notice until you are finished the texture and have it tiling across a floor. The few minutes it takes to recheck things like this make things much faster in the long run.

19. Use the Magic Wand to select the space between the stones and delete it. If you have wide spaces between your stones and want to work on the mortar between the stones by itself, then you can create a new layer and fill the selection in.

20. Create a new layer on the top of the stack and name it **stone material**.

21. Set your foreground color to black and the background color to white (D Key).

22. Filter > Render > Clouds.

23. Image > Adjustments > Brightness/Contrast—Contrast—50.

24. Filter > Render > Lighting Effects.
    Light Type—Spotlight
    Intensity—10
    Focus—69
    Gloss—42
    Material—56
    Exposure—0
    Ambience—10
    Texture Channel—Blue
    Height—87

See Figure 7-3 for the Lighting Effects dialog box and how to adjust the spotlight. In the window to the left you can see the small version of your texture and the circle that represents the spotlight.

Figure 7-3
The Lighting Effects dialog box in Photoshop CS.

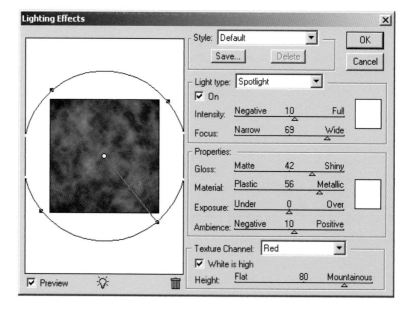

There are four squares along the edge of this circle. Drag the right-hand square out until the spotlight circle is completely outside the image.

25. You can run the Lighting Effects Filter once more if you want a rougher stone. I did not in this case. You can also run the Filter > Brush Strokes > Accented Edges to get a richer stone.
26. Save a copy of this base stone as a separate image in your asset library for later use.
27. Duplicate the layer.
28. Flip the layer vertically and horizontally (use Ctrl + T and right mouse click on the selection).
29. Offset this layer by 512 in both directions. We are doing this so the stones will look like they are made from random stones and not one sheet of stone.
30. Turn both these new layers off.
31. Activate the **stone** layer.
32. Select about half of the stones with the Magic Wand in a random pattern and invert the selection. I find that occasionally turning the layer off so you can see the selection by itself makes it easier to see the distribution of selected stones.
33. Activate the **stone material** layer and press Delete.
34. Deselect the layer and use Levels (Ctrl + L) and darken the stones slightly. Merge this layer with the **stones** layer.
35. Select a white stone on the **stone** layer and select Similar. Invert this selection.
36. Go to the other **stone material copy** layer and press Delete.
37. Merge these layers. You should have two layers: the stones and the background.
38. Add layer effects to the stones and change the following settings:
    Drop Shadow
    Use the default settings
    Outer Glow
    Blending Mode—Normal
    Opacity—54%
    Noise—20%
    Color—Black
    Size—27 px
    Inner Glow
    Blending Mode—Hard Light
    Opacity—60%
    Color—Black
    Noise—20%
    Size—40 px
    Bevel and Emboss
    Technique—Chisel Soft
    Soften—10 px
    Highlight Mode Opacity—60%
39. Copy the stone and background layers into a set and merge the copies.
40. Set your background color to black.
41. Filter > Brush Strokes > Accented Edges 2, 20, 4.
42. Filter > Noise > Add Noise—4%.

43. Filter > Brush Strokes > Accented Edges 2, 20, 4 (yes, again).

44. The stones already tile but you need to do two things to clean them up. First, use the Crop Tool to remove the excess pixels from outside the canvas area. When you merge a layer with an effect on it like Outer Glow with another layer, the effects cease to be a dynamic effect and become actual pixels outside the canvas area. If you can't visualize this, tile the image before you crop it and you will see what I mean.

45. Offset this image. You also need to use the Clone Brush to remove the line across the image where the effects were frozen.

If you want, you can create two versions of the stone layers as you did the above exercise, both offset exactly 50% from the other. They would be identical, but after they were merged the line that runs through the texture would be in different places on the textures. Just offset one of them and they will line up perfectly and then you just erase the hard line from the top image to expose the good part of the one below. I chose not to do this because, although my goal is speed on one hand, I also want things to look good and this was an opportunity for me to mix up the light and dark stones. The rendered lighting effects tend to lighten the middle stones. Your image should look like Figure 7-4.

Rough Stone Wall

We will use the pattern of the brick texture we created in the warehouse in the urban chapter and the stone material we created for the floor to create our stone wall.

1. Start by opening a copy of the brick pattern you created in the chapter on urban textures (**brick_pattern**), or go back and create it now. Save this file as **fantasy_stone_wall**.
2. Set the grid at 32 with "1 subdivisions".

Figure 7-4
The final stone floor texture.

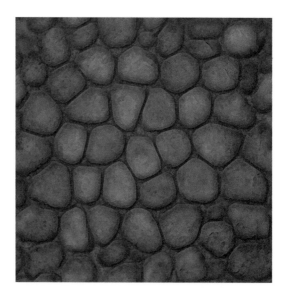

3. Go to the **Brick Shape** layer and use the Free Transform Tool and drag the bottom handle down until the bottom two rows of bricks are off the canvas.

4. Crop the image at its current size to remove the outer portions of the layer. Simply drag the Crop Tool across the canvas. Make sure you do not change the canvas size of the image.

5. The bricks are now vertically thicker and still tile perfectly. You may want to run the Offset Filter to make sure the image tiles perfectly.

6. We want to wear down the edges with a hard eraser like we did for the urban bricks. Turn off the grid and use a 13-pixel eraser and zoom into the image so you can work accurately. Be patient and subtle. Don't take too much off; we just want the bricks to look older and hand carved from stone. You will notice that you have more leeway to remove stone vertically because stretching the bricks made the mortar spaces wider horizontally, but not vertically. Your image should look like Figure 7-5 at this point.

7. Select the background layer and change the color to a dark gray RGB: 73,73,73.

8. Filter > Noise > Add Noise—5%.

9. Filter > Brush Strokes > Accented Edges—Edge Width 2, Edge Brightness 13, Smoothness 4.

10. Copy and paste a copy of the **stone_material** on the top of the stack from the stone floor image.

11. Duplicate the layer.

12. Flip the layer vertically and horizontally (use Ctrl + T and right mouse click on the selection).

13. Offset this layer by 512 in both directions.

14. Turn both these new layers off.

15. Activate the **Brick Stone** layer.

16. Select about half of the wall stones with the Magic Wand in a random pattern and invert the selection.

17. Activate the **stone_material** layer and press Delete.

18. Deselect the layer, use Levels (Ctrl + L), and darken the wall stones slightly. Merge this layer with the **Brick Stone** layer.

19. Add layer effects to the bricks and change the following settings:

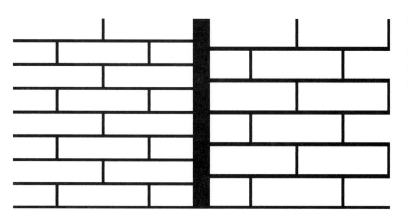

Figure 7-5
The bricks from the Urban Scene on the **left** and on the **right** after we stretch them down.

Drop Shadow
Use the default settings
Outer Glow
Blending Mode—Normal
Opacity—54%
Color—Black
Size—18 px
Bevel and Emboss
Technique—Chisel Soft
Size—5 px
Soften—4
Highlight Mode—Normal
Opacity—38%
Shadow Mode Opacity—40%

20. Add a new layer on top of the stack and name it **dirt**.
21. Filter > Render > Clouds.
22. Filter > Blur > Gaussian Blur—5 pixels.
23. Image > Adjustments > Brightness/Contrast—Brightness +25, Contrast −50.
24. Change the Blending Mode to Multiply and the Opacity to 45%. Depending on how and where you are using this texture, you might need to play with the Levels and the Brightness/Contrast. Your image should look like Figure 7-6.
25. Create a layer set and put the three layers into it we just created. You will have to duplicate the background layer to include it in the layer set.
26. Duplicate the layer set. And hide the original set. Flatten the new layer set (Ctrl + E).
27. Filter > Artistic > Sponge—Brush Size 2, Definition 2, Smoothness 11.
27. Fade this filter 50% (Ctrl + Shift + F).
28. Filter > Artistic > Poster Edges—Edge Thickness 4, Edge Intensity 5, Posterization 2.

Figure 7-6
This is what the stone wall looks like so far.

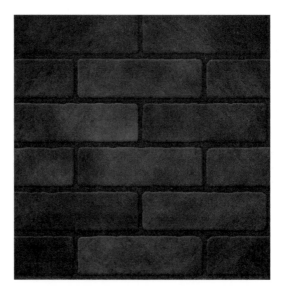

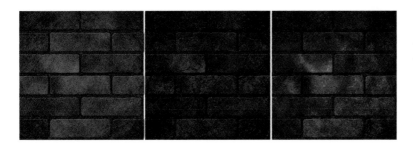

30. Fade this filter 25% and set the Blending Mode to Multiply.
31. Filter > Noise > Add Noise—Noise 5%.
32. Crop the image to remove the excess image that is outside the canvas and offset the image to check your tiling.
33. Your image should look like Figure 7-7.

Rough Wood Beams

We will base this texture on the wood fill from the warehouse. This will be used as a horizontally tiling beam, so we will make it longer and narrower, and add some detail.

1. Open a copy of the image **Wood_Fill_001**.
2. Change the Image size to 256, constrain proportions.
3. Duplicate the wood layer and make the Canvas Size 1024 in height. Keep the same width.
4. Tile this wood four times to fill the layer, and merge the four layers.
5. Liquefy this layer and create three or four knot holes and pinch the grain together in some spots along the beam.
6. Use the Burn and Dodge Tools to create an uneven, hewn, look to the beams' edges. Go easy; don't create any hotspots that will show up later when you tile the beam.
7. Check your tiling both ways. Even though this is designed as a vertically tiling beam, smoothing out the lines where the horizontal edges meet will make this texture easier to use and more versatile.
8. Use Levels to darken the wood slightly if you like. See Figure 7-8 for the steps I described here.

Plaster or Light Stucco

The plaster ceiling is based on the concrete texture we created in the warehouse. We will do a few things to make this concrete look like old stucco.

1. Open the image you created for the concrete with **pits** in it in the urban chapter, or go back to that chapter and create the image.
2. Colorize the image (Ctrl + U)—Hue 38, Saturation 6, Lightness −39.

Figure 7-8
The stages of the rough
hewn wooden beam.

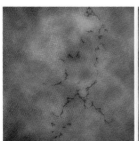

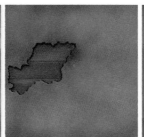

Figure 7-9
Variations of the stucco using
the same technique, but with
altered variables.

3. Create another layer on top of the stack and name it **cracks**.
4. Filter > Render > Clouds.
5. Filter > Artistic > Cutout—Number of Levels 8, Edge Simplicity 1, Edge Fidelity 2.
6. You can select and delete various parts of the resulting pattern. Depending on what you select and what you delete, you will get various crack patterns. The variations are endless. You can apply a variety of layer effects such as a very light Bevel and Emboss and Inner Glow to make the stucco have depth. Use the shape to mask off another image to get the effect that plaster is falling away from the wall and exposing the material behind it. Figure 7-9 shows the various effects I got using this method. I also used this cracked stucco as an overlay on the stone wall for the medieval version of this room at the end of the chapter.
7. Create a new layer on top and name it **dirt**.
8. Filter > Render > Clouds.
9. Filter > Render > Difference Clouds—two times.

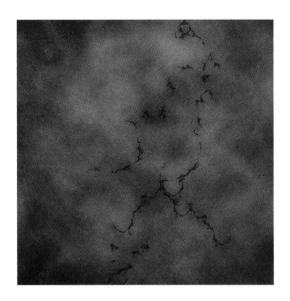

Figure 7-10
A harder, more defined crack using a different method.

10. Change the layer blending mode to Multiply and the opacity to 39%.

You can also create one strong crack in your stucco.

1. Use the Gradient Tool with a black to white gradient on a new layer named **crack**.
2. Filter > Render > Difference Clouds.
3. Adjust your Layer (Ctrl + L) by dragging the center arrow of the input to the left.
4. Zoom in and use the Magic Wand to select the darkest center of the crack and select Similar.
5. Invert the selection. Press Delete.
6. Now you can apply a Bevel and Emboss to the crack to add depth. See Figure 7-10.

There are several variables you can play with. The width and tightness of the gradient determine the chaos of the line. See Figure 7-11 for an illustration of this. You can also expand or contract the selection before you delete the pixels outside the crack.

Base Metals—Dark Iron, Pewter or Dull Silver, Gold

Dark iron, pewter, even a dull silver can simply be the base metal we created for the sci-fi hall.

1. Open a copy of **sci_fi_metal_base** and save it as **fantasy_metal_base**.
2. Image > Adjustments > Brightness/Contrast—Contrast—50%.

That's all you need to do. We will be using this base in various ways, and it works perfectly as a hand-crafted, beaten-up metal. As we use it, we will do specific things to the metal depending on where it

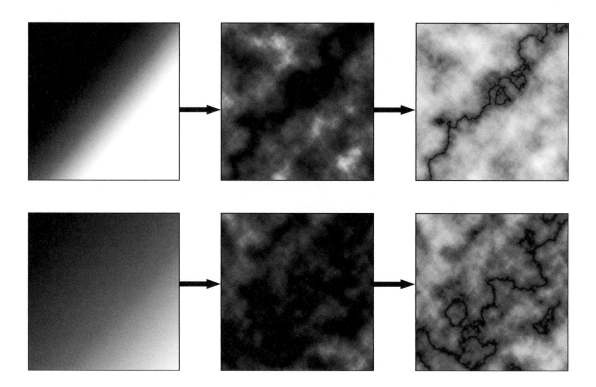

Figure 7-11
The width and tightness of the gradient determine the chaos of the line.

is and what it is used on. When we make the gold, it will be a very basic texture with a special shader applied to it.

Detail Textures

These detail textures will have a lot more detail in them than the previous textures and will require many steps to complete. We will start with the easiest and work up to the more complex textures.

Table Trim

In the concept art you can see the trim on the side of the table. This is simple and based on the wood we created for the heavy beams.

1. Open a copy of the wood beam texture and name it **fantasy_table_trim**.
2. Image > Rotate Canvas > 90 degrees.
3. Crop the image so it is 1024 wide and 128 high.
4. Create a new layer and name it **trim**.
5. Fill the layer with a color; it doesn't matter what color.
6. Using the grid and the circular selection tool, cut the arches out of the wood by pressing Clear and moving the selection. If you set the grid to 32, you can make the arches 7 units (224 pixels) with one unit between them all.
7. Use a hard, medium brush to make the circles (around 20 pixels).
8. Apply Layer Effects and change the following settings:

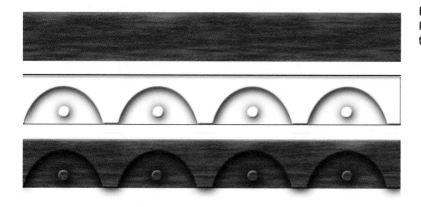

Figure 7-12
Progression of the table trim texture.

Fill—0
Drop Shadow
Size—25 px
Outer Glow
Blend Mode—Normal
Opacity—33%
Color—Black
Size—38 px
Bevel and Emboss
Highlight Mode Opacity—50%
Shadow Mode Opacity—60%

9. You can copy these layers and merge the copies so you can offset them to clean up the seams. See Figure 7-12 for a progression of the table trim.

Animal Fur Rug

The animal fur on the ground is a thick and plush bear skin rug. This requires a little hand painting but is easy and looks great. You do need to be patient and methodical, but you don't need very much artistic talent.

1. Open a new 512 wide × 1024 high image and name it **fantasy_bearskin**. Make sure your background is black.
2. Create a new layer and name it **bearskin**.
3. Fill this layer with a light brown RGB: 144, 109, 30.
4. Use the Lasso Tool and outline the general shape of half the bearskin. We are doing half because this texture can be mirrored on the 3D model it will be applied to, which saves texture memory. See Figure 7-13.
5. Invert the selection and delete.
6. Filter > Noise > Add Noise—10%.
7. Filter > Blur > Motion Blur - Angle 0, Pixels 32.
8. Filter > Brush Strokes > Angled Strokes—Direction Balance 6, Stroke Length 13, Sharpness 5.
9. Use the **Smudge Tool** and a 21-pixel soft brush and refine the outline of the bearskin by smudging the edge out. Your image

Figure 7-13
The general shape of half the bearskin.

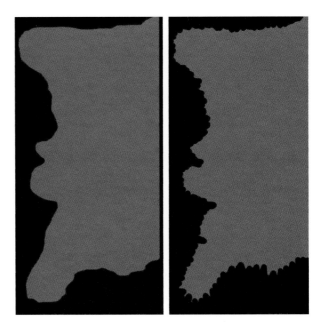

should look like Figure 7-14. Refer to Figure 7-14 as you work through the rest of this as it shows the fur at various stages of completion.

10. This is the fun part—actually, it's the tiresome part that is really fun when you are done because it looks so cool. We start by gradually outlining the general flow of the fur and will spend time building the fur up in layers—not hard, just a bit tedious. Since fur actually grows in layers and tends to clump, you don't have to draw individual hairs, and it looks great when you are done.

11. Use the Burn Tool—Midtones, exposure 38%—and a soft brush (13 pixels) and start by making basic lines and triangles defining the general pattern of how the fur grows from the pelt.

12. Use the Dodge Tool and a larger soft brush (27 pixels) and give each triangle a quick dash of highlight. You don't have to be too exact, just a general swoop down the middle.

13. Go back to the Burn Tool and select the "Spatter 39 pixels" brush.

14. Go to the Brushes Palette Tab and select the Shape Dynamics option; under the **Control** options to the right, select **Fade** from the drop-down box.

15. Enter the number 75 in the box to the right of this. This is the number of brush increments, not pixels, the brush takes to fade away. Therefore, a larger brush with the same value entered will take a longer distance to fade away.

16. This is where you need to be a bit more patient. Zoom in a bit and hit the [and] keys a few times to make the brush larger and smaller as you work. Start on the edges and work your way up.

17. Go back to step 14, only use the Dodge Tool this time.

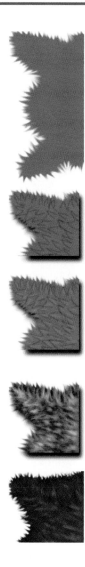

Figure 7-14
These are the stages of the bearskin rug. The fur looks great when it is done, but it starts with a simple layout that builds upon itself.

18. Go back to the Burn Tool and select a large, soft brush (100 pixels) and add a little depth by darkening the edges and a few major clumps of fur.
19. Do the same with the Dodge Tool, only highlight the areas you didn't darken.
20. Go back to the Burn Tool with the "Spatter 39 pixels" brush and the same Brush Dynamics settings. Go over the fur again to make it pop a little more. You don't need to do quite as much; use this opportunity to hit areas that may be a little too light. Do this with the Dodge Tool to pop the highlights and focus on the too-dark areas.
21. Filter > Artistic > Dry Brush—Brush Size 2, Brush Detail 10, Texture 1.
22. Fade this to 30% (Ctrl + Shift + F).
23. You are going to want to tweak a little with the Burn and Dodge Tools, and use the Smudge Tool again on the edges. The painted hairs may look like they are dead ending into the edge

Figure 7-15
The complete bearskin rug.

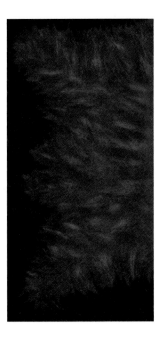

of the fur, and smudging them will blend the painted hairs into the edge. See Figure 7-15 for the final bearskin rug.

Chest

This chest is made of wood bound in heavy metal. We will use the base metal we created from the sci-fi metal. The beam we created in this chapter is actually a little too rough to use for the chest, so we will use the wood planks we created in the urban chapter.

In this exercise I will provide you with a UV template (Figure 7-16). This is an image that has all the parts of a 3D model that needs a texture laid out flat, and efficiently. The art of laying out a UV map efficiently and creating the texture for a UV mapped model is another book altogether. But I did want you to get a feel for what it is like to work with a UV map. Once you do this you will see the relationship between model and texture more clearly.

UV mapping a model before the texture is created is pretty common. It is also common for one artist to create both the texture and the model. The benefit is that the artist is able to switch among the texture, the UV editor, and the model, changing all three, and is not held to painting on one template. While that seems easier, UV'ing a model in advance and using the template is far easier and nets better results. Also, a lot of your work has been done for you if you are the texture artist getting the UV Map: you don't need to examine the model and do the tedious work of laying the UVs out and placing them in the square texture space in the most efficient way. This template may not be as efficiently laid out as possible (that wasn't my focus when I did it), but you will get a taste of creating

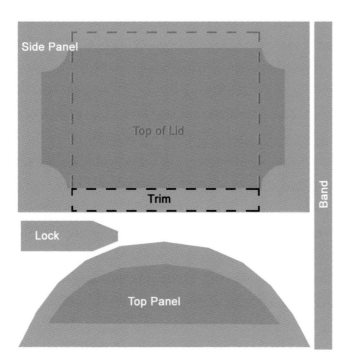

Figure 7-16
A typical template for a UV mapped model: in this case, our chest.

textures within boundaries. There are some quick, but major, efficient practices I did exercise. Notice that in this texture layout there are parts of the image that are used in repeated places on the model. The panels are repeated and the inner part of the panel is used as the top of the lid. The metal trim of the panel is used on all the small edges of the chest.

I always heard that guys like big chests in the fantasy genre, so let's give 'em what they want and make a big chest. The chest texture is composed of the following elements:

- The side panels
- The arched side panels on the top of the chest
- The lock
- The braided decorative band wrapped around the chest

These elements can all fit with room to spare on one texture, and we can make them all the same relative size. Relative sizing is important because if we made the side panels really big and then had to squeeze the lid panel in, making it smaller to fit, you would see the resolution difference on the final model.

1. Open the image from the DVD **fantasy_chest_UV_MAP** and save it as **fantasy_chest.**
2. I pasted **Wood_Planks_001** into the image and tiled four copies of it on the layer **wood.** The image **sci_fi_metal_base** is on the **metal** layer.
3. Turn off the **wood** and **metal** layers.

4. Open the layer set **UV Map.** This layer set has the UV map in it as well as a layer with text labels identifying what the parts are. There is also a layer with dashed lines that indicate where the parts of the chest are that we don't need to create art for, as they use parts of the existing texture. Select the layer with the UV map on it. You can turn the other layers off as you work.

5. Use the Magic Wand Tool and select the darker blue inner section of the chest lid and panel. These will be the wooden parts of the trunk.

6. Go to the **wood** layer, invert your selection, and press Delete.

7. Duplicate the **metal** layer and name it **panel frames.** Make sure this layer is on the top of the stack.

8. Go back to the UV Map and select the lighter blue outer portion of the panel and lid (the metal frame around the wood panels we just created) and the decorative plate in the center of the panel. Invert this selection.

9. On the **panel frames** layer, press Delete. If the **metal** layer is still visible, you won't see anything happen, so turn it off.

10. Apply Layer Styles with the following settings changed:
Outer Glow
Blend Mode—Linear Burn
Opacity—15%
Noise—13%
Color—Black
Size—62 px
Inner Glow
Blending Mode—Vivid Light
Opacity—45%
Noise—17%
Color—White
Size—35 px
Gradient Overlay
Blend Mode—Vivid Light
Opacity—29%
Bevel and Emboss
Technique—Chisel Soft
Contour—default
Texture—Scale—412%
Your image should look like Figure 7-17.

11. Create a new layer and name it **bolts.** Copy the layer styles from the **panel frames** layer and change the following settings:
Drop Shadow
Default Settings
Outer Glow
Opacity—24%
Size—29 px

12. Use a hard brush with a medium gray and place the large bolts on the corners of the chest frame and lid frame. I eyeballed this, but if you like you can use four guidelines to get them placed perfectly.

13. Duplicate the **metal** layer and name it **lock.**

14. Copy the layer style from the **bolts** layer and paste it on the **lock** layer.

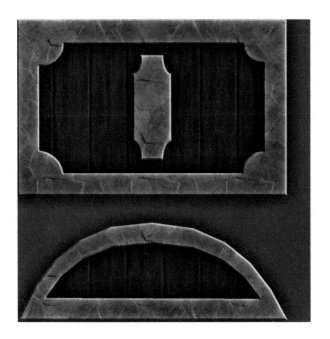

Figure 7-17
The beginnings of the chest with the major metal and wood parts in place.

15. Go to the **UV Map** layer, select the parts of the lock, and invert the selection.
16. On the **lock** layer, press Delete.
17. Duplicate the **bolts** layer and name it **lock bolts.** Clear this layer of pixels (Ctrl + A and Ctrl + X).
18. Use a small, hard brush and a medium gray and place the small bolts on the lock.
19. Change the following settings in the layer style:
    Drop Shadow
    Distance—4
    Size—6
    Outer Glow
    Opacity—35%
    Size—8 px
    Inner Glow
    Turn it off
20. Duplicate the metal layer and name it **band.**
21. Select the band on the **UV Map** layer and invert the selection.
22. On the **band** layer, press Delete.
23. Duplicate the **band** layer and name it **band top.** Press Delete on this layer, too. You should have two identical layers at this point: **band** and **band top.**
24. Copy the layer style from the **lock bolts** layer, paste it into the **band** layer, and change the following settings:
    Bevel and Emboss
    Size—9
    Soften—7
25. Copy the layer style from the **band** layer and paste it into the **band top** layer.
26. We need to cut the diagonal spaces into the **band top.** Use the grid and the Polygonal Selection Tool to create a diagonal

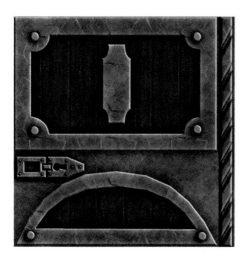 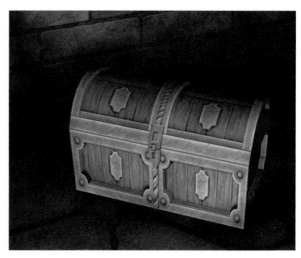

Figure 7-18
The final chest texture with a close-up of the chest from the fantasy scene.

selection, move it along the grid, and press Delete. You can see the chest in the final render, but Figure 7-18 shows the texture with a close-up of the chest. Notice that the top of the lid is the side panel texture, and the trim parts inside the metal frame are the trim from the metal bands on the lid.

Candlestick

The candlestick is actually three separate images.

- Candlestick—Metal, pewter with etched in leaves
- Candle Flame—Small, separate illumination mapped texture
- Candle Wax—Illumination mapped, but differently than the flame

Metal Candlestick

1. Open a copy of the base metal we made for the sci-fi setting. Change the image size to 512×512. Save this image as **fantasy_candlestick**.
2. Filter > Brush Strokes > Crosshatch—Stroke Length 10, Sharpness 6, Strength 1. This helps the metal look more worn and smoother than the rough base metal.
3. Duplicate this layer and name it **pewter**.
4. Duplicate it again and name it **ridges**. Make sure this layer is on top.
5. Using the grid and a hard brushed eraser (9 pixels), erase four evenly spaced horizontal lines. Don't forget that the top and bottom must have a half-line erased from each, or offset the image vertically and erase the line. We are doing this horizontally because not only is it much easier to work horizontally and rotate the texture on the model, we can zmore easily use this texture in other places with a horizontal orientation.
6. For this step you can apply layer styles including Bevel and Emboss or use the Burn and Dodge Tools to create the highlights and shadow on the metal. I opted to use Burn/Dodge

because at the end it looked better and was easier to tile. Here are the settings you need to change from the layer styles:

Outer Glow
Color—Black
Size—6 px

Inner Glow
Opacity—51%
Noise—13%
Color—White
Size—29 px

Bevel and Emboss
Depth—61%
Size—64

7. Link the **pewter** and **ridges** layers, create "new set from linked", and duplicate the layer set.

8. Hide one of the layer sets and merge the other.

9. Crop to remove the excess pixels outside the canvas area of the merged layer set.

10. Duplicate the layer and offset it 256 pixels in both directions. Use a large, soft brush to remove the seams.

11. Link these layers and merge them. The last thing we have to do is create the leaf pattern.

12. Create a new layer and name it **leaf**.

13. Use the Custom Shape Tool, select the "Leaf 3" shape, and make one big leaf on the new layer. Use the Free Transform Tool to size and rotate the leaf until it fits on about one fourth of the top band. Apply Layer Effects and change the following settings:
Fill—0

Outer Glow
Blend Mode—Color Burn
Opacity—45%
Noise—11%
Color—Black
Size—13 px

Bevel and Emboss
Style—Pillow Emboss
Depth—60 px
Size—12 px

Gradient Overlay
Blend Mode—Color Dodge
Opacity—58%

14. Duplicate the **leaf** layer and flip the leaf vertically adjust the two layers back and forth until the leaves look right, taking up about half the band (you want to fit four of them across eventually). See Figure 7-19. Change the following settings in the layer effects:
Color Overlay
Blend Mode—Overlay
Opacity—70%

15. Now that these two leaves look good, duplicate them and place them on the other half of the band. Keep duplicating leaves until you fill the texture. You can leave all these layers un-flattened and output the texture as you need it. Even if I flatten a texture before I output it, I always copy layers I may want to change later.

Figure 7-19
The candlestick metal with
the first leaves in place.

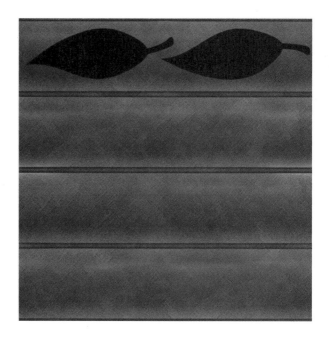

Figure 7-20
The final candlestick texture
with the model.

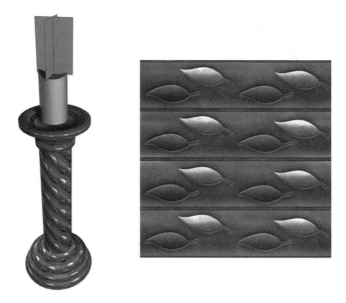

That's it. Here is the final texture with the model applied (Figure
7-20). The candle itself doesn't look good because we haven't
made the wax and flame yet.

Candle Flame

1. Create a new 256 wide by 512 high image with a black
   background and name it **candle_flame**.
2. Snap a vertical guideline to the center of the image.

3. Create a new layer and name it **orange**.
4. Use a large, soft brush (200 pixels) and put a big fuzzy orange circle at the bottom of the layer in the center. RGB: 255, 127, 0.
5. Use the Free Transform Tool and stretch this ball up by using the middle top handle. You will have to zoom way out to do this, and this will put a lot of nearly invisible pixels outside the canvas area, so you will want to crop the image to remove them. You should also clean the edges with a small, hard eraser and a larger, soft one if you see a hard line in the orange.
6. Create a new layer and name it **white**. Set your foreground color to white.
7. Use a smaller soft brush (65 pixels), open the Brushes Palette, and set the Shape Dynamics to Fade and the Fade Size to 55. Start very near the bottom and hold Shift to keep the flame straight and draw upwards. I also smudged the tip of the flame to get a better-looking flame tip.
8. Finally, I put a small black line in the center for the wick and brushed some white over the tip to blend it into the flame. See Figure 7-21 for the candle flame and its stages.
9. To create the **alpha channel,** simply duplicate the layer or the entire image, depending on how you need to handle the alpha channel, and desaturate it (Ctrl + Shift + U). Use the Hue/Saturation (Ctrl + U) to make the flame darker (Lightness −43) so it is more transparent. Use a white brush and make the wick solid white so it is not transparent at all.
10. To create an **Illumination Map,** copy the alpha image and use Hue/Saturation to make it much brighter. The Illumination Map makes areas of the object mapped with white fully bright and not affected by light, while black areas have no illumination and usually light normally, depending on the game engine or technology you are using. The lightness and darkness of the grayscale determine the amount of illumination.

Candle Wax

1. Create a new image 256 wide and 512 high. Name it **candle_wax.**

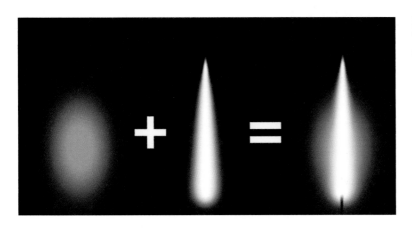

Figure 7-21
The stages of creating the candle flame.

Figure 7-22
The candle flame with and without the illumination map. Makes a big difference, doesn't it?

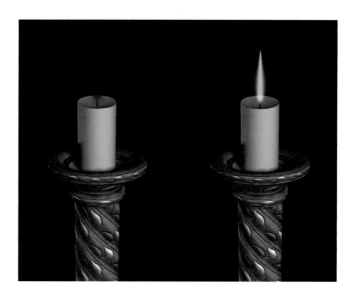

2. Create a new layer and name it **wax**.
3. Fill this layer with a desaturated light yellow RGB: 198, 184, 135.
4. Filter > Noise > Add Noise—20%.
5. Filter > Blur > Gaussian Blur—5 pixels.
6. Filter > Brush Strokes > Spatter—Spray Radius 6, Smoothness 6.
7. Filter > Render > Clouds.
8. Fade (Ctrl + Shift + F) Blending Mode—Overlay, Opacity 65%.
9. Use the Burn Tool and a large, soft brush (100 pixels) and darken the horizontal edges of the candle slightly.
10. Use the Dodge Tool and a smaller, soft brush (45 pixels) and do a faint line or two of highlight up and down the horizontal center of the candle. If you want the candle to look more like shiny wax, then also add another stronger, more narrow line to the highlights.
11. To get the dripping wax effect, create as new layer and name it **dripping wax**. Apply layer effects and change the following settings:
    Fill—0
    Drop Shadow
    Opacity—38%
    Distance—3 px
    Size—13 px
    Outer Glow
    Blend Mode—Color Burn
    Opacity—38%
    Color—Black
    Size—35 px
    Bevel and Emboss
    Size—16 px
    Soften—3 px
    Highlight Mode Opacity—60%
    Shadow Mode Opacity—31%
    Texture
    Pattern—Molecular

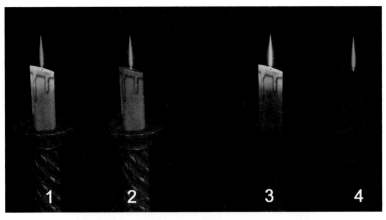

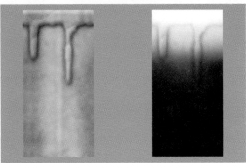

Figure 7-23
Candles 1 and 2 are in a brightly lit scene; but the illumination map still helps the candle look more authentic as the glow adds a perception of translucence to the candle. **Candles 3 and 4** are in a very low light scene; you can see the difference between the one with the illumination map and the one without. The **bottom left** image is the candle texture and the **bottom right** is the illumination map.

Scale—474%
Depth—+102%
Check the Invert box

12. To make the drips, use a soft 27-pixel brush, paint along the top, and draw a drip or two coming down the candle. Copy the layers and merge them so you can offset them and clean the tiling edge.

13. To make an illumination map, you do it the same way as the candle flame—copy the image, desaturate it, and adjust the darkness and lightness of the image in order to get the illumination effect you desire. In this case I used a black to white gradient (black starting at the bottom of the candle) and faded it to 70% and changed the blending mode to Linear Burn. I also tweaked the brightness at the top and the darkness at the bottom of the candle. This illumination map will make the candle appear to glow with the light of the flame. Figure 7-23 shows the candle with and without the illumination map in both a lit and nonlit scene.

Spell Book

Now we will create the spell book, which is a bit more complex. This book has a metal cover binding a dragon scale hide and is inset with gems. There is embossed writing and symbols on the cover and spine. For the writing we will use one of my favorite techniques—

fonts. I got permission from the fonts' creator to use it in the book and it is on the DVD, too. You will need to install this font (Tengwar-Gandalf) before you start this exercise. We will also be creating the unique shapes on the cover using paths. These shapes are also used on the door, banner, and map. Creating them using paths is flexible and you can drop the shapes into the other textures that use them. If you hand-paint the shapes on the texture, you will be repainting them every time you need them. Finally, we will create the decoration on the spin, the page edges, and the gems.

The spell book is similar to the chest in that we will be using a UV Map template. The main parts of the spell book on the UV map in Figure 7-24 are

- Metal binding, trim, and spine
- Dragon hide cover inset
- Page edges
- Gem

Metal Binding, Trim, and Spine

1. Open the image from the DVD **fantasy_spellbook_UV_MAP** and save it as **fantasy_spellbook.**
2. The **metal** layer has the **sci_fi_metal_base** already there for you.
3. Turn off the **metal** layer.
4. Open the layer set **UV Map.** This layer set has the UV map in it as well as a layer with text labels identifying what the parts are.

Figure 7-24
UV Map template for the spell book.

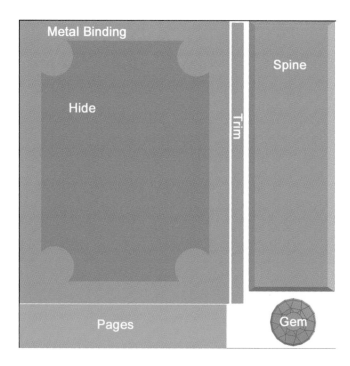

Select the layer with the UV map on it. You can turn the other layers off as you work.

5. Use the Magic Wand Tool and select the lighter blue sections of the book. These will be the metal bindings of the book. Make sure you get the book frame, trim piece, and all the parts of the spine.

6. Go to the **metal** layer, invert your selection, and press Delete.

7. Apply layer styles with the following settings changed:
Outer Glow
Blend Mode—Linear Burn
Opacity—15%
Noise—13%
Color—Black
Size—62 px
Inner Glow
Blending Mode—Vivid Light
Opacity—45%
Noise—17%
Color—White
Size—35 px
Gradient Overlay
Blend Mode—Vivid Light
Opacity—29%
Bevel and Emboss
Technique—Chisel Soft
Contour—default
Texture—Scale—412%

8. Filter > Brush Strokes > Crosshatch—Stroke Length 16, Sharpness 6, Strength 2.

9. Set your background color to gray RGB: 120, 120, 120.

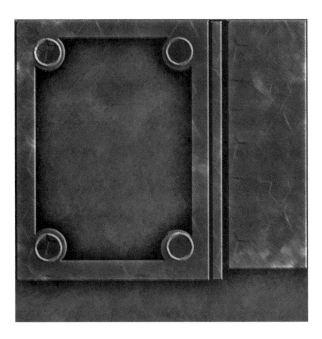

Figure 7-25
The metal binding of the book.

10. Filter > Artistic > Smudge Stick—Stroke Length 4, Highlight Area 12, Intensity 4.
11. You can create a place for the gems to be set in by duplicating the metal layer. Save it as **gem settings** and clear the layer contents. Set the Fill to 0 and use the circular selection to place a setting and Inner Stroke it.

Runes

The runes are very easy. First, make sure the Tengwar-Gandalf font from the DVD is installed.

1. Create a new layer set **runes** and a new text layer named **runes** and set the font to Tengwar-Gandalf. Make it about 42 pts.
2. Set the Tracking to −10 (tracking is the space between the letters).
3. Type whatever you want until the line of text fills the space between the gems.
4. Apply layer effects with the following settings changed:
   Inner Glow
   Blending Mode—Vivid Light
   Opacity—62%
   Noise—4%
   Color—White
   Size—10 px
   Bevel and Emboss
   Style—Outer Bevel
   Technique—Chisel Soft
   Depth—101%
   Size—2 px
   Contour—default
   Color Overlay
   Blend Mode—Normal
   Opacity—100%
   Color—RGB: 67, 90, 106
5. You can duplicate this layer and use the Free Transform Tool to rotate it to line up on the four sides of the book binding. You may have to delete or add letters to make a nice fit. You can also type different words if you want to make sure the runes look different on every side.
6. We also need to do the runes on the book spine, too. For this I pressed Return after each letter and made the font a little larger (about 60 pt) and adjusted the leading (the space between the letters vertically) to 35 pt. I linked all the runes so I could collapse them, but you can keep them separate if you think you will want to edit them later. Your image should look like Figure 7-26.

Spine Decoration

The decoration on the spine is broken down into three steps: top, middle, and bottom.

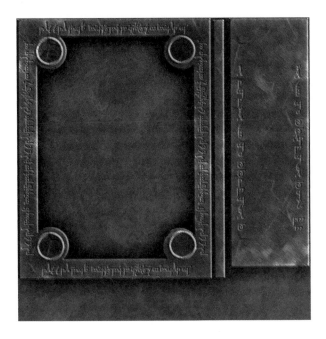

Figure 7-26
Runes on the cover and spine of the book.

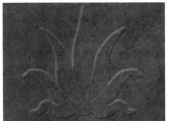

Figure 7-27
The progression of the creation of the top of the spine decoration.

1. Create a new layer set named **spine decoration**. Create a new layer named **top**.
2. Use the Shape Tool and select the shape "leaf 3" and start by making the center leaf; make it big to start with. The color doesn't matter.
3. Copy the leaf layer three times and use the Free Transform Tool (Ctrl + T) to flip and rotate the leaves into position. Use Liquefy and a very large brush to move the leaves around until they look good. Merge the layers together.
4. Duplicate this half you just created, flip it, line up the two halves, and merge them. Copy and paste the layer effects from the runes layer. Your image should look like Figure 7-27.
5. The middle of the spine decoration is a twist pattern. Select the Type Tool and set the font to **Eras Demi ITC.** Create a new text layer, type a capital "S", and make it pretty big.
6. **Rasterize** the layer and erase the ends of the **S**. Free Transform the curve down to a size small enough that you can stack them into the twist shape.
7. Snap a guide to the center of the resulting curve and copy the curve vertically using the guide to keep the curves centered.

Figure 7-28
The progression of the
creation of the curve for the
spine decoration.

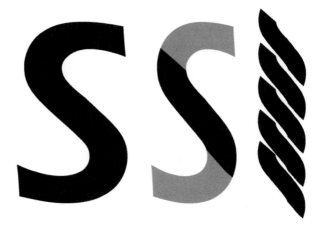

You can use the Free Transform Tool to manipulate the complete
twist to fit it into the spine the way you like it.

8. Copy the layer style from the **top** layer and paste it to this layer.
    See Figure 7-28 for the progression of the creation of the twist.
9. Create a new layer named **bottom** and copy the layer style from
    the **top** or **twist** layer and paste it to this layer.
10. Use the Shape Tool and select the **Fleur-De-Lis** and drag one
    out on this layer. You will need to use the Free Transform Tool to
    flip it vertically and resize it so it fits on the spine below the
    twist and between the runes. Figure 7-29 shows the finished
    book spine with runes and decoration.

Dragon Scales

Here I will introduce the Pen Tool. The Pen Tool creates paths, which
allow for the easy creation of smooth and complex curves. The great
thing about paths is that they are editable. You can lay them down
quickly without being too exact and then you can add and subtract
points, move them, and adjust the handles to get any curve you can
imagine. You can also save paths, fill them, stroke them, and more.

1. Create a new layer set and name it **scales**.
2. Create a new layer and name it **scale**.
3. Select the **Pen Tool**. I turned on the grid for this part of the
    project. See Figure 7-30 for the general placement of the
    anchors and points, the final path, and the final scale shape.
    a. Click somewhere in the upper left-hand side of the image.
    b. Click and **drag** a little in the lower left of the image to create
        an anchor point.
    c. Click and **drag** between the center line and the last anchor
        point.
    d. Click once on the center line.
    e. Hold Shift and move the line straight up and click once at
        the top center, at the same horizontal height as the starting
        point.
    f. Click once on the starting point to close the path off.

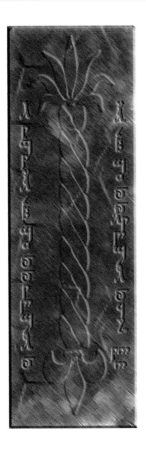

Figure 7-29
The finished book spine with runes and decoration.

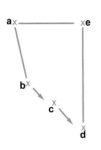 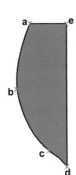 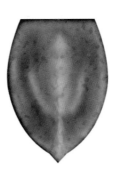

Figure 7-30
Initial path point placement, the final half-scale path, and the final full-scale shape. Note that you click and drag where the arrows appear. This creates curved lines instead of straight.

4. After you have created the path and adjusted it to your liking, go to the Paths Palette and save the path as **scale path** so it is still there after you close the file and reopen it later.
5. Fill the path with a medium green RGB:77,145,66. Right mouse click and choose Fill Path.
6. Turn off the path. Go to the Paths palette and click outside the path layer.
7. Go back to the Layers Palette and copy and paste the scale half. Flip it horizontally and line it up with the other half and merge the two layers. At this point you may not like the shape you

Figure 7-31
The progression of the painted scale.

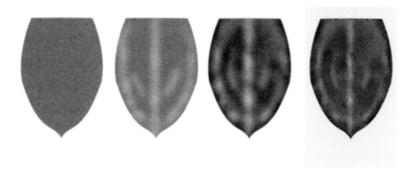

created. You can either use Free Transform or go back and adjust your path.

8. Filter > Noise > Add Noise—10%.

9. Filter > Blur > Gaussian Blur—1.5 pixels.

10. Now you will use your Dodge and Burn tools, just like we did on the banner in the warehouse and on the fur recently. Start by dodging a light line down the center of the scale using a soft, 45-pixel brush. Look at Figure 7-31 for a progression of the painted scale.

11. Dodge the edge of the scale. You can use short, choppy strokes if you don't have a graphic tablet or the ability to draw a continuous fluid line. Actually the lumpiness of a choppy line helps the scale look more organic than a smooth line. I dodged those two extra ridges in the sides of the scale to make it more interesting.

12. Burn the outer edge of the scale and in between the highlights to build up the depth of the scale. Go slow and use this opportunity to burn in between the bright spots to get a lumpy appearance, unless you want a smooth scale.

13. Set your background color to black.

14. Filter > Brush Strokes > Accented Edges—Edge Width 10, Edge Brightness 22, Smoothness 3.

15. Filter > Brush Strokes > Spatter—Spray Radius 8, Smoothness 8.

16. Filter > Artistic > Plastic Wrap—Highlight Strength 11, Detail 8, Smoothness 2.

17. I went back and strengthened some of the highlights and shadows with the dodge and burn again.

18. For this next step I turned off all other layers.

19. Create a copy of this layer and hide it. You want to keep one large copy of the scale in case you need it later.

20. Use the Free Transform Tool and size the scale down until you like the size. I made it about 200 pixels high.

21. Apply the layer effect **Drop Shadow** to the scale and change the following settings:
    Uncheck the "Use Global Light" option
    Opacity—25%
    Distance—12 px
    Size—10 px

22. I found it easier at this point to copy this layer and merge it with an empty layer to freeze the layer effects. You can also go

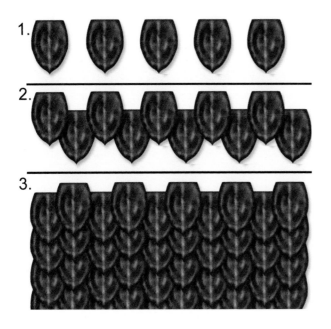

Figure 7-32
Scales laid out on the grid to create the cover. The top row of scales (1) is the first row you create. This goes at the bottom of your image. The second row (2) shows the duplicated layer placed above the first. The third row (3) shows the scales filling up the layer. You work from the bottom up, overlapping scales like a roofer laying tiles.

to the Layers Menu and Create Layers and merge the two as well. I am just in the habit of creating an empty layer and linking and merging faster than I can click through a menu.

23. Select All and use Ctrl + Alt to copy the scale on the layer. You don't want the first row of scales to touch or overlap. Lay them out on the grid with roughly half a scale space between them like in Figure 7-32. Start at the bottom and when you have a row, duplicate the layer and move it up half a scale and center it between the scales below.

24. Merge all the scale layers together and name the layer **finished scales**. I thought my scales were too bright personally, so I used Ctrl + U to lower the saturation and the lightness a bit.

25. Filter > Brush Strokes > Spatter—Spray Radius 8, Smoothness 8.

26. Filter > Artistic > Plastic Wrap—Highlight Strength 9, Detail 7, Smoothness 2.

27. Filter > Brush Strokes > Accented Edges—Edge Width 7, Edge Brightness 22, Smoothness 2.

28. Turn all the layers back on (except for the UV layer set and the saved scale). Mostly you want to see the **metal** layer and how the scales look under the metal frame of the book. Free Transform the scales until you like the size.

29. Go to the **metal** layer and select the empty inside of the cover with the Magic Wand and invert the selection.

30. Go to the **scales** layer and press Delete. You cover should look like Figure 7-33.

Cover Symbols

We will use paths again to create the symbols on the cover. These symbols will be used again on the map, banner, and door. When you

Figure 7-33
The cover with the finished scales.

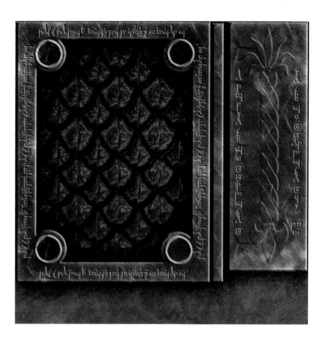

create these shapes, don't try to make them to fit the book cover; make them large so they can easily be reused.

1. Create a new layer set and name it **symbols**.
2. Create a new layer and name it **symbol**.
3. Select the **Pen Tool**. I turned the grid off for this part of the project.
   a. Click somewhere in the lower left-hand side of the image.
   b. Click and drag in the upper right-middle of the image to create an anchor point.
   c. Click to the right and a little lower of the last anchor point.
   d. Click down and a little to the left.
   e. Click and drag a little higher and to the left of the last point.
   f. Click once on the starting point to close the path off.
4. After you have created the first shape and adjusted it to your liking, go to the Paths Palette and save the path as **symbol path** so it is still there after you close the file and reopen it later.
5. Fill the path with any color. Right mouse click and choose Fill Path.
6. Turn off the path: go to the Paths palette and click outside the path layer.
7. Go back to the **symbol** layer and use the Magic Wand Tool and select the shape.
8. Select > Modify > Contract—select a number of pixels to contract the selection that looks good to you. Press Delete.
9. To create the circular shapes on the cover, create a new layer named **circle**. Create a circular selection and fill it.
10. Snap a guideline line to the vertical and horizontal center of the circle.
11. Drag out a circular selection centered on the circle using the guides and press Delete.

12. To make the half-moon shape, create a new layer named **half-moon** and drag out an oval selection. Make sure this selection is a little thicker vertically. Snap this selection to the center of the guidelines. Fill this selection.
13. Drag a circular selection out from the center of the guidelines that is a bit larger than the circle on the circle **layer**.
14. Press Delete to remove the middle of the oval and erase the remaining left-hand portion of the shape.
15. Now you have all the shapes you need to create the symbols on the cover. Duplicate the **symbols** layer set and name it **cover symbols**. Now all the original large versions of the shapes are there for you to create the other textures in the scene.
16. In the **cover symbols** layer, copy and manipulate the shapes until they look like the symbols on the cover and merge all the layers. See Figure 7-34 for the general placement of the anchors and points, the circular shapes, and the final shape.
17. Apply layer effects with the following settings changed:
    Fill—0%
    Outer Glow
    Blending Mode—Multiply
    Opacity—100%
    Color—Black
    Spread—9%
    Size—18 px
    Bevel and Emboss
    Style—Inner Bevel
    Technique—Chisel Soft
    Depth—131%
    Size—5 px
    Contour—default
    Color Overlay
    Color—White
    Opacity—50%
    Gradient Overlay—default

See Figure 7-35 for the book cover with the symbols in place.

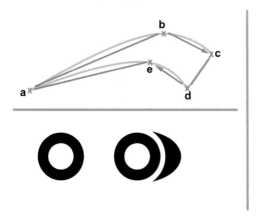

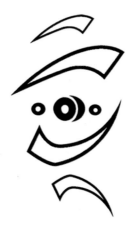

Figure 7-34
Initial path point placement, the circular shapes, and the final shape.

Figure 7-35
The cover with the symbols
in place.

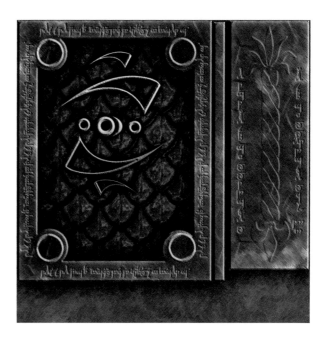

Page Edges

The book has old, well-worn page edges. These are easily
created.

1. Create a new layer set named **pages**.
2. Create a new layer named **pages**.
3. Go to the **UV Map** layer set and the **UV Map** layer and select the
   pages area with the Magic Wand Tool.
4. Go to the **pages** layer and move the selection up to the middle
   of the canvas and use the Select > Transform Selection
   command to rotate the selection 90 degrees.
5. Reset your colors (D key) to black and white.
6. Fill the selection with black.
7. Filter > Render > Fibers—Variance 10, Strength 15.
8. Colorize this (Ctrl + U)—Hue 45, Saturation 27, Lightness-57.
9. Reset your colors (D key) to black and white and swap them
   (X key).
10. Filter > Distort > Glass—Distortion 4, Smoothness 7, Scaling
    62%.
11. Rotate the pages back horizontally and position them over the
    UV area for the pages.
12. You can use the Burn Tool to darken the top, bottom, and side
    edges of the pages. See Figure 7-36 for the progression of the
    pages.

Gem

Finally, we need to make the gem for our spell book. Another easy
task.

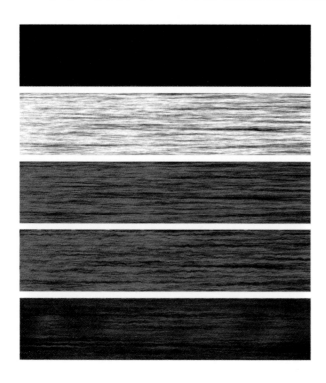

Figure 7-36
The progression of the pages.

1. Create a new layer set and name it **gem**.
2. Create a new layer and name it **gem**.
3. Go to the UV Map layer set and select the gem area of the UV map.
4. Go back to the gem layer and fill the selection with it with any color you want. You want to use a color not too close to black or white. A pretty saturated color works best.
5. Keep the selection active or lock the layer transparency.
6. Apply layer effects with the following settings changed:
   Inner Shadow
   Blending Mode—Multiply
   Color—Black
   Opacity—49%
   Distance—30 px
   Choke—7%
   Size—38 px
7. Use the Dodge Tool and lighten the lower edge of the gem.
8. Create a new layer and name it **highlights**.
9. Use a soft brush of various sizes and paint on some white highlights. Having the highlights on a separate layer allows you to edit them. Sometimes you may want to repaint them. If the highlights are too strong, you can apply a Gaussian Blur or take down the opacity. See Figure 7-37 for the stages of the gem.

A final step that makes the gem look great, in other contexts but not in this case since the gem will be mapped to geometry, is to the apply a large outer glow and a strong inner glow. Try these settings:

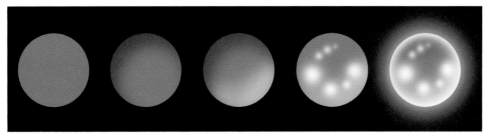

Figure 7-37
The progression of the creation of the gem. The last one on the right is the gem with added effects that look great in other contexts, but not here. It's a neat trick though.

Figure 7-38
The final spell book texture.

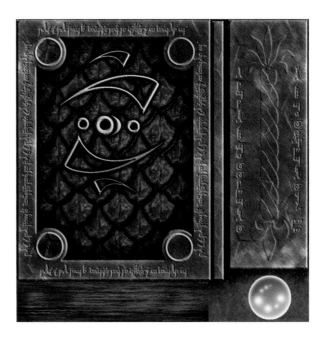

Outer Glow
Blending Mode—Normal
Opacity—75%
Color—The color you chose for the gem
Spread—10%
Size—250 px
Inner Glow
Blending Mode—Normal
Opacity—83%
Color—White
Choke—3%
Size—116 px

You are finished all the details of the spell book. Figure 7-38 shows the final spell book texture.

Old Map

Now we will create the old map on the table. This map is old dark parchment with burnt edges and faded ink. You can see the complex torn edges of the map and the holes in it as well. For this effect we will use an alpha channel.

1. Open a new 1024x1024 image and name it **map**. The background color should be black.
2. Create a new layer and name it **paper**. Fill this layer with the color RGB: 193,166,101.
3. Filter > Noise > Add Noise—15%.
4. Filter > Blur > Gaussian Blur—5 pixels.
5. Reset your colors to black and white (D key).
6. Filter > Render > Clouds.
7. Fade the clouds (Ctrl + Shift + F). Opacity 20%, Blending Mode—Multiply. See Figure 7-39.
8. Now we need to tear up the edges of the map. I started by making a square selection that had a 32-pixel border all the way around (I used the grid for this). Invert the selection and press Delete.
9. Use the eraser with a large, hard brush (40 pixels) and erase the general outline of the torn paper (Figure 7-40).
10. Use the 9-pixel "Drippy Watercolor" brush. You may have to load the "Wet Media Brushes" to make the brush a little larger and start eating away the edges of the paper. I experimented with a few brushes at various sizes to get different torn edge effects. One was the "Brush Heavy Flow Scatter".
11. Apply layer effects with the following settings changed:
    Inner Glow
    Blending Mode—Overlay

Figure 7-39
The parchment base.

Figure 7-40
The parchment with the
beginning of a worn edge.

Figure 7-41
The parchment with torn and
burnt edges.

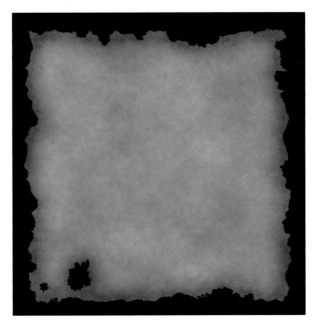

Opacity—52%
Noise—5%
Color—Black
Choke—9%
Size—90 px
See Figure 7-41.

12. Create a new layer named **terrain** and set the opacity to 49%
and the blending mode to Overlay. Use a small black brush (3–5
pixels) to draw some details on the map. Don't worry; they can

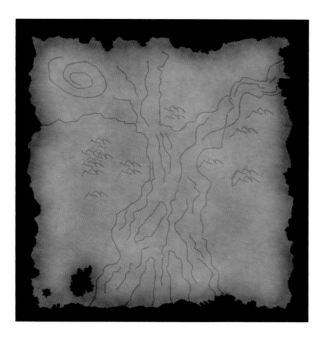

Figure 7-42
The terrain lines—don't have to be too good at this point.

be pretty simple. We will add more detail coming up. And don't worry if the lines don't look like the old ink you want it to, we will process that later. You can look at Figure 7-42 to see what I drew before it was processed.

13. Now go back to the spell book and copy the **symbol** layer into the map. Turn off all the layer effects and add a new one:
Stroke
Size—1 px
Position—Inside
Blending Mode—Overlay
Opacity—49%
Color—Black

14. Now you can copy and resize a few of these symbols about the map. You can erase portions of the symbols, flip them around, do whatever you think will look good.

15. Select the Text Tool, select the Tengwar-Gandalf font and make it 82 pt. Type whatever you want on the map. Make a few short lines of text, as if notes were written on the map. You may need to adjust the spacing between the letters and the lines of letters. Set the layer Fill to 0 and add the following layer effects:
Color Overlay
Blending Mode—Color Burn
Color—RGB: 92,45,45
Opacity—50%

16. Use the Free Transform Tool to rotate the text up on the right-hand side so it looks more handwritten.

17. Create a new layer and name it **dirt**.

18. Use the Color Picker to set your foreground color to a color close to the map's color. Just select anywhere on the map.

19. Filter > Render > Render Clouds.

Figure 7-43
The map getting dirty.

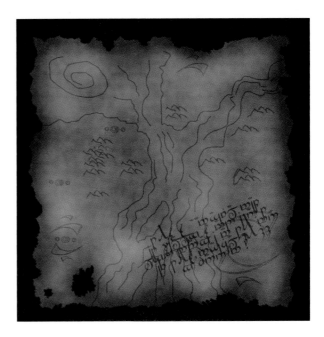

20. Filter > Render > Render Difference Clouds 2x.
21. Filter > Blur > Gaussian Blur—25 pixels.
22. Set the layer blending mode to Overlay and the opacity between 40 and 55% depending on how dirty you want your map. See Figure 7-43.
23. Link all the layers except for the background and create **Layer Set From Linked**.
24. Duplicate this layer set and unlink the text layer. Merge all the linked layers and make sure the text layer is on top.
25. Select the **paper** layer in the original, un-flattened layer set.
26. Selection > Load Selection—Press OK. The proper file name and layer should be the default when the correct layer is selected.
27. Hide the unflattened layer set.
28. Invert the selection.
29. Highlight the new flattened layer with the map on it and press Delete.
30. Filter > Brush Strokes > Spatter—Spray Radius 8, Smoothness 8.
31. Filter > Distort > Ocean Ripple—Ripple Size 12, Ripple Magnitude 4.
32. Filter > Brush Strokes > Accented Edges—Edge Width 4, Edge Brightness 24, Smoothness 4.
33. Turn the text layer back on. See Figure 7-44.
34. Create a new layer, name it **alpha**, and fill it with black.
35. Select the **paper** layer in the original, un-flattened layer set.
36. Selection > Load Selection—Press Okay.
37. Turn off every layer but the new alpha layer.
38. Select the **alpha** layer and fill the selection with white (right mouse click, Fill).

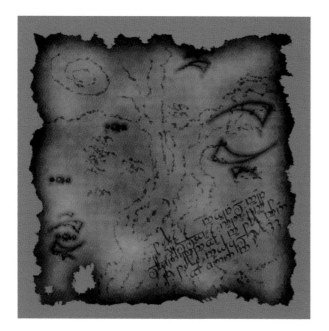

Figure 7-44
The final old and worn map.

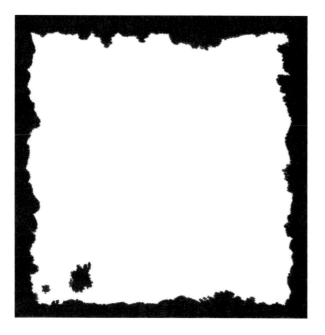

Figure 7-45
The alpha channel for the map.

Windows

The windows are bright based on the light shafts and the glass looks clean and unbroken. The colors are yellow and blue based on the sun and moon symbols. The seams are the bulgy lead seams typical of stained glass. We will create an illumination map, which is simply a grayscale image based on the complete texture to be used in a shader.

Figure 7-46
UV Map template for the window.

1. Open the 512x512 image **fantasy_window_UV.psd** on the DVD. See Figure 7-46.
2. This image is a UV template like the chest, only not nearly as complex. This image is rather simple to create and really simple to map onto a piece of geometry. You will notice some space to the right of the window shape and that is semi-wasted space. In a real-world scenario we could use this for the candle flames, or find another use for this space. Here the focus is creating the art itself and not laying out UV coordinates as efficiently as possible. I wanted you to be aware of this fact so in real practice you could address this issue.
3. Use the Magic Wand to select the shape.
4. Create a new layer and name it **lead**.
5. Look at Figure 7-47. You can see the pattern of the lead seams very clearly. Correcting for the angle of the drawing and given the fact that we are working from a template, we should be able to recreate this fairly easily. Also, there is no reason for this unique, one-of-a-kind texture to be tileable, on the grid, or exact in any way. That makes recreating it a lot easier.
6. The easiest thing to create first is the frame that surrounds the glass. If your selection is not still active, use the Magic Wand again to select the shape and activate the newly created **lead** layer.
7. Stroke the inside of the selection with a 5-pixel black line.
8. Snap a guideline to the vertical center of the window frame and one to the horizontal center. Look at the concept art. The next easiest thing to do would be to draw the line that runs up the center of the window. Refer to Figure 7-48 for a progression of the lead seams as they are drawn.
9. Select a hard, 5-pixel brush and draw the line up the center and go a little beyond where the guidelines meet.

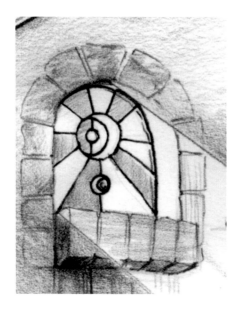
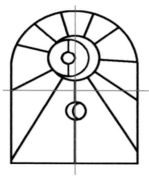

Figure 7-47
The stained-glass windows from the concept sketch, and the finished frame we created in Photoshop.

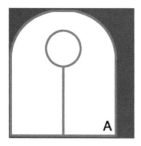
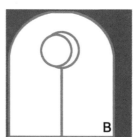
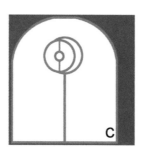
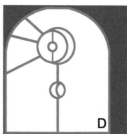

10. Use the Circular Marquee and hold down the Alt and Shift Keys to make the marquee symmetrical and to make the start point the center of the selection. Make the circular selection about 160 pixels and vertically centered on top of the straight line we just drew, like a lollipop (Figure 7-48-A).
11. Make another circular selection as we just did, only make it about 130 pixels and move it to the left and press delete before stroking it 5 pixels (Figure 7-48-B).
12. Select a 5-pixel hard brush and draw the line dividing this new circle in half.
13. Make a new circular selection about 43 pixels in the center of this line, press Delete, and stroke it 5 pixels (Figure 7-48-C).
14. There is a cool moon/crescent moon below the large moon we made first. Make a circular selection that is 70 pixels, centered on the vertical line, and just a tad under the horizontal line (Figure 7-48-D).
15. Press Delete to remove the line, stroke this 5 pixels/inside, and then move the selection over to the right until the left edge snaps to the center guideline.
16. Stroke the 5 pixels on the **outside** of the selection.
17. Deselect and use a hard eraser and erase the unwanted outer ring of the moon. Be careful erasing where the two rings overlap.

Figure 7-48
A progression of the lead seams being drawn for the stained-glass window (A-D).

18. All that's left to do is create those raylike lines coming from the main moon/sun. Choose a hard, 5-pixel brush and click a dot where you want the line to start, hold Shift, and click where you want it to end and you will have a straight line between the two points.

We will apply the layer effects to the lead seams after the glass panes are in place. Logically, we need to see what's below the lead seams before we are able to tweak and adjust their layer effects.

1. The glass is easy to make now that the frame is made. Activate the **lead** layer and use the Magic Wand to select the areas in the frame where the darker, blue glass will be. Look at the concept art for this.
2. Create a new layer and name it **panes**. Fill the selection with blue RGB:74,90,171.
3. Go to the **lead** layer and select the remaining areas inside the frame except for the small moon inside the larger moon at the top of the window and the large crescent to the right. Activate the **panes** layer and fill these spaces with yellow RGB:175,172,89.
4. Go back to the **lead** layer and select the small moon inside the larger moon and the large crescent. Activate the **panes** layer and fill these two spaces with white (Figure 7-49).
5. Deselect the selection.
6. Reset your colors to black and white (D key) and switch them (X key) so black is your background color.
7. Filter > Noise > Add Noise—10%.
8. Filter > Distort > Glass—Distortion 8, Smoothness 4, Texture Frosted, Scaling 100.
9. Fade Filter 50%.

Figure 7-49
The window glass, colored.

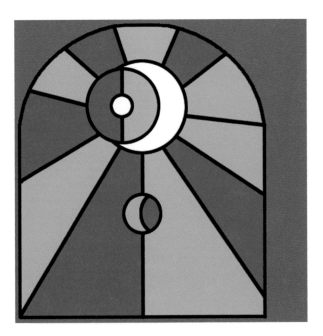

10. Filter > Artistic > Sponge—Brush Size 2, Definition 2, Smoothness 1.
11. Filter > Distort > Glass—Distortion 2, Smoothness 7.
12. Filter > Artistic > Plastic Wrap—Highlight Strength 13, Detail 5, Smoothness 2.
13. Fade Filter 50%, Blending Mode Vivid Light.
14. Filter > Blur > Gaussian Blur—1.5 pixels.
15. Filter > Distort > Glass—Distortion 3, Smoothness 3, scale 58%.
16. Add the following layer effects and change these settings:
    Inner Shadow
    Distance—6 px
    Size—10 px
    Inner Glow
    Blending Mode—Multiply
    Opacity—59%
    Noise—5%
    Color—Black
    Size—24 px
    Gradient Overlay
    Blend Mode—Vivid Light
    Opacity—29%

At this point I was happy with the blue and yellow glass, but the parts we left white still looked too plain to me so I selected their spaces on the **lead** layer and ran the Ink Outlines filter on the **panes** layer—Stroke Length 12, Dark Intensity 6, Light Intensity 9.

Meanwhile back at the lead seams . . .

1. Turn on the **lead** layer and apply the following layer effects.
   Drop Shadow
   Default settings
   Outer Glow
   Blending Mode—Multiply
   Opacity—47%
   Noise—2%
   Color—Black
   Size—32 px
   Bevel and Emboss
   Technique—Smooth
   Depth—111%
   Size—1 px
   Contour
   Cone—Inverted
   Texture
   Scale—127%
   Depth—371%
   Gradient Overlay
   Blend Mode—Normal
   Opacity—50%
   Style—Radial
   Scale—65%
   See Figure 7-50 for the final window texture.

Figure 7-50
The final window texture.

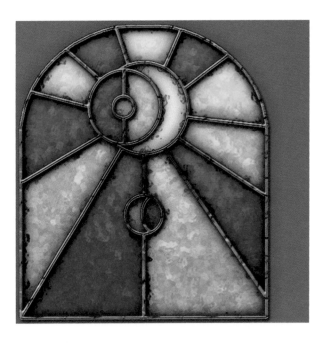

Figure 7-51
The illumination map for the window and the texture in a dark room with and without the illumination map.

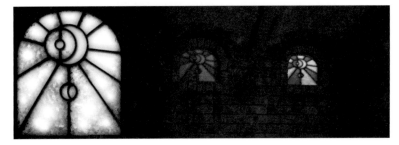

The illumination map is nothing more than a grayscale image. Black is dark and white is fully illuminated.

1. Duplicate the window image and name it **fantasy_window_illumination**.
2. On the **lead** layer turn off the Bevel and Emboss layer effects and apply a solid black Color Overlay Layer Effect.
3. Go to the **panes** layer and desaturate it (Ctrl + Shift + U).
4. Image > Adjustments > Brightness/Contrast—+ 22 brightness, + 48 contrast.
5. You will still need to use a large, soft brush of various sizes to airbrush the centers of the panes white and leave only a small amount of darkness at the edges. Figure 7-51 shows the illumination map with the texture in a dark room with and without the illumination map.

Banner

The banner is cloth and the colors are the same as the window, but these colors will be more desaturated based on the material, the

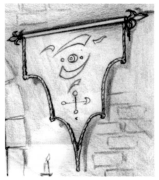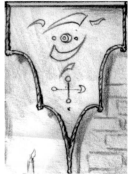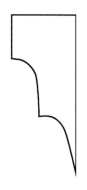

location of the banner, and its assumed adventuring history. In this exercise we will use the shapes we created for the spell book cover like we did on the map. We will also create new paths to define the outline of the banner. Finally, we will create the alpha channel for this banner and put a faked shadow in it. The great thing is that if you don't want the shadow, you can turn it off.

1. Open a new 1024x1024 image and name it **fantasy_banner**.
2. Create a new layer and name it **banner outline**.
3. Look at the shape of the banner in the concept sketch. We will create half of the banner using paths and then flip it. See Figure 7-52 for the shape breakdown of the banner.
4. Drag a vertical guide out to the 400-pixel mark on the canvas. Hold down Shift and the guide will snap every 10 pixels. We don't want to build the shape in the exact center because we want to leave some space for the alpha channeled objects.
5. Select the Path Tool and drag out the shape of the banner. I detailed the creation of a shape using the Path Tool a few times previously in this chapter. If you don't know how to use the Path Tool, go back to those sections and practice on those shapes. See Figure 7-53 for the banner path drag and click points.
6. Once you have half the banner outlined, you can save the path if you wish, make sure you are on the **banner outline** layer, and still have the Direct Select Tool selected and right mouse click to fill the banner with blue RGB: 62,98,163.
7. Turn off the path. Duplicate this layer and flip it horizontally.
8. Line up the two halves, link them, and merge them. Make sure the resulting shape is solid and that there is no seam between the two pieces. Also make sure there is enough space at the bottom between the end of the banner and the edge of the banner if you plan to put a drop shadow in.
9. Filter > Noise > Add Noise—5%.
10. Filter > Brush Strokes > Crosshatch—Stroke Length 31, Sharpness 10, Strength 1.
11. Filter > Artistic > Poster Edges—Edge Thickness 1, Edge Intensity 1, Posterization 3.
12. Filter > Blur > Gaussian Blur—1.5 pixels.
13. Filter > Artistic > Paint Daubs—Brush Size 6, Sharpness 0, Brush Type Dark Rough.

Figure 7-52
The breakdown of the banner shape. From **left** to **right**; the banner cropped from the concept sketch, the straightened version, the half-banner path line, and the final shape.

Figure 7-53
The click and drag points of
the banner path.

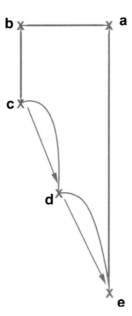

Figure 7-54
The progression from basic
shapes to the final banner
decoration. Using shapes
previously created saved us a
lot of time presently.

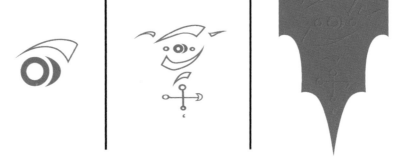

14. Open the spell book file and find the **symbols** layer that has the original, large version of the shapes you created for the cover of the spell book. Copy this layer into the banner image. If you didn't copy the entire layer set, create a new layer set so all the shapes and symbols are easily collapsed and organized later.

15. Refer to the concept art and start the process of laying the banner shapes out with the symbol shapes you already have. I was able to create all the shapes by copying the original shapes and using Free Transform. The only shape I needed to create by hand were the cross bars in the lower symbol. I took some time and filled in the circles and erased them, making them look a little more organic or handmade. See Figure 7-54 for the progression from basic shapes to the final banner decoration.

16. Collapse all the symbols onto one layer and apply layer effects with the following settings.
    Fill—0%
    Outer Glow
    Blending Mode—Multiply

Opacity—71%
Color—Black
Noise—8%
Spread—5%
Size—29 px
Bevel and Emboss
Style—Inner Bevel
Technique—Chisel Hard
Depth—81%
Size—5 px
Contour—default
Texture—default
Color Overlay
Color—Yellowish RGB: 178,166,38

17. The next thing we need to make is the fringe that borders the banner. Create a new layer and name it **fringe**.
18. Go to the **banner outline** layer and use the Magic Wand to select the area outside the banner and invert the selection.
19. Go back to the **fringe** layer and stroke the selection: Inner Stroke and 16 pixels.
20. Remove the very top line of the stroked outline using a hard eraser or the Selection Tool (pressing the Delete key).
21. Copy the layer effects from the **symbols** layer and paste them into the layer.
22. Duplicate the **fringe** layer. Now we can erase the gaps in the top layer to make the border fringe look wound. You can eyeball this with a small, hard eraser or use the grid with a selection, moving the selection and pressing Delete, if you want the gaps perfectly spaced.
23. Duplicate one of the **fringe** layers, make sure it is on the top of the other two, and clear the contents from this layer (Ctrl + A and Ctrl + X). Change the following settings in the layer style of this layer.
    Bevel and Emboss
    Technique—Smooth
    Size—21 px
24. Use a 40-pixel hard brush and put the balls on the ends of the banner points. Your image should look like Figure 7-55.
25. Link all the layers except for the background and **Create Layer Set From Linked**.
26. Duplicate this layer set and name it **banner flat** and flatten it. Hide the original un-flattened layer set.
27. Filter > Noise > Add Noise—5%. I also took the saturation and contrast down just a little on the banner.
28. Filter > Artistic > Dry Brush—Brush Size 3, Brush Detail 5, Texture 1.
29. Filter > Brush Strokes > Accented Edges—Edge Width 4, Edge Brightness 26, Smoothness 2.
30. To create the alpha channel, and to make the drop shadow part of the texture, you need to go to the original un-flattened **banner** layer set and duplicate it. Name it **alpha**.
31. Turn off all the outer glow layer effects in the layer set, but leave the rest of the layer effects on. Flatten the **alpha** layer set.

Figure 7-55
The banner with fringe on it.

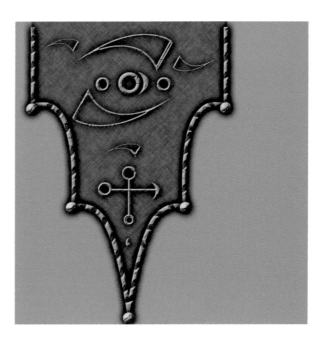

32. Select > Load Selection > say OK and go back to the banner layer. Invert the selection and press Delete. The outer glow should disappear—make sure this is the only active layer if you don't see this happen.
33. We also need to create the end cap. Create a new layer and name it **end cap**.
34. Use the Shape Tool with the Fill Pixel option chosen and set your foreground color to a medium gray.
35. Choose the Fleur-De-Lis shape and drag out a shape that fills in part of the empty space. This doesn't have to be too big and doesn't need to be constrained using the Shift key. I made mine a little longer than wide.
36. Erase the bottom three smaller tips of the shape and apply the following layer style and settings:
    Bevel and Emboss
    Style—Inner Bevel
    Technique—Chisel Soft
    Depth—111%
    Size—27 px
    Soften—3 px
       Contour—default
       Texture—Pattern: Satin, Scale—341%, Depth + 34
    Color Overlay
    Color—Yellowish RGB: 178,166,38
37. Duplicate the **end cap** layer and link it to the **alpha** layer and merge them.
38. Put a solid black Color Overlay on the alpha layer and a Drop Shadow to your liking. I only changed the distance (17 px) and the Size (21 px). If your background layer is black, you won't see any of this so make it a light gray.

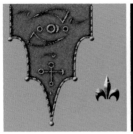

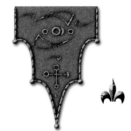

Figure 7-56
Left to right; the banner, the alpha channel and the banner with the alpha enacted showing the faked drop shadow.

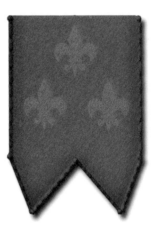
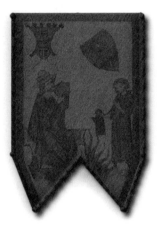

Figure 7-57
A couple of variations on the banner using the same technique (I used an overlay of an image for the one on the right).

39. Create a new layer and link it to the alpha layer and merge them so the effects are baked in and become pixels rather than an effect.
40. Select > Load Selection > OK.
41. Go to the Channels tab and create a new alpha channel and fill the selection with white. You should only have to right mouse click in order to do this here.
42. Now the alpha channel contains the fake drop shadow. Figure 7-56 shows the banner, the alpha channel, and the banner with the alpha enacted with the faked drop shadow. And Figure 7-57 shows a couple of variations on the banner using the same technique (I used an overlay of an image for the one on the right).

Magic Door

The door is metal and intricately carved with symbols and writing. The symbols and writing have a magical glow. The door was easier to do than I originally anticipated. By the time you get to this point in the fantasy setting you have all the shapes, symbols, and magical writing you need for the door. Plus the curves you see in the door are not made by you with paths; they are part of the model and, hence, part of the UV map.

1. Open the image from the DVD named **fantasy_door_UV_Map.psd**. See Figure 7-58.

Figure 7-58
UV Map template for the magic door.

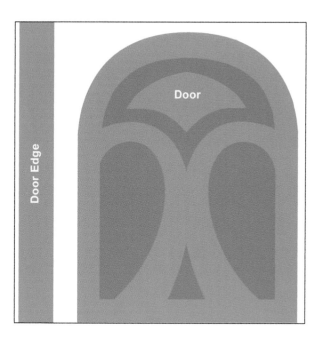

2. You see the familiar setup, the UV map, and the labels for the parts.
3. Paste the base metal in you made for the fantasy setting on the top of the stack of layers and name it **metal**.
4. Duplicate the **metal** layer and name it **door frame**.
5. Turn both layers off and go to the UV map and select the frame, select similar, and invert the selection.
6. Select the **door frame** layer to turn it on and press Delete.
7. Apply layer styles with the following settings changed:
   Drop Shadow
   Blend Mode—Multiply
   Opacity—53%
   Distance—6 px
   Size—18 px
   Outer Glow
   Blend Mode—Linear Burn
   Opacity—19%
   Noise—17%
   Color—Black
   Size—65 px
   Bevel and Emboss
   Technique—Smooth
   Depth—151%
   Size—9 px
   Highlight Mode Opacity—57%
   Shadow Mode Opacity—57%
   Texture—Pattern = Molecular, Scale = 537%, Depth = +95
8. Now we will create the magical writing all over the door. Create a new layer set and name it **writing**.
9. Select the Text Tool and the Tengwar-Gandalf font. Make it 35 pt.

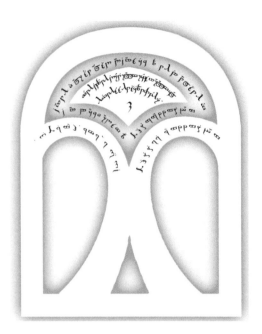

Figure 7-59
Placing the text on the door
is a trial and error process,
but well worth the effort.

10. Type whatever you want and then use the Warp Text Tool to fit
the text into the spaces in the door. This is a trial and error
process. You have to experiment with more or fewer letters and
different warp settings. I also used the Character Palette and
adjusted the tracking (horizontal spaces between letters) and
moved the letters closer to each other. See Figure 7-59 for the
layout of the text on the door.

11. When you have placed all the text, pick one layer and apply
layer styles with the following settings changed:
Outer Glow
Blend Mode—Color Burn
Opacity—24%
Color—Black
Technique—Precise
Size—9 px
Bevel and Emboss
Style—Outer Bevel
Technique—Chisel Soft
Depth—127%
Direction—Down
Size—2 px
Highlight Mode Opacity—69%
Shadow Mode Opacity—74%
Color Overlay
Blend Mode—Normal
Color—RGB: 167,255,239

12. Link all the text layers, copy the layer style from the initial text
layer, and **Paste Layer Style to Linked.**

13. The shapes on the door are the last thing to do. You can open
the shapes you saved elsewhere and paste them into a layer set
named **shapes** and manipulate them with the Free Transform

Figure 7-60
The layout of the shapes on the door.

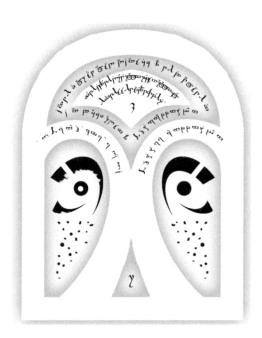

Tool and Liquefy, or you can easily create these shapes using paths, or even the circular selection tool. For the little shapes toward the bottom, I used a few brushes so there would be variety and interest there. See Figure 7-60 for the layout of the door shapes.

14. Once one side of the door is complete, you can duplicate the layer, flip it horizontally, position it, and alter it a little so it looks more interesting and not like a perfect mirror of the other side.

15. Copy the layer style from the text layers, paste it onto this layer, and change the following settings:
    Color Overlay
    Blend Mode—Vivid Light
    Opacity—47%

16. See Figure 7-61 for the final door. You may notice that there is the door edge to the left; that is a simple layer shape based on the UV map with the layer Fill set to 0 and a Bevel and Emboss applied.

Pitcher and Goblet Set

The pitcher and goblet are of fine metal with inset gems. Although highly polished, these vessels have seen their share of use and bear many dents and scratches.

In order to get a reflective gold metal that has bumps and scratches in the surface—that look real—we need to use a shader. Shaders are becoming very common—very prevalent at this point. In fact, as I am finishing this book I have started a job using a commercial game engine creating a next-generation game and virtually every

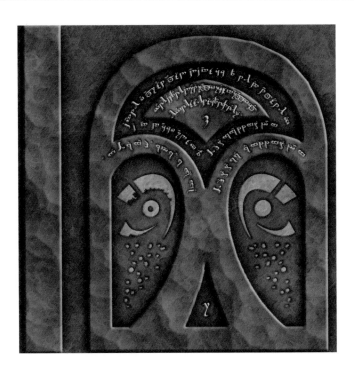

Figure 7-61
The final magical door texture.

surface has a shader of some sort on it. We discussed shaders way back in the beginning of the book, defining what they are and looking at some visual examples of them. I noted that as artists we are most often concerned with the input and the output of the shader and not the code itself. One of the primary tasks you will perform as an artist will be to create several images that the shader will use to process various real-time effects. You will often redo these images and adjust them until you get the visual results you want. We will use this part of the fantasy scene to take the creation of a basic shader step by step. If you are not familiar with shaders you may be surprised how simple some of them can be. Not to oversimplify a potentially very complex topic, but most of the common shaders are fairly easy to work with. In this case we will be using a common shader that uses the following map types.

- Diffuse (or color) map—Contains almost exclusively color information
- Bump Mapping—Grayscale image that simulates bumps and scratches
- Environment (or Cube) Map—A series of images used to fake a reflection
- Environment Mask—Grayscale image that alters the reflective value of the Cube Map

I will not step you through the creation of these maps. Based on their simplicity and what you have already learned in this book, making them should be easy for you. Let's look at the pitcher before any visual information is applied. In Figure 7-62 you can see that this is relatively a simple mesh.

Figure 7-62
The pitcher mesh before we apply any visual information.

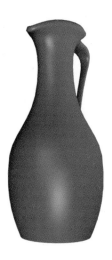

Figure 7-63
The diffuse map and the diffuse map applied to the pitcher. Notice how plain it is. Now that shaders process many visual details in real time; we don't need to add this detail to the texture.

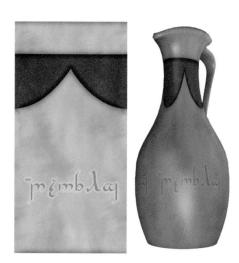

Diffuse Map

The diffuse map is what most people are talking about when they use the word "texture." Previously, the diffuse map contained virtually all the visual information that would be applied to the 3D geometry of a game. The diffuse map is still referred to as a texture, but more commonly it is again being referred to as the diffuse map, or color map, since it now contains virtually nothing but color information. See Figure 7-63 for the diffuse map and the map applied to the pitcher. Notice how plain it is.

In this book we created textures that contained all of the visual information pertaining to an object or surface: color, highlight, shadow. Having all this visual information painted into the image, and therefore static or nonreactive to the environment, is often referred to as "baking," as in, "The shadows are baked into this texture." The techniques in this book don't bake the visual information into the source image; therefore, you can easily go back and split the visual information out before flattening the PSD file to make maps for a shader. Learning to paint a texture is the best way to get the strong basis you will need to create effective shaders. You can't rely on technology; shaders are a tool and not a replacement for artists.

Bump Map

Bump mapping makes the surface of the texture appear to be — bumpy. White on the bump map represents the highest parts of the surface and black the lowest. You can use bump maps to simulate etched letters with solid black and hard edges, or dents with lighter gray and soft edges. The bump map adds detail that makes the geometry look far more detailed than it really is. See Figure 7-64 for the bump map of the pitcher and the pitcher with the bump map applied. Notice the letters are solid black with hard edges and the dents are softer and lighter in color so they are not so harsh and deep as the letters. You can also see in Figure 7-65 the effect of using a high- and low-resolution image for the bump map.

Environment or Reflection Map (Cube Mapping)

We will create a reflective surface on our pitcher using an environment or reflection map. The environment map uses a series of images called a cube map to fake the reflection on the surface of an object. Cube maps are so named due to the fact that the reflections you see are actually six images arranged in a cube. These images are rendered from the spot the reflective object is located, so the cube map reflects the object's surroundings accurately. These six images cover all directions: up, down, front, back, left, and right. Ideally they all line up, meaning the images meet at the edges so

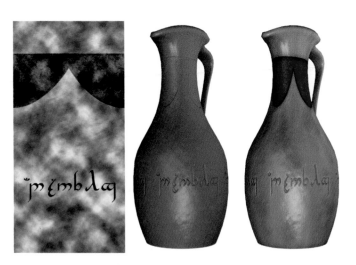

Figure 7-64
The bump map for the pitcher and the pitcher with the bump map applied. White represents the highest parts of the surface and black the lowest. To the far right is the pitcher with the diffuse and bump map applied.

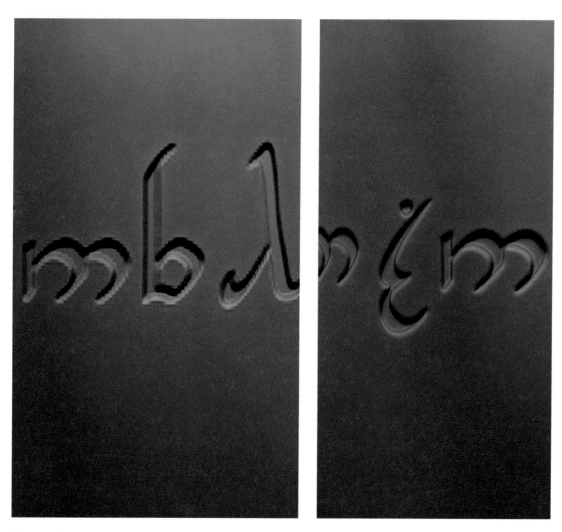

Figure 7-65
The resolution of the bump map image affects the outcome. A low-resolution image was used for the bump map on the **left** and a high-resolution image for the one on the **right**.

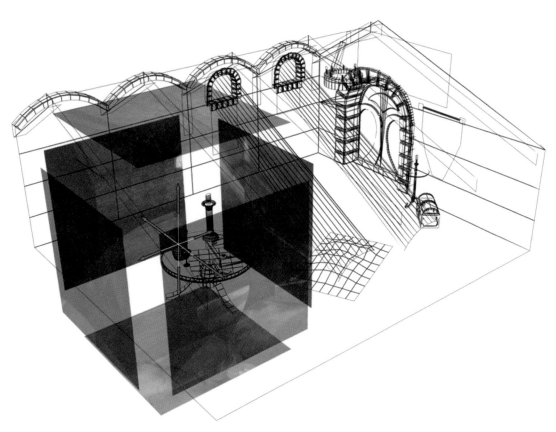

Figure 7-66
The six images that form the cube map were rendered from the location of the pitcher so the metal looks as if it is reflecting its surroundings.

the reflection is seamless. The images of the cube map are most commonly static, meaning they are always the same. If you are looking into a reflection created by a static cube map, you won't see yourself (or in-game character). This is the most efficient way to handle cube mapping, but there are also other techniques for generating real-time reflections. One of those techniques is called Dynamic Cube Mapping. This method redraws the six images in the cube map every frame. If the object mapped with the environment map moves, or something in the environment around it moves, the cube maps are updated to render an accurate reflection in real time. See Figure 7-66 for an illustration of the (static) cube map as it was created for this scene and Figure 7-67 for the cube maps arranged as if the cube were folded open like a box. If you don't have access to a 3D package, you can also use an image of clouds, or a blurry nondescript image, for a cube map. Figure 7-68 shows the pitcher with only the cube map applied in its initial state. The cube map is clear and reflecting at 100%.

Figure 7-67
The six images that form the cube map arranged as if the cube were folded open like a box.

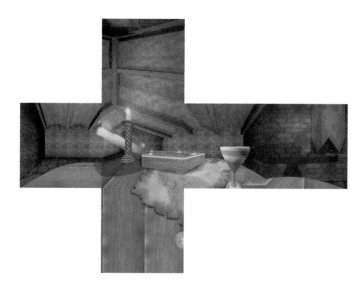

Figure 7-68
The pitcher with only the cube map applied in its initial state. The cube map is clear and reflecting at 100%.

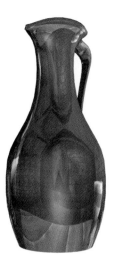

Since this metal pitcher has seen a good deal of use, the metal shouldn't reflect like a mirror so there are several things we can do to make this reflection look much more realistic. First I blurred the cube maps so the reflection appears not so crisp and mirror-like. I also desaturated the images a little. Figure 7-69 shows the pitcher with a blurred and desaturated cube map.

At this point if you turn on your color and bump map, you will see the pitcher taking shape.

The last step adds a final level of realism that finishes this surface off nicely is a mask for the reflection. This mask determines how strong various parts of the reflection are based on grayscale values.

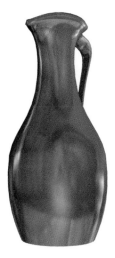

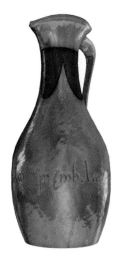

Figure 7-69
The pitcher with the blurred and desaturated cube map.

Figure 7-70
The pitcher with the color map, bump map, and reflection active.

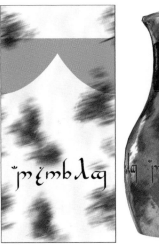

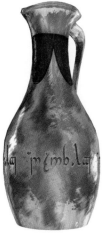

Figure 7-71
The pitcher with the final detail, masking the reflection.

White is fully reflective and black is matte, or nonreflective. I used some light gray areas so the pitcher looks well worn. Figure 7-71 shows the progression of the pitcher from simple mesh to finished product. You will notice the gems in the concept art and the final scene. These were smaller, red diffuse maps, but used the same environment map as the pitcher.

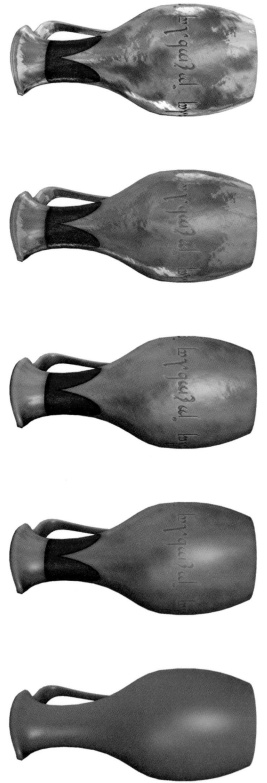

Figure 7-72
The progression of the pitcher shader.

The Complete Scene/Variation

That's the end of the fantasy setting. Here is the complete scene using all the textures you created (Figure 7-73). And as I mentioned in the beginning of the chapter, the medieval setting is simply the fantasy setting stripped down (Figure 7-74).

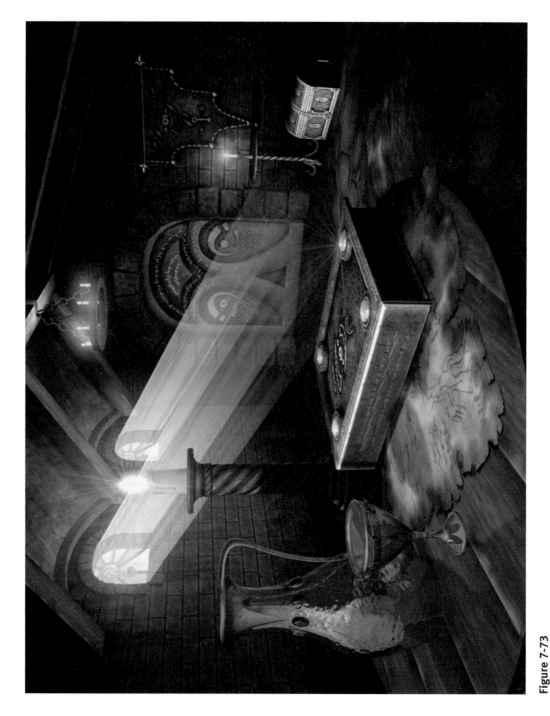

Figure 7-73
The final scene using all the textures created in this chapter.

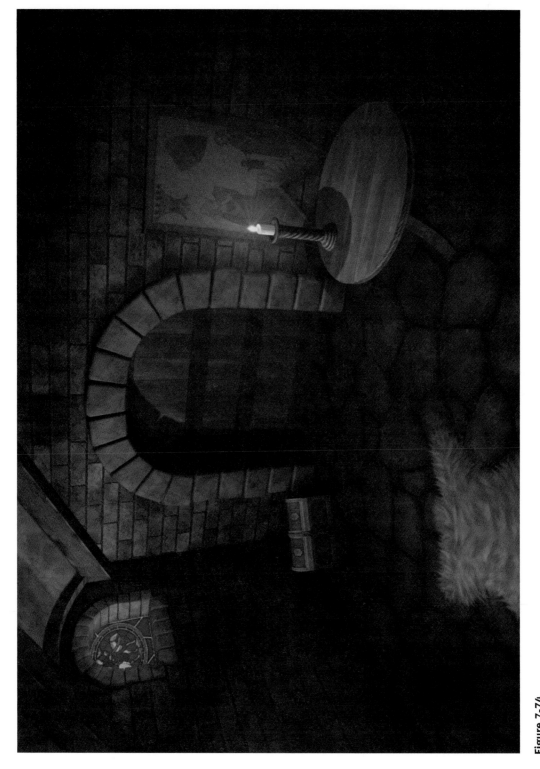

Figure 7-74
A scene variation of the fantasy setting, the medieval setting.

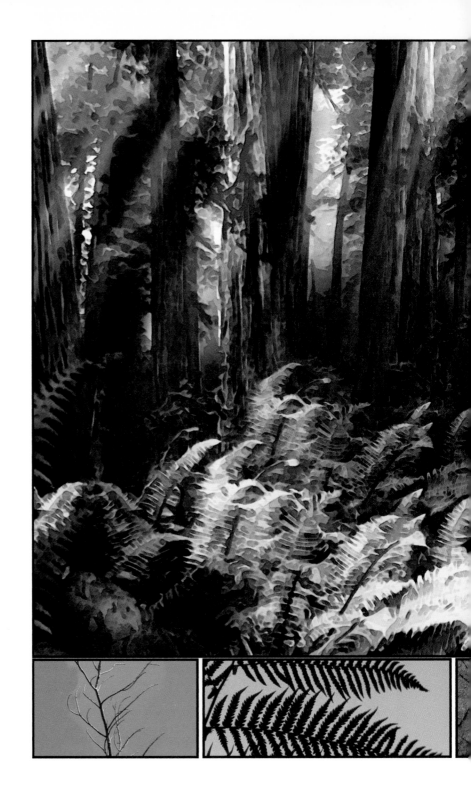

Chapter 8

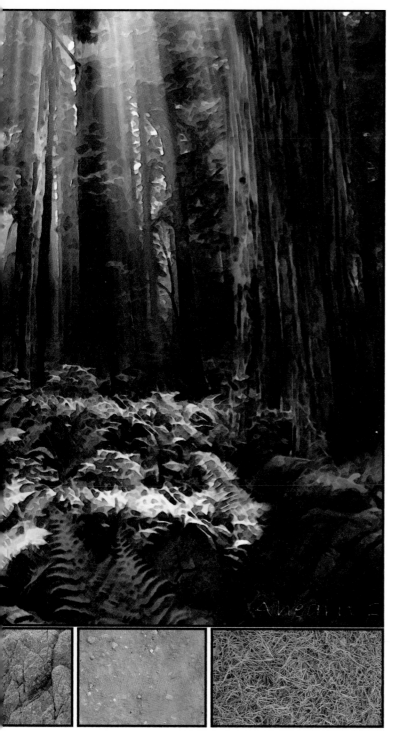

Introduction

In this chapter we will create a set of textures for a forest that can be altered to look spooky, friendly, or fanciful. Using the basic approach presented here, you can also create a similar simple set of textures for any outdoor environment: jungle, desert, etc. I will also introduce the use of photo source in texture creation. I mentioned in the very beginning of the book that the use of photo source to create textures is not only common but preferred. It makes your job faster and easier and gives your textures an extra layer of richness that can take a lot of time to achieve otherwise. I find that using overlays when creating assets for the outdoor environment is particularly useful. The surface of a rock, the bark on a tree, the veins in a leaf are all challenging to create for most, whether by hand or in Photoshop, or time-consuming at the very least. Using an overlay of a real leaf over a solid leaf shape will create a better texture quicker than either hand-creating the leaf or trying to manipulate a digital image into a workable asset.

Forest Concept 2005 by Luke Ahearn

The Outdoor Setting

With overlays you still use the same work flow as in all of the previous chapters. While working with overlays may take the most time and tweaking, they are generally added later in the creation process, after a good foundation is laid. Using digital imagery will greatly enhance and speed up your work, but you don't want it to be a crutch that you will always lean on. Using photo source should primarily be looked upon as the icing on the cake, not the whole meal. After you finish this chapter, a good exercise would be to go back and open the textures you created for any one of the previous settings and experiment with overlays. You can start with the resource images on the DVD of this book or go on Google and find an almost unlimited supply of them. Remember, a good piece of photo source can make a mediocre texture a great one or a good texture a bad one if used incorrectly. To avoid some of the most common mistakes when overlaying images, keep these points in mind.

You Are Creating One Material

Two base materials usually don't layer on top of each other well. Bricks made have a top layer of cement or plaster falling off of them, but laying stone on top of brick will look horrible. Usually, you will have your (tiling) base material as the bottom layer in your Photoshop file and your overlays dirt, cracks, stains, etc. stacked on top of it.

The Overlay Should Be Logical

What type of surface is this? Stucco and concrete walls can have long wandering cracks in them, but brick walls tend to have cracks that follow the mortar lines. Glass shatters, dirt craters, wood chips, and metal dents. How would the material you are creating respond to the conditions of the world it is to be placed in? Materials darken when they are wet and often glisten. A very dry climate might have desaturated colors, even a hint of dust, on the material surface.

How will the material be used, or applied to the surface? If you are creating a wall texture, don't use an overlay from a surface that has a different orientation unless you correct for it. If an image of the ground has leaves and loose material in it and you don't correct this, it will look as if this stuff is glued to the wall. One trick I use to fix the problem of incompatible overlays, especially when overlaying on bricks, is to use the method from the fantasy chapter. Basically, if you have a pattern you want to use as an overlay on a brick wall, but the pattern has elongated aspects to it that would cross over individual bricks, you can select alternating bricks in the pattern and use the Free Transform Tool to simply flip and rotate them. This way the material is still completely compatible, but looks good as it is unique to each brick. This is easy to do if you have built your texture from a clean pattern, but even if you are working over a flattened image, you can still use the Marquee Selection Tool instead of the Magic Wand (with a slightly feathered edge) to make the selections. The exceptions to this are drips and stains that would logically cross over brick boundaries.

Color Trouble?

I often Desaturate my overlays or take the saturation down. This way I am not fighting with conflicting colors and can focus on the color of the base material on its own layer and use the overlays for their intended purpose—to add detail; cracks and drips can usually be desaturated and often work better that way. You can also desaturate the base material and use an overlay to add color. This might be a good option if you are trying to color match a large number of textures in a set.

Be Subtle

Too many overlays tend to muddy an image. Overlays that are too prominent or strong tend to tile. The best overlays are subtle. From far away subtlety blends in and the texture appears to be mostly one color, which helps reduce tiling. When the player gets close to the surface, the subtle details like cracks and stains come into view. On the note of subtlety, there is no rule that says you have to use the entire layer as an overlay. If there is a specific drip or crack you like, it blends well, but the rest of the overlay is messing up the image, go in and erase the rest of the image except for the crack.

Do You Need to Create an Overlay?

Are you trying to overlay patterns, cracks, highlights, or other surface properties best created with a shader or another technique?

You Can Work Out of Context

You don't want stone on top of brick to clash and you don't want a wooden castle door to look like a digital photo of your veneer computer desk from Costco (complete with flash burn), but you can use an overlay of stone with brick if the primary material is supported as previously discussed. The veneer office desk may have a great wood grain pattern you can subtly lay over the base wood you are using, but probably can't be used as the base material itself (and if you have a flash burn on an image you took, then go back and read the beginning of the book you skimmed through ;)).

Experiment

Try all the blending modes, opacity settings, and other tools in Photoshop you can until you get the result you are looking for.

The Concept Sketch

Creating assets for the outdoor setting can be fun because it can actually be simpler in some ways and net more impressive results. We are just now beginning to experience truly impressive outdoor environments in games due to technological advancement. Remember when 3D games were set in confined spaces such as hallways? As computers become more powerful, things will keep opening up and we will continue to see more of the outdoors. Already we are seeing impressive outdoor spaces being built for games, with expansive terrain and high poly-count models, and things are only getting better.

These large, impressive, and elaborate environments can be challenging to create in many ways, but they are also actually easier to create compared to just a few years ago. Partly this is due to the fact that most outdoor environments consist of similar elements (grass, dirt, leaves, bark, and stone), and a good set of assets can go a long way if they are used correctly with newer technology. A relatively small set of textures can be mapped to an equally small set of meshes and then the models placed, rotated, scaled, and arranged to produce an enormous amount of variety. This alone gives us the ability to create a more convincing forest or jungle. But the major reason that creating outdoor environments is now easier is that the tools are more powerful, more refined, and more user-friendly. As I mentioned in the chapter on prepping for texture creation, some game engines allow for the combining of multiple layers of textures on terrain in a manner similar to how Photoshop handles layers. This allows the terrain textures to be composed predominantly of one material, and therefore easier to tile. Add to this the fact that we are also able to use much larger textures and you can get some really great-looking outdoor environments.

It used to be that the terrain mesh was tiled with one (smaller) texture and if you wanted something like a road or dirt patch, you had to create various versions of that one texture to place on specific polygons on the terrain where you wanted the road to run or the dirt patch to appear. This was limiting to say the least; roads ran in straight lines and right angles and you had to create a separate texture for any unique terrain detail. Now we can create a few large textures of a specific terrain material (packed dirt, grassy dirt, dried dirt, grass, dead grass) and paint them onto the terrain. You can lay down a base layer of grass on your terrain and paint on darker grass patches, add an organic winding dirt road—you can create any type of terrain you can imagine. Painting and erasing layers on terrain are easy and the results superior than any previous technique.

The front plate shows a pretty typical forest with towering trees and ferns. In addition to the obvious tree bark and ferns, we also need to create assets for the rocks, branches, the ground, and the end of the log in the lower right-hand corner. You can even see the sky so we will need to create that, too, and that involves a bit more planning and a different technique than typical texture mapping.

I did a few quick color studies of this environment. The goal with the initial concept was to create a neutral location, just a plain forest. These variations are to explore the potential of the environment using various color schemes. I would use one of these color studies as a guide when texturing and lighting a scene to recreate the feel of the study. In addition to spooky/dark/desaturated and happy/bright/colorful, I created a bleak, dreary place that is more emotionally disturbing than scary. Altering the concept art was easier than altering all the textures and loading them into a game editor or 3D application to see the results, Figure 8-1.

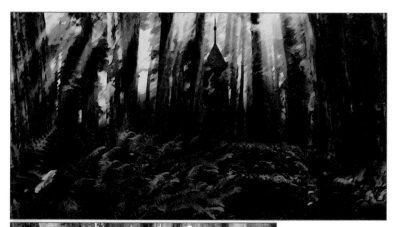

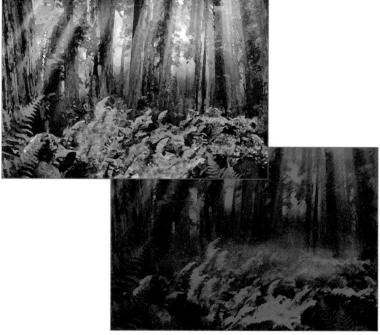

Figure 8-1
A few quick color studies. **Upper** image, a bleak dreary place that is more emotionally disturbing than scary. **Middle,** happy/bright/colorful and **bottom** spooky/dark/desaturated.

Breaking Out the Materials in the Scene

This set will contain

- Forest Floor
- Tree Bark
- Tree Branches
- End of Log
- Rock
- Ferns

Forest Floor

This concept art is a visual guide for the look and feel the environment should have, but it isn't a game-specific piece of art. Sometimes, as a specific location of a world is being designed, you will start creating assets for it and will only have information based on a piece of art that is a representation of the look and feel of the game. We need to anticipate and create the assets most likely needed for a game world based on a look and feel piece. So, although you can't see it, the ground needs to be created because it is pretty likely that in a game the player will see the ground.

In a dense forest like this, the ground tends to be covered with a dark, moist, matted blanket of rotting vegetation. For this texture I started with an image of the ground after rain. I added an image of some dead grass on top of this. Even though the grass looks dead and dry in the original image, it worked great because of the contrast. When overlaid, it looks as if the grass occasionally grew, but died and matted down with the rest of the forest floor. In addition, I created a texture I could use as a path through the trees. A path will be worn, with packed dirt, but it also needs to blend into the scene in terms of color, contrast, etc. I created a new image and used a third image of some packed dirt with small rocks in it on top of a copy of the forest floor texture. I blurred the forest floor to get the overall color and general feel of the ground (the subtle pattern of the forest floor remains). See Figure 8-2. I made this image a bit lighter because it is dirt in the open and would be drier. You also need a little contrast so the path stands out.

Tree Bark

Tree bark is actually a bit hard to digitally photograph. It is usually in less than ideal lighting conditions, and it is wrapped around a cylindrical shape. This means that even though you can see about half of the trunk facing you, only a small portion of the bark is actually positioned facing you straight on. I used the Fiber Filter, stretched the image vertically, used Liquefy to make some fine adjustments (like we did with the wood crate in the urban chapter), and colorized the image. See Figure 8-4 for the progression of the tree bark.

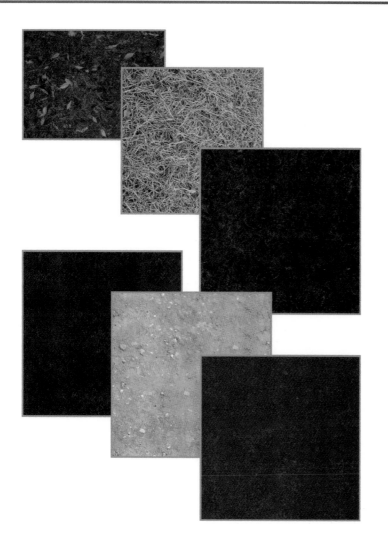

Figure 8-2
The progression of the forest floor and path texture.

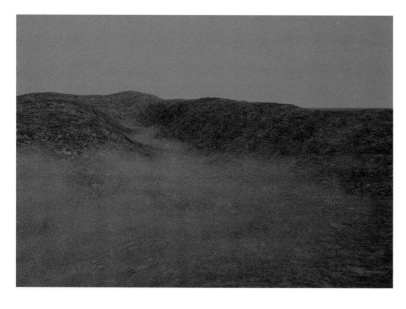

Figure 8-3
The beginning of the scene with only the terrain in place.

Figure 8-4
The progression of the tree bark.

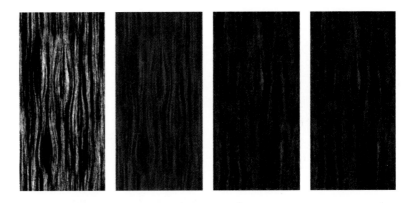

Figure 8-5
The next stage, trees. They are usually added after the branches are on them, but I wanted you to see the stages of the texturing.

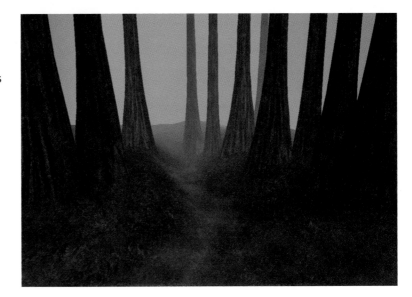

Tree Branches

For the tree branch I used a digital photo of a branch with no leaves on it that I was able to capture with only the contrasting blue sky behind it. I used the Extraction Tool (under the Filter menu) and took the background out. I did have to do a little clean up with the eraser, but not too much and I colorized the branch. I took another digital image of a close-up of the redwood needles and did the same. I copied and pasted this only a few times. I made an alpha channel by selecting the transparency of the merged branch elements the way we have done previously. See Figure 8-6 for the progression of the branch and the evolving scene.

At this point I started to adjust my color and lighting a bit to more closely match the concept art. I tend to work on the dark side. As you build textures you may find that you have certain pitfalls that you gravitate toward, so be sure to refer to the concept art often to make sure you are on track (Figure 8-8). I also added the tree line

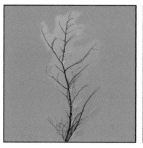
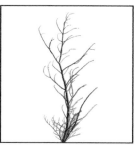
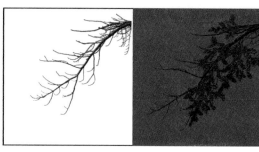

Figure 8-6
The progression of the tree branches. **Left:** the original image; **second:** the extracted branch; **third:** the cleaned-up and rotated branch; **far right:** the final branch texture.

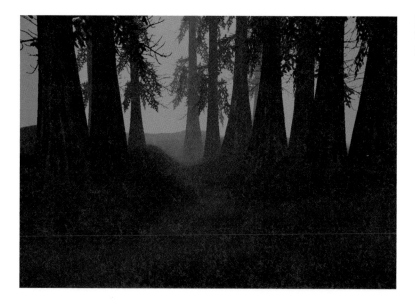

Figure 8-7
The evolving scene with the branches added to the trees.

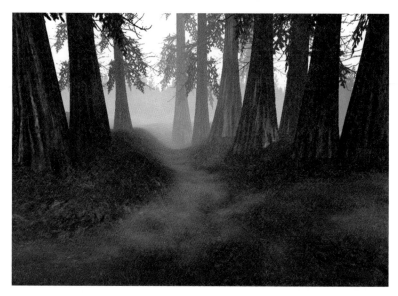

Figure 8-8
The scene with the tree line backdrop added and some color corrections to more closely match the concept art.

Figure 8-9
The tree line backdrop; a
photo, the Extract Tool, and
a little bit of work with the
eraser.

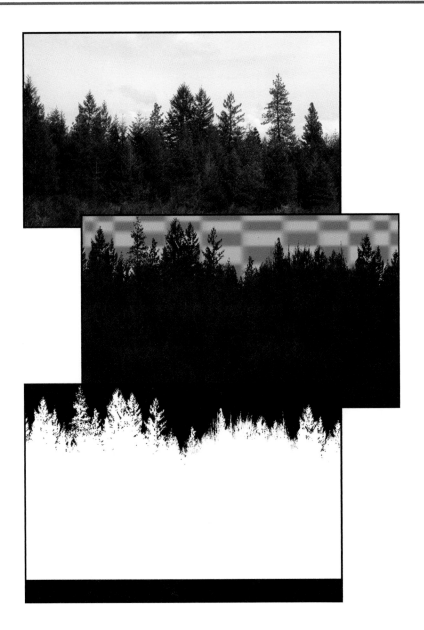

backdrop. I used a photo and the same steps as I used to create the
branch, Figure 8-9. In order to work, a tree line backdrop must be
where the player can never get to it and usually needs to be
desaturated and darkened to emulate the color and luminance we
lose with distance.

End of Log

To create the end of the log, I used a digital image of a—that's
right—the end of a log. I enhanced the image with the sketch filter
(circles); see Figure 8-10.

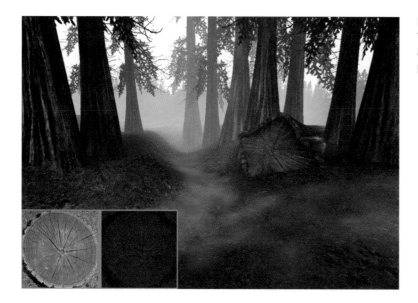

Figure 8-10
The scene with the fallen tree added and the end of log progression inset.

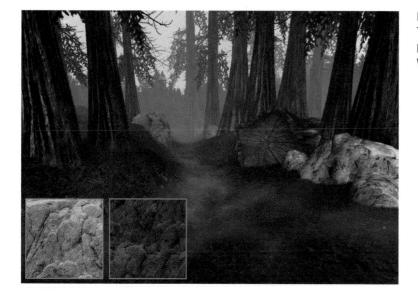

Figure 8-11
The stone texture progression and the scene with boulders in place.

Rock

The rock texture was simply a colorized image of some rock. I lowered the contrast and saturation, and I made it tile. Actually, I made it seamless. It technically doesn't tile because I left the bottom of the texture darker to simulate shadow and moisture, as if the boulders were sitting in the ground a long time. If this texture were tiled across a large surface, you would see the repeating pattern. This texture was made specifically to be wrapped around the boulders, Figure 8-11.

Ferns and the Complete Scene

The ferns were all made from one fern leaf just like the tree branch (Figure 8-12). I went outside, digitally photographed a fern leaf, extracted it in Photoshop, and created an alpha channel. Here is the final scene with the ferns in place, Figure 8-13.

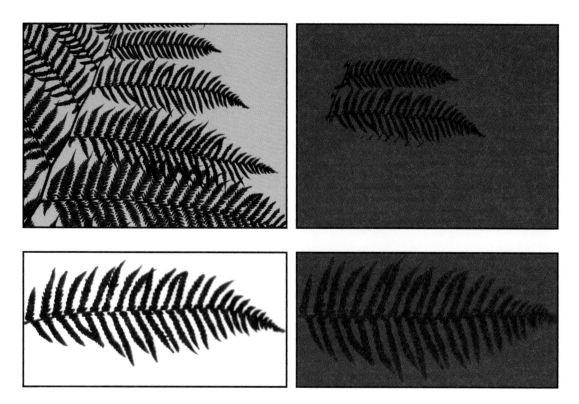

Figure 8-12
The fern texture progression. **Upper left:** the original image; **upper right:** the extracted fern; **lower left:** the cleaned-up fern frond; **lower right:** the final fern texture.

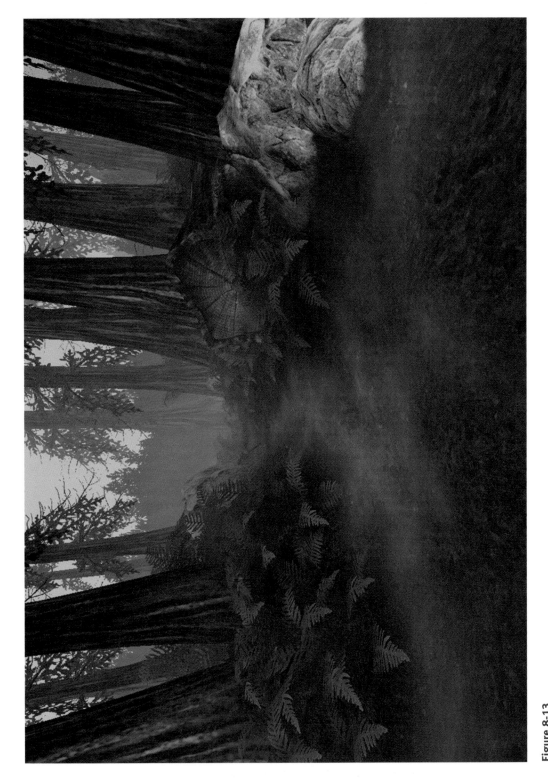

Figure 8-13
The final scene with the ferns in place.

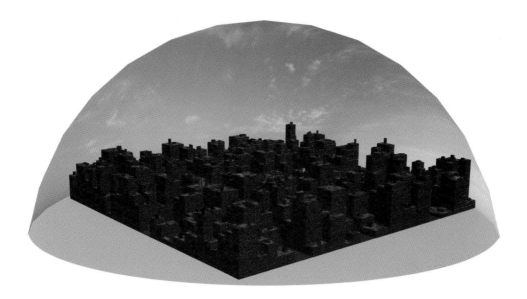

Additional Information: The Sky

A good sky adds a lot to the feeling of depth and atmosphere in a virtual world even if only glimpsed through trees in a scene like this one, but it's *almost* not worth having one at all if it is poorly implemented. If there are mistakes in the sky (the player can see seams, etc.), the illusion is shattered. Typically, in a game, the sky is handled a few ways:

- Single image
- Sky dome
- Skybox

The single image technique is used in only a few, generally older, games that have a limited view of the world. Most older 3D games and many driving games kept players on a certain path. You were in some form of a 3D world, but your view was restricted to a 2D plane, you could only look left and right but not up and down (you could often walk up and down stairs, just not tilt the camera to look up at the sky). These games used an equally limited technique for the sky, a single image only moved left to right and up and down as the player moved about the world. I won't step you through this technique simply because it is rarely used, if at all, in any quality game. With mobile gaming exploding it may well become prevalent again; nevertheless, if you can create one panel of a skybox, then you have the required asset for this technique.

The sky dome technique is simply a fixed model that is part of the game map and is large enough to encase the entire world. This approach is referred to as a sky dome because typically a dome shape looks best using this approach, but you can also use a simple cube (if it works) and save a lot of polygons. Mapping a texture to a

Figure 8-14
The sky dome is simply a fixed model that is part of the game map and is large enough to encase the entire world. This approach is called sky dome because typically a dome shape looks best with this approach, but you can also use a simple cube (if it works) and save a lot of polygons.

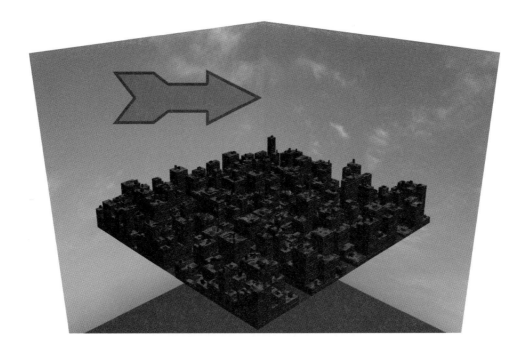

Figure 8-15
The sky dome using a cube.
The seam can often show.

dome is easier whereas a cube requires more tweaking to get things to look right. See Figure 8-14 for an illustration of the sky dome and Figure 8-15 for an example of a skybox with a seam showing. Personally, I don't like the sky dome method for several reasons; it's harder to work in the map with the sky in the way, and if I hide the sky dome the level doesn't look like it will in the game and it's harder to accurately judge the work I am producing. In the game the dome is also a physical limit, and the player has to be kept away from it. This isn't at all conducive to the larger worlds we are able/required to create today, especially those worlds on the scale of a present-day/near-future MMO.

The skybox technique is actually a separate area in a map (like a little room) with only the sky elements in it. There is a camera centered in the area that doesn't move but swivels in the same direction the player looks. What this camera sees in the sky box is composited with what the player sees and the result is impressive. I like this method because it is easier to work with, you get better results, and the player can walk forever and never reach it, or view it from an angle where it doesn't look its best. Since the sky moves with the player, you can control precisely how it looks to them. It is easier to get a skybox looking perfect from one angle than every conceivable angle. See Figure 8-16 for an illustration of how the skybox works.

Conclusion

That concludes the asset creation for the outdoors. Next we will look at effects in games.

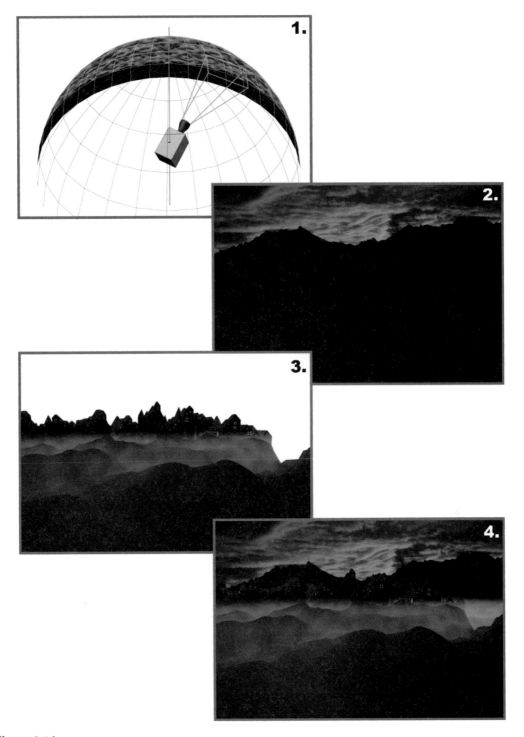

Fikgure 8-16
Number 1: The camera is in its own location and swivels to look where the player looks, but doesn't move.
Number 2: The view of what the skybox camera sees. **Number 3:** The players' view with no sky. **Number 4:**
The sky and players' view composited together.

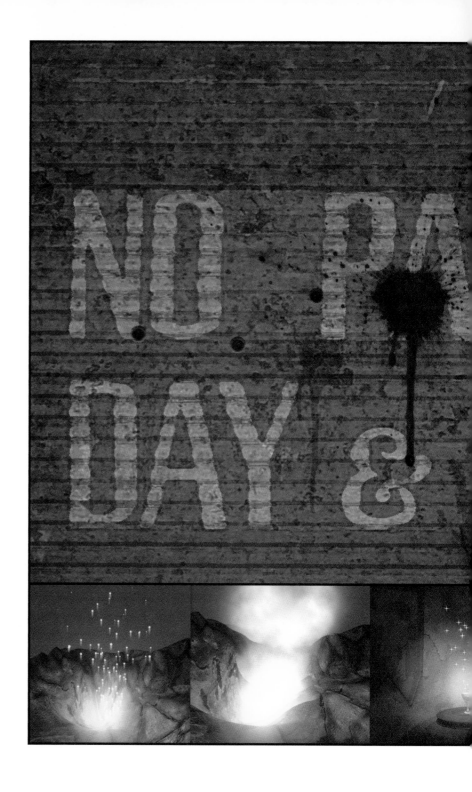

Chapter 9

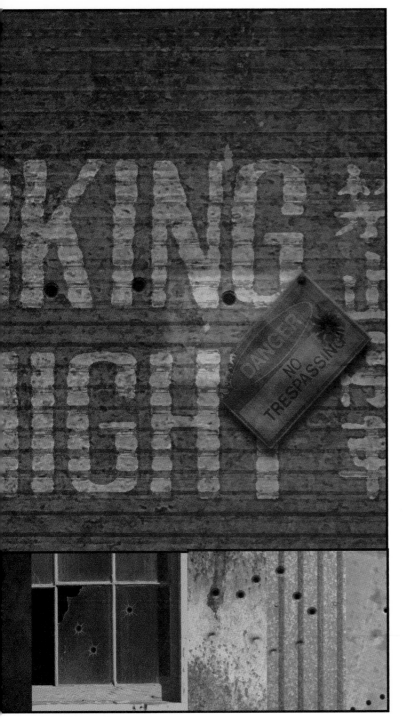

Introduction

Games are full of visual effects, probably even more than you realize. These effects are important, not just as eye candy, but for giving the player clues and information on what is happening in the game world. These effects also add a great deal to the level of immersion a player will experience in a game. For example, in some games you can shoot at a wall and nothing will happen—did a bullet come out of your gun? In another you can shoot a wall and a few pixels may fly from the point of impact; how satisfying is that? Shoot a gun at a wall in a recent game of any quality and you will see a hole or abrasion on the wall, a small shower of debris fly from the point of impact, and a puff of dust dissipate into the air. Typically, if you shoot at any surface in a game—wood, metal, concrete, and their variations—you will see and hear a different effect for each surface. Effects also include the glow around a candle, light shafts from a window, even rain drops—and a whole lot more. The assets for these effects are fairly easy to create. Actually, asset creation is the easy part of creating effects in a relative sense. It does take work to create the art and it must look good, but it's the systems that run the effects that can be complex and challenging to work with.

Game Effects

There are generally three types of effects you will create assets for:

- Static
- Animated
- Particle

Static Effects

Most effects are based on a fairly simple texture and mesh set; the texture and mesh of the static effect don't move. Effects like the light beams streaming from the windows in the warehouse and fantasy settings and the glow around the candles in the fantasy setting are static effects. Some of the most common static effects are the marks left on a wall after the impact of a bullet like those in the front plate of this chapter. The various impact marks on each of the different surfaces are all created in this chapter. See Figure 9-1 for an illustration of the bullet hole image (with alpha) mapped to a two-triangle polygon to create the decal, and how it looks when placed in the world. Effects like the bullet holes are called decals because they are displayed like a decal on a surface in the game world. A bullet hole is easy to make; it's the programmers who have the difficult job of getting the decal to appear at the right time, display correctly on the surface, and fade away after a certain amount of time, and other numerous variables. Some game engines rotate the image, cycle through different images for each bullet hole, and even animate the images on the decal. While usually simple, these effects add a lot to the game world they appear in.

Animated Effects

Animated effects are based on the texture/mesh arrangement, only the texture is animated and plays like a mini-movie on the face of

Figure 9-1
An illustration of a bullet hole decal. A simple texture with an alpha channel applied to a two-triangle polygon. Below a row of bullet decals placed on a wall.

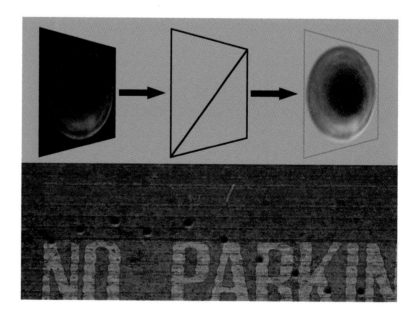

the mesh. There can be a few to many frames in an animated progression, and the frames can exist on one large image or as separate images. In one case the separate frame images are displayed one after the other, and in the other the frames are all on one image and the game engine displays the various areas of the image in order. The program flips through these frames and plays the images like a movie. Animated sequences were usually used as fire in previous games, blinking lights on a console, oozing blood, and many other effects. Fire was created by using a flat plane that always faced the camera and the animated sequence was mapped to it. Animated effects can also be applied to nonmoving models, like the lights of a computer console, Figure 9-2. I put the entire console image in the figure so you can see the animation in context, but for a game the lights would be a separate image with an alpha channel to save memory. Some current games, and probably all future games, are increasingly using nonanimated particles because the particle systems and the hardware have evolved enough that a much higher degree of control can be achieved, more particles and emitters can be used, and now effects exist that process in real time that make the particle systems look much better than a static, or pre-rendered asset.

Animated effects are still used to animate some decals such as a weapons blast. Imagine the burst of energy from a blaster hitting a metal wall beside you in a space station. The blast mark is bright from the heat of the blast and the glow fades and shrinks as it quickly cools; see Figure 9-3. This animated sequence was made quickly in Photoshop. Animated images are a little more challenging to work with, and the job of creating a 2D animation for an effect often falls to the artist who may not be used to traditional animation, or have access and the knowledge to use a 3D package. Animated effects are commonly used in the muzzle blast from a gun and are often used for explosions and smoke, so you will most likely see them around a little while longer. You can use ImageReady to create and test animated effects.

Particle Effects

A particle system is a system that can display an assigned asset in great numbers (the asset is usually a small polygon—two triangles—with an applied texture that has alpha transparency on it). The system tracks the particles in 3D space using a set of parameters that the artist can change. These parameters typically alter the rate, size, speed, position, and life span of the particle as well as telling the particle to shrink, fade, or always face the camera (which it usually does). Particles can even physically interact with the game world; colliding and bouncing off surfaces. Figure 9-4 shows the same scene with the same particle system in use with a different texture used in each scene. Actually, the particle used for all of the effects (except the sparks in the upper left-hand corner) is mapped with the same texture; however, in each case the texture has simply been colorized with a different hue and saturation. The texture itself is simple to create.

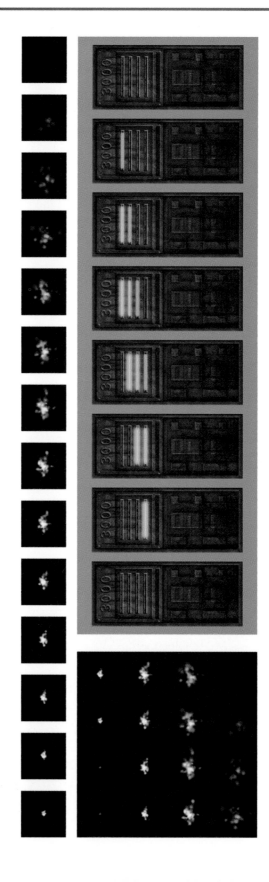

Figure 9-2
Animated effects are based on the texture/ mesh arrangement, only the texture plays like a mini-movie. There are several frames in the animated progression, and the frames can exist on one large image or as separate images. The computer console is an example of an animated sequence in context.

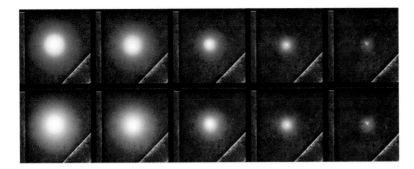

Figure 9-3
The creation of an animated particle or decal doesn't always have to be difficult. This laser blast was made quickly in Photoshop.

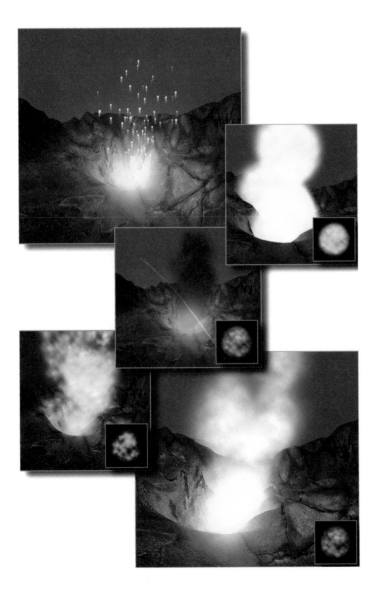

Figure 9-4
Particles are used in these scenes to create various effects such as sparks (**upper left**), gaseous flames (**upper right**), volcanic smoke or ash (**middle**), poisonous gas (**lower left**), and steam (**lower right**). These scenes use the same particle system with a different texture used in each scene. Actually, the particle used for all of the effects (except the sparks in the upper left-hand corner) is mapped with the same texture. In each case the texture has simply been colorized with a different hue and saturation.

- Create a 512 × 512 image, black background
- Create a new empty layer
- Drag out a circular selection with a 22-pixel feather centered in the image
- Render clouds
- Select > Load Selection—Load the transparency of the layer
- Dodge, Burn, Airbrush, and/or Colorize this image to get the effect you want.

A particle system can be used to simulate a wide variety of effects from smoke to a flock of birds. Traditionally, the use of particle systems with a large number of particles coming from it was too big a drain on a computer, so the effects game developers were able to achieve were limited. But as software gets more complex and game hardware more powerful, smoke and fire and other impressive effects are being very effctively generated using a much larger number of particles.

Dealing with particle systems can be the most difficult part of effects work. Understanding and effectively using the systems that drive the particles, especially a good system with lots of options, can take a lot of time and patience. But even a complex particle system usually uses the same simple texture and geometry setup for the visual particles. See Figure 9-5 for the progression of a static magical sparkle. And Figure 9-6 shows a simple particle system. In the upper set of images the particles are represented by crosses (so you can see what the particle system is actually doing) and in the

Figure 9-5
A magical spell starts with a small static sparkle.

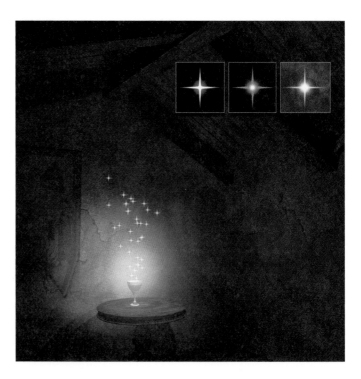

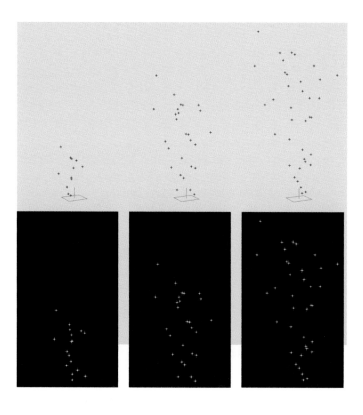

Figure 9-6
This is an illustration of a simple particle system, a magical spell. The upper set of images shows the particles represented by crosses so you can see what the particle system is actually doing, and the lower images are the same as the upper, only with the sparkle image attached to each particle.

lower images are the same as the upper, only with the sparkle asset attached to each particle.

The point at which the particles are spawned, or appear, is called an emitter. An emitter can be of any size. A small emitter with lot of particles coming out in a spray may be what you would use for a garden hose, whereas a very large emitter high in the sky of your game world with a few particles falling from it might be used for rain or snow. See Figure 9-7 for the effect of using different emitter sizes. Often special particle systems are written for specific uses. Specific particle systems that handle weather effects, for example, are commonly created because weather systems have a more limited function but cover a larger area than a typical full-featured particle system usually does. These special versions of a particle system allow the developers to make them run more efficiently. This is achieved partly by simply dropping many of the features a typical particle system has that are not needed for a more specific use particle system. Emitters are typically represented by some sort of icon in the game editor, but are invisible in the game—you only see the assets spawning at the emitter point being controlled by the particle entity they are attached to. Usually the game artist, when placing an emitter, makes sure it looks as if the particles are coming out of something and not just from thin air.

While a simple particle system may only contain an emitter, a polygon, and a texture, more complex particle systems can contain multiple emitters and multiple textures and use 3D meshes as

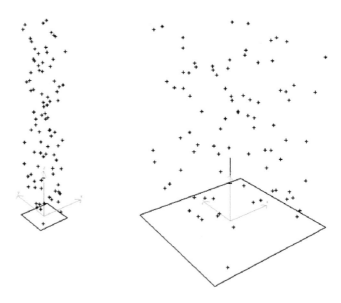

Figure 9-7
Emitters are where the particles come from and can be of various sizes. The same number of particles is coming out of both emitters in the figure, but the wider emitter has spread the particles out over a larger area.

particles. An explosion is usually composed of a quick ball of fire and a spray of debris, then smoke that drifts from the blasted area and dissipates into the air. This is typically created using a blast decal and several systems, one for each effect: flash, debris, and smoke. Additionally, particle systems are usually associated with sound events. Sound adds a lot to the effect a particle system has. What would rain be without the rumble of thunder? How effective would a silent explosion be? When a fire crackles as you get near it, it adds another level of realism and immersion to a game.

We will start with some simple weather effects and then tackle some of the more common effects for a game, such as lighting and weapons effects.

Weather

As complex as nature can be, the particles for the most common weather effects are easy to create. Rain and snow are both tiny simple images. Notice the images are blurred a little. The rain is blurred toward the back of the drop to simulate the blurring of a real rain drop as it falls to the ground. You can see the effect a few hundred of these tiny particles can have on a scene; see Figure 9-8.

Lighting

If you understand the math and science of light, then more power to you. But most of us mortals can only understand this stuff on a basic level—it can get really complex. Of course, it helps to understand how light works, but it is absolutely no guarantee that you can create the art that makes a light look good in a game. In fact, an artist is probably better served by observing a variety of

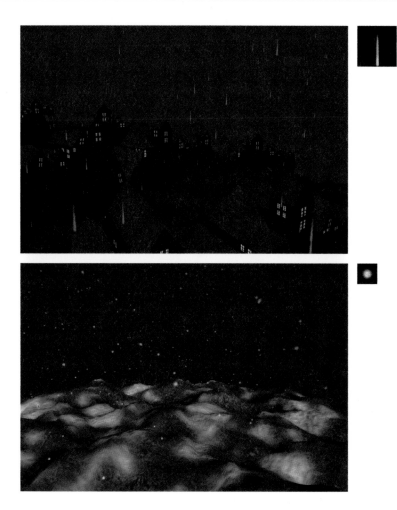

Figure 9-8
The particles for the most common weather effects are easy to create. Rain and snow are both tiny simple images. You can see the effect a few hundred of these tiny particles can have on a scene.

light sources in various situations and studying them at a purely visual level than trying to wrap her mind around a subject that may have driven them to art in the first place. Fortunately, we are artists and we have to make things look good, not write the code that controls the particle. Several of the more common lighting effects are easy to understand and recreate in a game setting. These effects are accomplished with a simple mesh and texture set. You have already seen a few of these effects in the previous chapters.

Light Shafts

Do you remember the shafts of light that streamed in from the windows in the warehouse and the windows in the fantasy setting? In the real world, light shafts are created when light passes through the atmosphere and reflects off tiny floating particles. Light shafts are prevalent in games because they look cool, but they can also be important visual clues. Presently light shafts are created using the simple mesh/texture set. In the future they will probably be rendered in real time, but for now . . . see Figure 9-9 for the

Figure 9-9
The components of the light shaft are a simple mesh and texture.

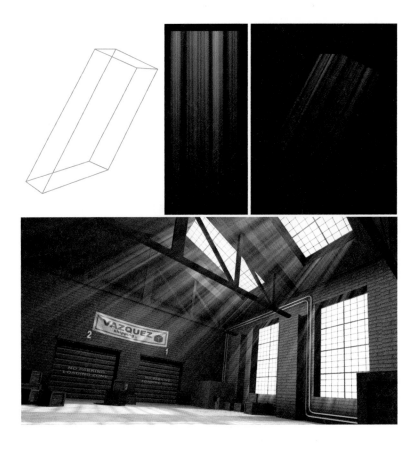

components of the light shafts as I created them for the scenes in this book.

To create that texture I simply created an image that was 256 wide and 1024 high. I turned on the Fade option in the Shape Dynamics for the brush and drew a few white lines with a soft brush from top to bottom. Then I Motion Blurred it down a few times and Gaussian Blurred it a little, too.

If you are able to use these textures in a 3D application, keep the following points in mind:

- Exclude the geometry from being affected by the light sources in the world so it doesn't cast a shadow.
- Turn the full-bright (or illumination) on the texture all the way up. When you do this, the texture displays at full brightness and seems to glow. Since light shafts are located near a source of light that is brighter than the surrounding (relative) darkness, they look great and will never be in a situation where they are bright for no reason (well I guess you can make a door close and the light shafts will remain, but you shouldn't do that).
- Turn collision off so your light shafts don't block anything (like real light) and the collision process is a processor hit, so it's

always a good idea to turn collision off anything that doesn't need it.

I have seen this effect augmented in some creative ways; with animated textures that make the shafts seem to waver or shift, with particle systems that simulate dust drifting through the light shaft, a projected shadow like I used on the floor of the warehouse so it appears that the light is actually casting a shadow.

Candle Glow/Corona

At night, light sources often seem to have a glow or halo around them. This effect, in the real world, is caused by the light, the atmosphere between the light source and the viewer, and the viewer. As the light hits water droplets in the air, it is broken up into various colors based on the many variables that can exist in the light source (distance, color, brightness), the atmosphere (amount of moisture in the air, pollutants), and even the viewers' eyes. While a game might have one corona for many light sources, occasionally creating a few special case coronas for drastically different-colored light sources, in reality each corona you see is unique because of the many variables involved. Fortunately, a game is usually designed around a theme or setting, which allows for the use of a smaller, more focused, set of assets—coronas being one of them.

In the fantasy setting we had a glow around the candle flame, which is also a corona, but has a different texture made to look like a candle glow rather than an electric light source (see Figure 9-10). While the light shafts are static, a corona needs to move. To simulate a glow around a light source effectively, many games rely on a technique that uses a moving polygon with a simple corona or glow image mapped to it. The corona entity allows the artist to control several parameters that make the corona image shrink,

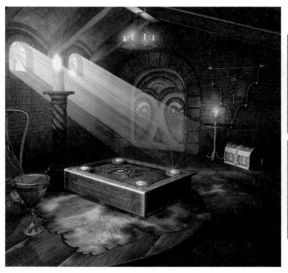
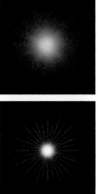

Figure 9-10
The fantasy setting uses a glow around the candle flame, which is also a corona entity with a texture made to look like a candle glow rather than an electric light.

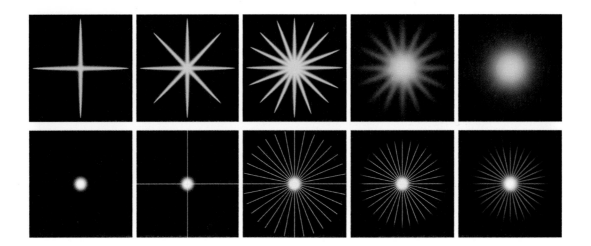

Figure 9-11
The progression of the candle glows.

grow, and fade in and out as the player moves toward and away from it.

I actually created two glows for the candles in the fantasy scene, one that was more diffuse and faint for the background candle, and a brighter, more fanciful glow for the candle on the table in the foreground to give the impression that it is magical. See Figure 9-11 for the progression of both glows. The steps are as described ahead.

Candle Glow, Faint and Diffuse

- Create a new image, 1024 × 1024. I work this large so I can get finer gradation in the glows. You do lose some of that when you resize, but I find it makes the corona smoother.
- Make a layer named **center** filled with black and snap two guides to the horizontal and vertical center of the image.
- Create a new layer named **lines**.
- Use a small, soft brush with the Fade option set at about 75 pixels.
- Draw yellow-orange lines from the center to all four points of the compass. Copy, paste, and rotate this four times.
- Filter > Blur > Gaussian Blur—20 pixels.
- Filter > Blur > Radial Blur—Amount 100, Quality Best.
- Create the alpha channel in the same manner as you did for the candle flame in the fantasy chapter.

Candle Glow, Brighter and More Fanciful

- Create a new image, 1024 × 1024.
- Make a layer named **center** filled with black and snap two guides to the horizontal and vertical center of the image.
- Create a new layer named **lines**.

- Use a smaller, soft brush and set the foreground color to a very desaturated yellow RGB: 255,248,218.
- Set the foreground color to white and reduce the brush size a few steps and put a white center in the yellow circle.
- Create a new layer named **lines**.
- Invert your colors and use the desaturated yellow and a small, hard brush, 5 pixels.
- Draw lines across the canvas until you have a complete circle of tight thin lines. You can draw two lines using the guides and then copy, paste, and rotate them. Merge all the line layers together when you are done.
- Use an inverted circular selection with a 42 feather to remove the ends of the lines.
- Gaussian Blur this 4 pixels.
- Radial Blur this, too. Amount 100, Blur Method Zoom.

Traditional Corona

The traditional corona is a little more involved than a candle glow. You can use the Render > Lens Flare filter to get a variety of effects that are great reference when creating a corona, but you can't use the resulting lens flare as a corona texture because you can't render the effect on an empty layer, which makes the creation of a decent alpha channel a challenge. Also, the lens flare is meant to simulate the flare from a camera lens, not the glow from a light source, so there is a good deal of extra visual information in the effect that would be next to impossible to remove. The steps to create a corona start as the candle glow.

- Create a new image, 1024 × 1024.
- Make a layer filled with black, and snap two guides to the horizontal and vertical center of the image.
- Create a new layer named **center**.
- Use a large, soft brush and set the foreground color to white. Put the center white glow in.
- Coronas can have many colors in them, but they should be subtle. We will start by creating a faint circle in the background. Create a layer named **brownish circle** behind the glow on the **center** layer. Use a circular marquee with a 22-pixel feather and fill it with a brown RGB: 80,71,59.
- Create a new layer named **ring1** under the **center** layer.
- Set your foreground color to RGB: 40,47,40.
- Use the circular marquee with the 22-pixel feather still on it and stroke an 8-pixel line outside of the brownish circle.
- You have the option of adding a circle or two more if you like. Ultimately, the corona's color and intensity will be based on the setting it is in.
- Either paint or smudge the white lines out from the center. Note that the lines are fewer than the fanciful candle glow and are of varying lengths.
- Finally, Gaussian Blur this about 4 pixels. See Figure 9-12.

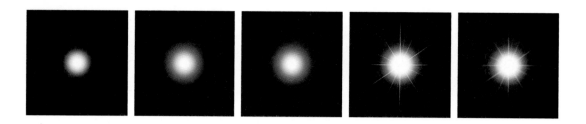

Figure 9-12
The progression of the
traditional corona.

Weapons

Now we are going to tackle weapons effects. These can be the most involved and complex effects to set up, given the number of weapons in a typical game, the number of effects each weapon has associated with it, and the effect the weapon's projectile might produce when impacting any given surface of the game world. While these effects are usually complex and involved to set up, the assets they use are fairly easy to create.

Muzzle Blasts

The plume of fire that discharges from the barrel of a weapon is called a muzzle blast. In reality, every type of weapon has a distinct muzzle blast, but most people can't distinguish between the muzzle blasts from similar firearms to any great degree. A muzzle blast from a rifle will do the job for most rifles in a game, but a muzzle blast from a rifle on a handgun might be noticeable. While the muzzle blast from various weapons will have various patterns and sizes, currently they are all made in the same basic fashion. They are a combination of geometry and texture. First, let's look at the elements of the typical muzzle blast in Figure 9-13 and the complete muzzle blast in front of a backdrop.

Here are the steps to create the muzzle blast. See Figure 9-15 for a visual progression of the steps below. To create the circular part of the muzzle blast:

- Open a new 512 × 512 document in Photoshop with a black background.
- Create a new layer named **orange**.
- Set your foreground color to orange RGB: 255, 150, 0.
- Use a very large soft brush (300 pixels) and put a large orange circle in the middle of the image using a horizontal and vertical guide.
- Use a smaller, soft brush (200 pixels) and put a white circle in the middle of the orange circle.
- Use the Smudge Tool (27 pixels, 74%) and smudge out the color from the center of the image.
- Filter > Distort > Ripple—Amount 75%, Size Large.
- Filter > Blur > Radial Blur—Amount 10, Blur Method Spin, Quality Good.

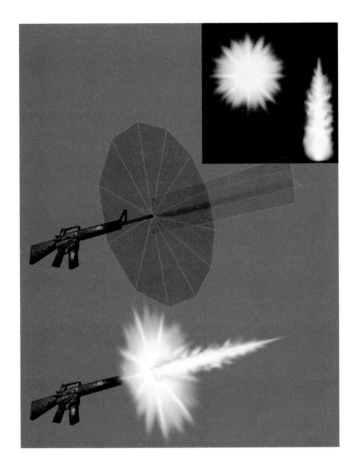

Figure 9-13
The plume of fire that discharges from the barrel of a weapon is called a muzzle blast. They are created with a combination of geometry and texture. **Upper right,** the muzzle blast texture. **Middle,** the model of a gun with the geometry for the muzzle blast in place. **Bottom,** the muzzle blast with the texture and geometry together.

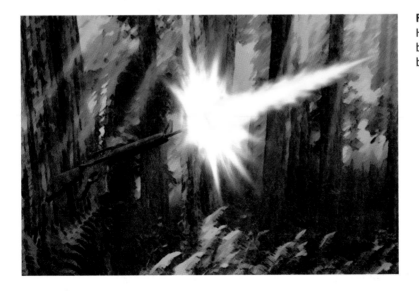

Figure 9-14
Here is the completed muzzle blast in front of a colored backdrop.

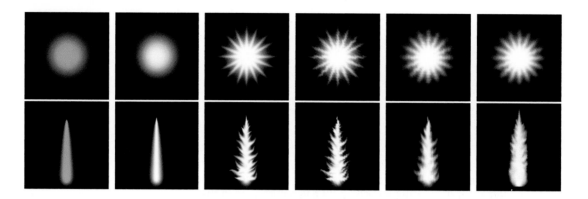

Figure 9-15
The progression of the steps to create the muzzle blast.

- Filter > Blur > Radial Blur—Amount 25, Blur Method Zoom, Quality Good.

To create the elongated part of the muzzle blast:

- Open a new 512 × 512 document in Photoshop with a black background.
- Create a new layer named **orange**.
- Set your foreground color to orange RGB: 255, 150, 0,
- Use a large, soft brush (100 pixels) and set the Shape Dynamics to Fade—25 pixels. Drag a long orange line from the bottom to the top.
- Use a smaller brush (50 pixels) and set the Shape Dynamics to Fade—55 pixels. Drag a white line from the bottom to the top of the image.
- Use the Smudge Tool (27 pixels, 74%) and smudge out from the center of the image and upwards.
- Filter > Distort > Ripple—Amount 75%, Size Large.
- Filter > Blur > Motion Blur—Angle 90, Distance 25 pixels.
- Filter > Blur > Radial Blur—Amount 25, Blur Method Zoom, Quality Good.
- I did a little more smudging to strengthen the flames.

Impact Effects: Bullet Holes and Debris

When you fire a gun in a game, the muzzle blast may be notable, but it's the effect the bullet or projectile has on the surface it strikes that is really satisfying. If little to nothing happened when you fired a weapon, you wouldn't feel as immersed or excited by the game. The effect is not only cool, but it also is an important interaction with the game world. In fact, a player is usually made aware of the effect his interaction has on the game world (other players being part of the game world) through visual effects. Impact effects give you important visual clues as to how close you are to hitting the target you are aiming at. It is a particularly tense event in a game to hear the sound of a bullet impact near you and see the hole and debris and realize that you are the target. In a stealth shooter, where you are both hunter and prey, this is an important part of game play. Of course, auditory and even tactile effects (vibrating controller) play an important role, too, but you can more easily play a game without speakers than without a monitor.

This section is entitled *Impact Effects* with the added *Bullet Holes and Debris* because almost any interaction with a game world is an impact that spawns an effect: weapons effects are just a subset of impact effects. But weapons effects are usually the most commonly needed and complex effects created for a game. I am limiting the examples of impact effects in this chapter to basic weapons effects because the same principles apply to the creation of virtually all other effects. The bloody hole and red spray from a gunshot wound, the tracks left behind and dust kicked up by a vehicle's tires in the desert, a swarm of insects, and most other effects are all created in the same manner as other effects created in this chapter.

Some effects are relatively simple: you fire a gun and blow dirt from the ground or leave a hole in a metal panel. But some can be pretty dramatic. In some games you can shoot a window and blow the glass pane into a thousand shards. If you are in the position to create effects such as these for a game, you will quickly realize that you need a spreadsheet to track the weapon types, ammunition or projectile, world surfaces, and the description and needed assets for each impact effect. This spreadsheet can also include the associated sound files and even special case events like malfunctions and misfires. Here I will walk you through the basics of creating impact effects for an average bullet on the most common surfaces.

First, we list the most common surfaces in an average game world:

- Cloth
- Concrete/Plaster/Brick
- Dirt
- Glass
- Grass
- Metal
- Water
- Wood

For each of these surfaces we must create a texture that the game engine can display over the surface (like a decal) and look as if a bullet left a mark at the point of impact. We also need to create a particle/debris image for each surface and variations for some of the surfaces. For example, a bullet hitting the thin metal of a tin garden shed might simply put a neat hole right through the metal with little to no debris coming from the point of impact, but the same bullet slamming into the heavy metal of a blast door may only slightly dent the metal but send a shower of debris, even red-hot sparks, flying from the point of impact.

Although you may come up with a neat list of the materials in your world, these materials may all look vastly different. For example, heavy metal can be rusted or freshly painted, wood can be old (desaturated and brownish) or new (brightly painted furniture or highly polished panels). The challenge here is to create a bullet hole decal for a certain material (wood, for example) that will work equally well in many situations (old wood, painted wood, etc.). I find that a grayscale image with good light, shadow, and alpha treatment works best as it tends to blend with the material it is displayed on top off. This method also allows you to focus your efforts of how a given material will react to a bullet impact regardless of the color or condition of the material. For example, wood generally splinters, glass shatters, metal is dented or punctured, etc. By leaving the color information out, you can create an effect that will adopt the color of the surface it is displayed on and spew the appropriate particles for the material type. The key to creating a good impact and debris set is to consider the physical properties of the material first; how hard, brittle, squishy, etc. is the material, and how will it react to the impact of the specific projectile that will be hitting it? Then focus on the highlight and shadow of the hole and debris. Experiment with the effects in Photoshop and in-game and adjust the alpha channeling to obtain the best results. A deeper hole may be small with an almost solid black center while a shallow dent may be wider and almost transparent with only a hint of light and shadow.

Here are the basic surfaces I usually work with in a game. They are listed alphabetically and not by importance.

Cloth

If you kick in the door of the average crack house and start blazing away with your nine, chances are you will hit a sofa, stained mattress, or some dope shag carpeting. When you are taking down that stained mattress, you want to know it's really dead, so the game artist better give you some good visual feedback.

Cloth tends to rip and tear and leave strings or fibers when it is destroyed. To create the impact and particles for cloth, I started with a simple stringy pattern and applied the Bevel and Emboss layer style and finally added some additional strings and darkened the hole to give it depth. See Figure 9-16 for the progression of the cloth bullet hole and Figure 9-17 for the bullet hole, debris, and the effects in context.

Figure 9-16
The progression of the steps to create the bullet hole for cloth.

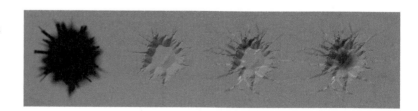

Concrete/Plaster/Brick

These three materials are very common in game worlds and similar in their effects. The holes and debris are almost interchangeable, but you may want to differentiate between light concrete, heavy reinforced concrete, and/or bricks and heavy ceramics because of the frequency and wide variety of these types of materials.

Light concrete or plaster will leave a cleaner hole and produce a more wispy puff of debris. See Figure 9-18 for the light concrete/plaster effects set. This effects set was created as most of the other effects were, using various brushes and the Bevel and Emboss layer style as a beginning.

For the heavier, reinforced concrete, I made the holes shallower and rougher and the debris essentially the same as the lighter concrete. I also added a puff of dust to the context image. We created the puff earlier in the chapter in the section on Particle Effects, so you could see a more complete example of an effect (Figure 9-19).

For the bricks I went with a simple circular hole as if the brittle brick was blown out in a large shallow circle. I think the shallow carved-out look works for most brittle brick and tile surfaces. I made the debris contain some small chunks since it seemed the brick would be blasted outward, whereas the concrete would powder under the impact (Figure 9-20).

Dirt

Dirt tends to crater when impacted so I created a wider, shallower, crater-like hole and a longer, wider, spray of dirt grains (see Figure 9-21).

Glass

In general, one of two things can happen when glass is impacted in a game world, a hole and debris are spawned or the glass shatters into pieces and falls out of the frame. For the glass to break and fall usually involves the glass disappearing and being replaced with a particle system of falling glass shards. This involves less asset creation and more technical setup. We will look at the hole and debris option. Often, when glass is impacted by a projectile, it doesn't shatter but a spidery hole appears. This can be the case for thick, reinforced, or bulletproof glass. For this set the hole is a black circle with a faint inner glow for some depth and thin white lines emanating out from the center (use the Fade option for this). The glass debris are some simple shapes I dodged and burned. See Figure 9-22.

Grass

I created the grass effects set based on the techniques used for the cloth and dirt set. The hole created when grass is shot wouldn't be a clear hole, but a dark patch where the grass was displaced with a few blades overhanging. The debris would be dirt and grass blades. I colored the debris greenish so it would look like grass blades, but could have left it desaturated if I needed it to be more versatile. See Figure 9-23.

Metal

Metal is another potentially big category. I created three basic scenarios: the light metal with a clean hole, the heavier metal that will get dented inward and punctured when shot, and the dense metal that will only dent when impacted. Each hole is a variation on a bevel and emboss with some dodging and burning. See Figure 9-24 for the light metal, Figure 9-25 for the heavier metal, and Figure 9-26 for the dense metal.

Water

When water is shot is sprays upward and outward. Here I show you the simple decal/debris version we have been working with. Some games make the water splash more complex, resembling the muzzle blast of the gun we look at earlier. See Figure 9-27 for the water impact and splash.

Wood

Wood will splinter when shot, so I created a simple hole similar to the grass impact. There is a depression with splinters that overhang the hole. The debris is obviously splinters or chips of wood. See Figure 9-28.

Conclusion

That's a basic rundown of in-game effects. The asset creation is the easy part; it's working with the various systems to get the effect you want that is the real challenge. This chapter has provided you with a basis to create the assets for any effect you may be required to create for a game.

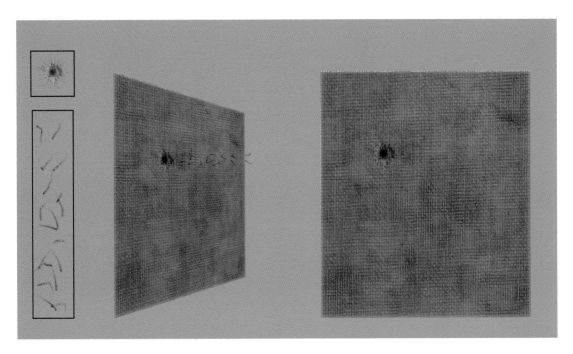

Figure 9-17
The cloth bullet hole, debris, and the effects in context.

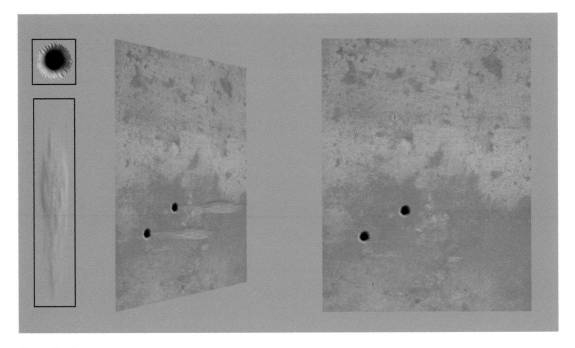

Figure 9-18
The light concrete/plaster effects set and the effects in context.

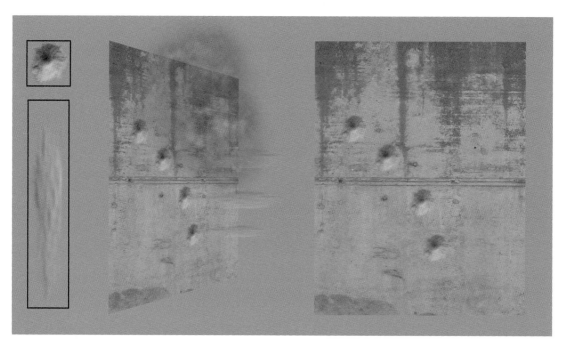

Figure 9-19
The heavier concrete effects set and the effects in context, with a puff of dust that drifts away after the initial impact. We created the puff earlier in the chapter, in the section on particle effects.

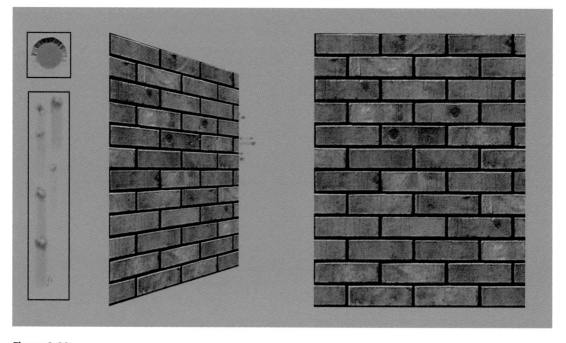

Figure 9-20
The brick effects set and the effects in context.

Figure 9-21
The dirt effects set and the effects in context.

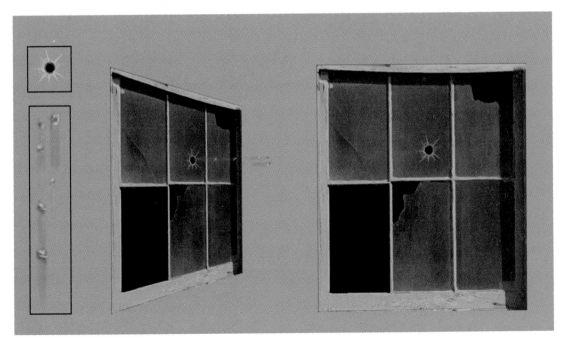

Figure 9-22
The glass hole and debris effects set and the effects in context.

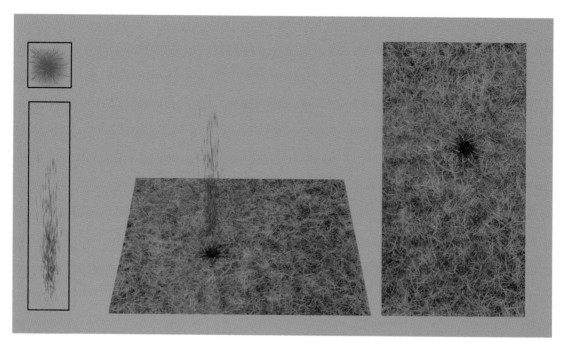

Figure 9-23
The grass effects set and the effects in context.

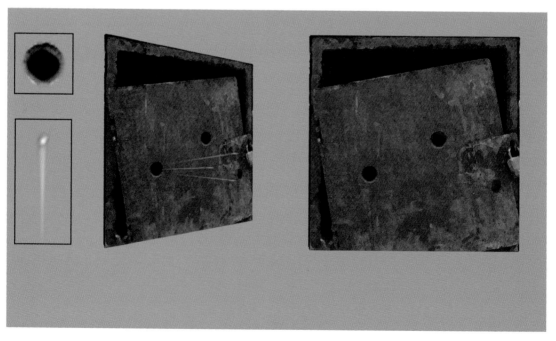

Figure 9-24
The light metal effects set and the effects in context.

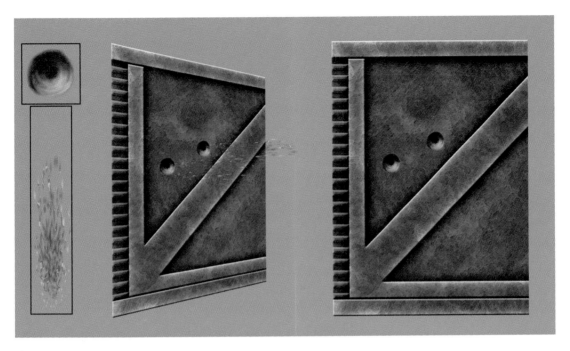

Figure 9-25
The medium metal effects set and the effects in context.

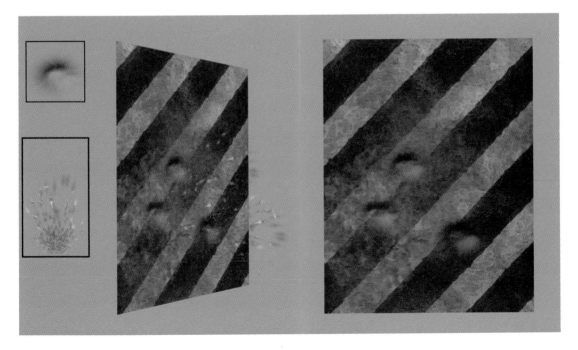

Figure 9-26
The dense metal effects set and the effects in context.

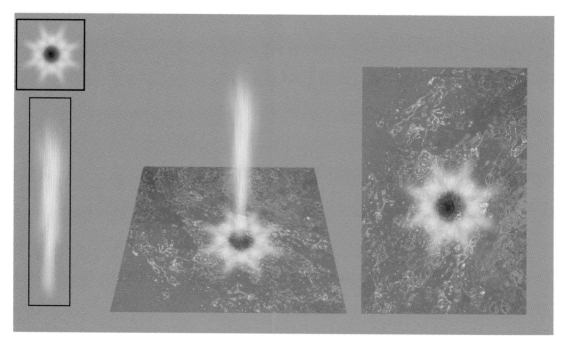

Figure 9-27
The water effects set and the effects in context.

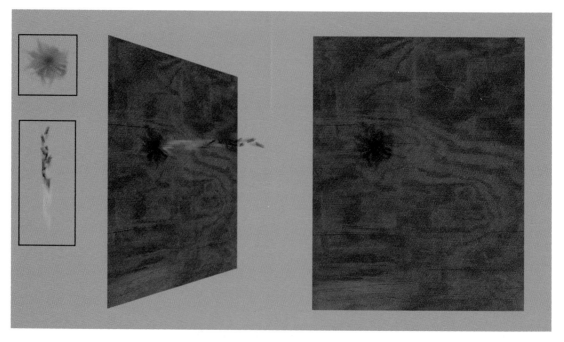

Figure 9-28
The wood effects set and the effects in context.

INDEX

ELSEVIER SCIENCE DVD-ROM LICENSE AGREEMENT

PLEASE READ THE FOLLOWING AGREEMENT CAREFULLY BEFORE USING THIS DVD-ROM PRODUCT. THIS DVD -ROM PRODUCT IS LICENSED UNDER THE TERMS CONTAINED IN THIS DVD -ROM LICENSE AGREEMENT ("Agreement"). BY USING THIS DVD-ROM PRODUCT, YOU, AN INDIVIDUAL OR ENTITY INCLUDING EMPLOYEES, AGENTS AND REPRESENTATIVES ("You" or "Your"), ACKNOWLEDGE THAT YOU HAVE READ THIS AGREEMENT, THAT YOU UNDERSTAND IT, AND THAT YOU AGREE TO BE BOUND BY THE TERMS AND CONDITIONS OF THIS AGREEMENT. ELSEVIER SCIENCE INC. ("Elsevier Science") EXPRESSLY DOES NOT AGREE TO LICENSE THIS DVD -ROM PRODUCT TO YOU UNLESS YOU ASSENT TO THIS AGREEMENT. IF YOU DO NOT AGREE WITH ANY OF THE FOLLOWING TERMS, YOU MAY, WITHIN THIRTY (30) DAYS AFTER YOUR RECEIPT OF THIS DVD -ROM PRODUCT RETURN THE UNUSED DVD -ROM PRODUCT AND ALL ACCOMPANYING DOCUMENTATION TO ELSEVIER SCIENCE FOR A FULL REFUND.

DEFINITIONS

As used in this Agreement, these terms shall have the following meanings:

"Proprietary Material" means the valuable and proprietary information content of this DVD-ROM Product including all indexes and graphic materials and software used to access, index, search and retrieve the information content from this DVD-ROM Product developed or licensed by Elsevier Science and/or its affiliates, suppliers and licensors.

"DVD-ROM Product" means the copy of the Proprietary Material and any other material delivered on DVD-ROM and any other human-readable or machine-readable materials enclosed with this Agreement, including without limitation documentation relating to the same.

OWNERSHIP

This DVD-ROM Product has been supplied by and is proprietary to Elsevier Science and/or its affiliates, suppliers and licensors. The copyright in the DVD-ROM Product belongs to Elsevier Science and/or its affiliates, suppliers and licensors and is protected by the national and state copyright, trademark, trade secret and other intellectual property laws of the United States and international treaty provisions, including without limitation the Universal Copyright Convention and the Berne Copyright Convention. You have no ownership rights in this DVD-ROM Product. Except as expressly set forth herein, no part of this DVD-ROM Product, including without limitation the Proprietary Material, may be modified, copied or distributed in hardcopy or machine-readable form without prior written consent from Elsevier Science. All rights not expressly granted to You herein are expressly reserved. Any other use of this DVD-ROM Product by any person or entity is strictly prohibited and a violation of this Agreement.

SCOPE OF RIGHTS LICENSED (PERMITTED USES)

Elsevier Science is granting to You a limited, non-exclusive, non-transferable license to use this DVD-ROM Product in accordance with the terms of this Agreement. You may use or provide access to this DVD-ROM Product on a single computer or terminal physically located at Your premises and in a secure network or move this DVD-ROM Product to and use it on another single computer or terminal at the same location for personal use only, but under no circumstances may You use or provide access to any part or parts of this DVD-ROM Product on more than one computer or terminal simultaneously.

You shall not (a) copy, download, or otherwise reproduce the DVD-ROM Product in any medium, including, without limitation, online transmissions, local area networks, wide area networks, intranets, extranets and the Internet, or in any way, in whole or in part, except that You may print or download limited portions of the Proprietary Material that are the results of discrete searches; (b) alter, modify, or adapt the DVD-ROM Product, including but not limited to decompiling, disassembling, reverse engineering, or creating derivative works, without the prior written approval of Elsevier Science; (c) sell, license or otherwise distribute to third parties the DVD-ROM Product or any part or parts thereof; or (d) alter, remove, obscure or obstruct the display of any copyright, trademark or other proprietary notice on or in the DVD-ROM Product or on any printout or download of portions of the Proprietary Materials.

RESTRICTIONS ON TRANSFER

This License is personal to You, and neither Your rights hereunder nor the tangible embodiments of this DVD-ROM Product, including without limitation the Proprietary Material, may be sold, assigned, transferred or sub-licensed to any other person, including without limitation by operation of law, without the prior written consent of Elsevier Science. Any purported sale, assignment, transfer or sublicense without the prior written consent of Elsevier Science will be void and will automatically terminate the License granted hereunder.

TERM

This Agreement will remain in effect until terminated pursuant to the terms of this Agreement. You may terminate this Agreement at any time by removing from Your system and destroying the DVD-ROM Product. Unauthorized copying of the DVD-ROM Product, including without limitation, the Proprietary Material and documentation, or otherwise failing to comply with the terms and conditions of this Agreement shall result in automatic termination of this license and will make available to Elsevier Science legal remedies. Upon termination of this Agreement, the license granted herein will terminate and You must immediately destroy the DVD-ROM Product and accompanying documentation. All provisions relating to proprietary rights shall survive termination of this Agreement.

LIMITED WARRANTY AND LIMITATION OF LIABILITY

NEITHER ELSEVIER SCIENCE NOR ITS LICENSORS REPRESENT OR WARRANT THAT THE INFORMATION CONTAINED IN THE PROPRIETARY MATERIALS IS COMPLETE OR FREE FROM ERROR, AND NEITHER ASSUMES, AND BOTH EXPRESSLY DISCLAIM, ANY LIABILITY TO ANY PERSON FOR ANY LOSS OR DAMAGE CAUSED BY ERRORS OR OMISSIONS IN THE PROPRIETARY MATERIAL, WHETHER SUCH ERRORS OR OMISSIONS RESULT FROM NEGLIGENCE, ACCIDENT, OR ANY OTHER CAUSE. IN ADDITION, NEITHER ELSEVIER SCIENCE NOR ITS LICENSORS MAKE ANY REPRESENTATIONS OR WARRANTIES, EITHER EXPRESS OR IMPLIED, REGARDING THE PERFORMANCE OF YOUR NETWORK OR COMPUTER SYSTEM WHEN USED IN CONJUNCTION WITH THE DVD-ROM PRODUCT.

If this DVD-ROM Product is defective, Elsevier Science will replace it at no charge if the defective DVD-ROM Product is returned to Elsevier Science within sixty (60) days (or the greatest period allowable by applicable law) from the date of shipment.

Elsevier Science warrants that the software embodied in this DVD-ROM Product will perform in substantial compliance with the documentation supplied in this DVD-ROM Product. If You report significant defect in performance in writing to Elsevier Science, and Elsevier Science is not able to correct same within sixty (60) days after its receipt of Your notification, You may return this DVD-ROM Product, including all copies and documentation, to Elsevier Science and Elsevier Science will refund Your money.

YOU UNDERSTAND THAT, EXCEPT FOR THE 60-DAY LIMITED WARRANTY RECITED ABOVE, ELSEVIER SCIENCE, ITS AFFILIATES, LICENSORS, SUPPLIERS AND AGENTS, MAKE NO WARRANTIES, EXPRESSED OR IMPLIED, WITH RESPECT TO THE DVD-ROM PRODUCT, INCLUDING, WITHOUT LIMITATION THE PROPRIETARY MATERIAL, AND SPECIFICALLY DISCLAIM ANY WARRANTY OF MERCHANTABILITY OR FITNESS FOR A PARTICULAR PURPOSE.

If the information provided on this DVD-ROM contains medical or health sciences information, it is intended for professional use within the medical field. Information about medical treatment or drug dosages is intended strictly for professional use, and because of rapid advances in the medical sciences, independent verification of diagnosis and drug dosages should be made.

IN NO EVENT WILL ELSEVIER SCIENCE, ITS AFFILIATES, LICENSORS, SUPPLIERS OR AGENTS, BE LIABLE TO YOU FOR ANY DAMAGES, INCLUDING, WITHOUT LIMITATION, ANY LOST PROFITS, LOST SAVINGS OR OTHER INCIDENTAL OR CONSEQUENTIAL DAMAGES, ARISING OUT OF YOUR USE OR INABILITY TO USE THE DVD-ROM PRODUCT REGARDLESS OF WHETHER SUCH DAMAGES ARE FORESEEABLE OR WHETHER SUCH DAMAGES ARE DEEMED TO RESULT FROM THE FAILURE OR INADEQUACY OF ANY EXCLUSIVE OR OTHER REMEDY.

U.S. GOVERNMENT RESTRICTED RIGHTS

The DVD-ROM Product and documentation are provided with restricted rights. Use, duplication or disclosure by the U.S. Government is subject to restrictions as set forth in subparagraphs (a) through (d) of the Commercial Computer Restricted Rights clause at FAR 52.22719 or in subparagraph (c)(1)(ii) of the Rights in Technical Data and Computer Software clause at DFARS 252.2277013, or at 252.2117015, as applicable. Contractor/Manufacturer is Elsevier Science Inc., 655 Avenue of the Americas, New York, NY 10010-5107, USA.

GOVERNING LAW

This Agreement shall be governed by the laws of the State of New York, USA. In any dispute arising out of this Agreement, you and Elsevier Science each consent to the exclusive personal jurisdiction and venue in the state and federal courts within New York County, New York, USA.